THE SAINSBURY COLLECTION

WHOLEFOOD COOKING

THE SAINSBURY COLLECTION

WHOLEFOOD COOKING

Published exclusively for J Sainsbury plc
Stamford House Stamford Street
London SE1 9LL
by Martin Books
Simon and Schuster Consumer Group
Fitzwilliam House
32 Trumpington Street
Cambridge CB2 1QY

First published 1991

© 1991 Woodhead-Faulkner (Publishers) Ltd

ISBN 0 85941 639 9

Recipes and photographs in this book (except chapter frontispiece photographs) have previously been published in various titles in the Sainsbury's Recipe Library series.

Recipes by Alex Barker, Carol Bowen, Mary Cadogan, Roz Denny, Liz Downing and Pete Smith, Caroline Ellwood, Clare Gordon-Smith, Carole Handslip, Lorna Rhodes, Lyn Rutherford, Jane Suthering, Michelle Thomson and Rosemary Wadey

Design: Ken Vail Graphic Design

Cover and chapter frontispiece photographs: David Burch

Other photographs by Martin Brigdale, Laurie Evans, James Jackson, James Murphy, Roger Phillips, Andy Seymour, Charlie Stebbings, Clive Streeter, Grant Symon, Sara Taylor and Paul Williams

Origination by Colthouse Repro Ltd, Bournemouth

Printed and bound by Printer Trento, Trento, Italy

Cover recipe: Paprika Bean Casserole (page 100)

Notes

Ingredients are given in both metric and imperial measures. Use either set of quantities, but not a mixture of both, in any one recipe.

All spoon measurements are level:
1 tablespoon = one 15 ml spoon
1 teaspoon = one 5 ml spoon.

Preheat the oven to the temperature specified.

Freshly ground black pepper is intended where pepper is listed.

Eggs are standard size 3 unless otherwise stated.

Fresh herbs are used unless otherwise stated. If unobtainable, dried herbs can be substituted in cooked dishes but halve the quantities.

Contents

Vegetables and Vegetarian Meals

A wholefood diet gives plenty of scope for making the most of the bountiful range of vegetables now available. With their high nutritional values – vegetables are one of the best sources of most of the important vitamins and minerals, as well as being good sources of dietary fibre – and their wonderful range of tastes and textures, vegetables are the ideal wholefood.

In this chapter you will find a wide assortment of vegetable accompaniments and vegetarian main courses, from simple salads, soups and starters to substantial dishes that are meals in themselves. Covering a range of vegetables from the best of seasonal produce to exotic imports, these recipes provide vegetable dishes for every occasion.

Right (clockwise from top left): Tomato and Basil Salad, Cashew Nut Curry (page 34), Summer Green Salad (page 10), Spiced Red Cabbage with Pine Kernels and Apricots

Tomato and Basil Salad

Serves 6
Preparation time: 15 minutes, plus making dressing and marinating
Freezing: Not recommended

500 g (1 lb) extra-large tomatoes, sliced thinly	*25 g (1 oz) pine kernels*
small bunch basil, chopped roughly	*1 tablespoon coarse-grain mustard*
	6 tablespoons French dressing (page 9)

1 Arrange the tomatoes and basil on a plate. Sprinkle with the pine kernels.
2. Add the mustard to the dressing and shake well to blend. Spoon over the salad, cover and leave to stand for at least 20 minutes. Serve lightly chilled.

Spiced Red Cabbage with Pine Kernels and Apricots

Serves 4–6
Preparation time: 5 minutes
Cooking time: About 30 minutes
Freezing: Recommended

This is a good light lunch or supper, or a tasty accompaniment to a main course.

2 tablespoons sunflower oil	*grated rind and juice of 1 orange*
375 g (12 oz) red cabbage, shredded	*1 tablespoon raspberry vinegar*
50 g (2 oz) pine kernels	*150 ml (1/4 pint) dry cider*
75 g (3 oz) dried apricots, chopped	*salt and pepper to taste*
1 teaspoon ground cumin	*TO GARNISH:*
1 teaspoon ground coriander	*kumquat slices*
	coriander sprigs

1. Heat the oil in a pan and stir in the cabbage until coated in the oil. Add the pine kernels, apricots, spices, and salt and pepper and sauté for 6 minutes.
2. Add the orange rind and juice, raspberry vinegar and cider. Bring to the boil, then cover and simmer for 25 minutes.
3. Transfer to warmed serving plates and garnish with kumquats and coriander. Serve with bread and cheese.
VARIATION
Serve raw as a salad: Place the cabbage, nuts and apricots in a serving bowl. Add the spices, orange rind, and salt and pepper. Blend the oil, orange juice and vinegar together, pour over the cabbage and toss well. Omit the cider.

Top: Spiced Rice Salad (page 52)

Fennel with Red Pepper Sauce

Serves 4–8
Preparation time: 15 minutes
Cooking time: 12–14 minutes
Freezing: Recommended for sauce only

A delicious, vibrant red sauce is the perfect partner for simply steamed fennel. Serve as a starter, or an accompaniment to fish and chicken dishes.

2 bulbs fennel
15 g (¹/2 oz) butter (optional)
FOR THE SAUCE:
2 red peppers, cored, seeded
*   and sliced thinly*

1 tablespoon lemon juice
salt and pepper to taste

1. First, make the sauce. Place the red peppers and 150 ml (¹/4 pint) water in a pan, cover tightly and bring to the boil. Cook for 10 minutes, stirring once. Drain, then place in a food processor or blender. Add the lemon juice and work to a purée. Return to the pan and add salt and pepper.
2. Meanwhile, trim the fennel bulbs, reserving any fronds for garnish, and cut lengthways into quarters. Place in a metal colander or steamer, cover tightly and steam over boiling water for 12–14 minutes, until just tender.
3. Gently reheat the sauce and serve with the fennel, dotted with the butter if you wish. Garnish with the reserved fennel fronds.

Garden Salad

Serves 4
Preparation time: 20 minutes
Freezing: Not recommended

The vegetables chosen here are in season in the spring and summer; in winter you could use old potatoes, celeriac, beetroot, leeks and cauliflower.

250 g (8 oz) courgettes
175 g (6 oz) carrots
175 g (6 oz) baby turnips
125 g (4 oz) young spinach
*   leaves*
500 g (1 lb) small new
*   potatoes, boiled*

500 g (1 lb) shelled broad
*   beans, cooked*
¹/2 quantity French Dressing
*   (page 9)*
2 tablespoons natural yogurt

1. Coarsely grate the courgettes, carrots and turnips.
2. Place the spinach leaves on 4 dinner plates and arrange all the vegetables in small piles on top.
3. Mix together the dressing and yogurt and drizzle over the salads just before serving.

Stuffed Squash Rings

Serves 4
Preparation time: 30 minutes
Cooking time: About 25 minutes
Freezing: Recommended

A moist nut and cottage cheese mixture makes a tasty filling. When in season, use marrow instead of squash.

1 butternut squash or marrow, weighing about 1 kg (2 lb)	125 g (4 oz) fresh breadcrumbs
600 ml (1 pint) vegetable stock	4 tablespoons chopped herbs (including parsley, marjoram and thyme)
25 g (1 oz) butter	
2 tablespoons oil	1 tablespoon tomato purée
375 g (12 oz) onions, chopped	
125 g (4 oz) mushrooms, chopped	227 g (8 oz) carton cottage cheese
50 g (2 oz) almonds, chopped	dash of Tabasco
25 g (1 oz) desiccated coconut	salt to taste

1. Cut the squash or marrow into 8 rounds and remove the seeds. Place in a single layer in a large shallow pan, add the stock and simmer for 10–15 minutes, until almost tender; cook in 2 batches, if necessary. Drain, reserving the stock, and set aside.
2. Meanwhile, heat the butter and oil in a pan, add the onions and fry gently until light golden. Add the mushrooms and almonds and fry gently for 5 minutes.
3. Remove from the heat, stir in the remaining ingredients and moisten with 8 tablespoons of the reserved stock.
4. Place the squash rings on a baking sheet and fill with the nut mixture. Cook in a preheated oven, 200°C/ 400°F/ Gas Mark 6, for 25 minutes, until tender. Serve hot.

French Dressing

Makes 175 ml (6 fl oz)
Preparation time: 5 minutes
Freezing: Not recommended

Virgin olive oil, which is green in colour, is superior in flavour to ordinary olive oil and improves dressings enormously. Use 1 or 2 cloves garlic, according to personal taste. Any left-over dressing can be stored in the refrigerator for up to 2 weeks.

125 ml (4 fl oz) olive oil	1½ teaspoons clear honey
4 tablespoons lemon juice	1–2 cloves garlic, crushed
1½ teaspoons coarse-grain mustard	salt and pepper to taste

Top: Lentil and Coriander Cannelloni (page 52)

Place the ingredients in a screw-topped jar and shake well to blend. Use as required.

VARIATIONS

Soy Sauce Dressing: Replace the lemon juice with soy sauce. Omit the honey and mustard, and add 2.5 cm (1 inch) piece crushed fresh root ginger. A tasty dressing, ideal for rice and bean sprout salads.

Herb and Peppercorn Dressing: Add 2 teaspoons each chopped parsley, thyme and chives, and 1 tablespoon green peppercorns. Use with leafy green salads, mushroom salads, and tomato salads.

Orange and Mint Dressing: Replace the lemon juice with fresh orange juice. Add 1 teaspoon wine vinegar, 2 tablespoons chopped mint and 1 tablespoon chopped marjoram. A nice refreshing dressing and a perfect complement for chicory, cucumber and watercress salads.

Crudités with Caribbean Dip

Serves 4–6　　　Cooking time: About 7 minutes
Preparation time: 30 minutes　　　Freezing: Not recommended

Use a selection of colourful fruits and vegetables for the crudités; some suggestions are given here – you might try pieces of carrot and celery, sliced bananas or grapes.

FOR THE DIP:	1 tablespoon light soy sauce
125 g (4 oz) creamed coconut	salt and pepper to taste
125 ml (4 fl oz) water	FOR THE CRUDITÉS:
1/2 teaspoon each chilli powder, ground cumin and ground coriander	1/2 fresh pineapple, skin and core removed
1–2 cloves garlic, crushed	1 slice watermelon, weighing 250 g (8 oz)
3 tablespoons crunchy peanut butter	1 each red and green pepper, cored, seeded and sliced lengthways
2 spring onions, chopped	

1. First prepare the dip. Put the coconut and water in a pan and bring slowly to the boil, stirring constantly. Stir in the chilli powder, cumin and coriander, then the garlic and peanut butter.
2. Cook, without boiling, for 5 minutes, stirring constantly. Remove from the heat and stir in the spring onions, soy sauce, and salt and pepper. Leave to cool.
3. If the dip seems too thick, stir in a little cold water. Spoon into a serving bowl and place on a large plate. 4. Cut the pineapple and watermelon into pieces.
5. Arrange the fruits and vegetables around the dip and serve immediately, as an appetizer.

Potato, Egg and Anchovy Salad

Serves 6　　　Freezing: Not recommended
Preparation time: 20 minutes

Serve this delicious dish with a green salad. If you like the flavour, blend an anchovy fillet with the mayonnaise.

500 g (1 lb) small or new potatoes, boiled in their skins	2 tablespoons natural fromage frais
2 hard-boiled eggs	50 g (2 oz) can anchovy fillets, drained
2 tablespoons mayonnaise	salt and pepper to taste
	paprika to garnish

1. Halve or quarter the potatoes and eggs and arrange on a serving platter or in individual serving dishes.
2. Blend together the mayonnaise, fromage frais, and salt and pepper and spoon over the potatoes and eggs.
3. Arrange the anchovy fillets on top in a lattice. Sprinkle with paprika. Serve chilled.
Pictured on page 84

Summer Green Salad

Serves 4　　　Freezing: Not recommended
Preparation time: 10 minutes

This is one of those 'flexible' salads, into which you can throw any leaves you have available – the following is merely a suggestion.

1/2 Cos or crisp lettuce	1 quantity French Dressing (page 9)
1/2 feuille de chêne lettuce	
few roquette or sorrel leaves	2 tablespoons chopped mixed herbs, e.g. mint, chervil, tarragon, marjoram
few young spinach leaves	
frisée leaves	

1. Roughly tear the leaves and place in a bowl. Mix together lightly with the fingers.
2. Pour over the dressing just before serving, toss lightly and sprinkle with the herbs.
Pictured on page 7

Cauliflower Salad

Serves 6
Preparation time: 15 minutes   Freezing: Not recommended

Very lightly blanched cauliflower with celery and a Stilton dressing makes a happy combination. If you want a more substantial salad, add some crumbly Wensleydale cheese.

1 small cauliflower, broken into florets	*125 g (4 oz) smetana*
2 celery sticks, sliced thinly	*2 tablespoons chopped parsley*
50 g (2 oz) blue Stilton cheese	*salt and pepper to taste*

1. Blanch the cauliflower in boiling salted water for 2 minutes. Drain and place in a mixing bowl with the celery.
2. Mash the cheese with a fork and gradually add the smetana to make a smooth paste, seasoning with salt and pepper.
3. Pour over the cauliflower, add the parsley and mix until completely coated. Transfer to a serving bowl.

Curried Potato Salad

Serves 6
Preparation time: 35 minutes, plus making dressing
Freezing: Not recommended

A lovely combination of egg and potato with a lightly curried creamy sauce.

750 g (1½ lb) new potatoes	*1 teaspoon concentrated curry paste*
2 tablespoons French Dressing (page 9)	*2 hard-boiled eggs, cut into 8 wedges*
6 spring onions, sliced thinly	*salt to taste*
150 g (5 oz) smetana	
2 teaspoons tomato purée	

1. Cook the potatoes in their skins in boiling salted water for about 20 minutes, until tender. Drain well, cut into chunks and place in a bowl with the French dressing and spring onions.
2. Mix together the smetana, tomato purée and curry paste until smooth.
3. Pour over the potatoes, add the eggs and mix well until coated. Transfer to a serving dish.

Carrot and Ginger Soup

Serves 4

Cooking time: 30 minutes

Preparation time: 10 minutes

Freezing: Recommended

750 g (1½ lb) carrots	salt and pepper to taste
1 litre (1¾ pints) water	TO GARNISH:
600 ml (1 pint) chicken stock	1 tablespoon chopped parsley
2.5 cm (1 inch) piece fresh root ginger, peeled and grated	1 tablespoon porridge oats, toasted
1 tablespoon orange juice	

1. Cut the carrots in half, or quarter if very large. Place in a large pan with the water and a little salt and cook for about 20 minutes, until very soft. Drain, reserving 300 ml (½ pint) of the cooking liquid.
2. Place the carrots, reserved liquid and the chicken stock in a blender or food processor and work until smooth. Return to the pan.
3. Add the remaining ingredients, bring to the boil, then simmer for 10 minutes. Check the seasoning.
4. Pour into individual soup bowls and sprinkle with parsley and oats to serve. Serve hot or cold.

Courgette and Herb Soup

Serves 4

Preparation time: 15 minutes

Cooking time: 13 minutes

Freezing: Recommended, at end of stage 1

Make this soup in the summer months when courgettes are cheap and plentiful. Served cold, it is a delicious, refreshing starter.

750 g (1½ lb) courgettes, grated	2 teaspoons cornflour
600 ml (1 pint) chicken stock	150 ml (¼ pint) skimmed milk
1 tablespoon lemon juice	salt and pepper to taste
3 tablespoons chopped mixed herbs or 2 teaspoons mixed dried herbs	TO SERVE:
	4 tablespoons natural low fat yogurt

1. Place the courgettes, stock, lemon juice and herbs in a pan and cook for about 10 minutes.
2. Blend the cornflour with a little of the milk. Stir in the remaining milk, then whisk into the courgette mixture. Bring back to the boil and cook for 1 minute, until thickened. Season with salt and pepper.
3. Pour into individual soup bowls and swirl a spoonful of yogurt onto each one. Serve hot or cold.

Parsnips with Onion and Mustard Confit

Serves 4–6
Preparation time: 10 minutes

Cooking time: 4–5 minutes
Freezing: Not recommended

Hot buttered parsnips with a rich creamy confit of onion and coarse-grain mustard make an excellent accompaniment to many vegetarian dishes, grilled steaks and sausages, and roast meats.

375 g (12 oz) small parsnips, scrubbed and sliced thickly
25 g (1 oz) butter
2 onions, halved and sliced very thinly
3 tablespoons white wine

1 tablespoon coarse-grain mustard
2 tablespoons double cream or Greek-style yogurt
salt and pepper to taste
chopped parsley or parsley sprigs to garnish

1. Place the parsnips in a pan, just cover with boiling water, cover and cook for 4–5 minutes or until just tender. Drain well, then return to the pan with half of the butter and keep warm.
2. Meanwhile, melt the remaining butter in a frying pan, add the onions and fry gently for 4–5 minutes, until soft and just beginning to brown. Stir in the wine and mustard and cook over a high heat for a few seconds.
3. Lower the heat and add the cream or yogurt, stir well and season with salt and pepper. Transfer to a warmed serving dish, arrange the parsnips on top and garnish with parsley.

Corn Cobs with Flavoured Butters

Serves 4
Preparation time: 15 minutes, plus chilling
Cooking time: 8–10 minutes
Freezing: Recommended; freeze butters and corn cobs separately

Manageable-sized pieces of corn-on-the-cob and a selection of savoury butters is especially good served as a accompaniment to grilled or barbecued meat and fish, and many vegetarian dishes.

125 g (4 oz) butter, softened
4 corn cobs
CURRIED LEMON BUTTER:
¼ teaspoon garam masala
grated rind of 1 lemon
pepper to taste

HORSERADISH AND CHIVE BUTTER:
1 teaspoon creamed horseradish
2 teaspoons snipped chives
CHILLI AND GARLIC BUTTER:
½ teaspoon mild chilli powder
½ clove garlic, crushed

1. First prepare the butters. Divide the softened butter into 3 equal portions. Blend with the remaining ingredients in 3 separate small bowls.
2. Form the curried lemon butter into a ball, flatten onto clingfilm or greaseproof paper and wrap loosely.
3. Roll the horseradish and chive butter into a cylinder shape and wrap in clingfilm.
4. Shape the chilli and garlic butter into a rectangle brick shape and wrap in clingfilm.
5. Chill all the butters for at least 1 hour.
6. Cut each corn cob into 3 pieces, place in a steamer and sprinkle with pepper. Steam over boiling water for 8–10 minutes, until tender.
7. Meanwhile, using small fancy cutters, cut shapes from the curried lemon butter. Cut the other butters into slices. Arrange on small serving plates.
8. Arrange the corn cobs on a warmed serving dish and serve with the butters.

Salsify with Hazelnut and Lemon

Serves 4–6   *Cooking time: 4 minutes*
Preparation time: 10 minutes   *Freezing: Not recommended*

Salsify has a delicate flavour which is often likened to that of oysters. It is best, therefore, cooked simply, as here with lemon and nut oil. Serve as a contrast to rich foods such as game or to complement chicken and white fish dishes.

500 g (1 lb) salsify   *1 tablespoon lemon juice*
2 tablespoons hazelnut oil   *salt and pepper to taste*
40 g (1½ oz) hazelnuts,   *shredded lemon rind to*
    chopped roughly   *garnish*

1. Peel the salsify and cut into 5 cm (2 inch) lengths. Drop into water with a few drops of lemon juice added to prevent discolouring.
2. Heat the oil in a frying pan, add the salsify and hazelnuts and sauté gently for 4 minutes, stirring constantly, until the salsify is tender and the hazelnuts well browned.
3. Transfer to a warmed serving dish and add the lemon juice and salt and pepper. Garnish with the lemon rind.

Leek and Broad Bean Ragoût

Serves 4
Preparation time: 30 minutes
Cooking time: 25-30 minutes
Freezing: Recommended

Although this is fine as a complete meal, for non-vegetarians it can also be served as a substantial accompaniment for grilled meats or sausages.

50 g (2 oz) butter or   *1 teaspoon chopped thyme*
    margarine   *1 kg (2 lb) fresh broad beans,*
750 g (1½ lb) potatoes, cut   *or 500 g (1 lb) frozen*
    into 1 cm (½ inch) thick   *2 leeks, sliced thickly*
    slices   *284 ml (10 fl oz) carton*
2 cloves garlic, crushed   *soured cream*
25 g (1 oz) plain flour   *2 tablespoons chopped parsley*
300 ml (½ pint) vegetable stock   *salt and pepper to taste*

1. Melt the butter or margarine in a large heavy-based pan, add the potatoes and fry until lightly coloured. Add the garlic and cook for 1 minute.
2. Add the flour and cook for 1 minute, stirring well. Gradually add the stock and cook, stirring, until thickened. Add the thyme, cover and cook for 10 minutes.
3. Add the beans, leeks, soured cream, and salt and pepper and stir well. Cover and cook for 15–20 minutes, until the vegetables are tender. Sprinkle with parsley just before serving.

Baby Corn with Mange tout

Serves 3–6
Preparation time: 2 minutes

Cooking time: 3 minutes
Freezing: Not recommended

1 tablespoon groundnut oil
1 tablespoon sesame oil
375 g (12 oz) baby corn cobs
125 g (4 oz) mange tout,
  topped and tailed

2 spring onions, cut into 2.5
  cm (1 inch) lengths
2 tablespoons light soy sauce
salt and pepper to taste

1. Heat the oils in a wok, add the corn cobs, mange tout and spring onions and stir-fry for 3 minutes. Add the soy sauce, and salt and pepper.
2. Transfer to a warmed serving dish to serve.

White Radish with Red Pepper and Black Beans

Serves 3–4
Preparation time: 10 minutes

Cooking time: 2 minutes
Freezing: Not recommended

White radish (mooli) is a long white milder version of our familiar red radish. Its mild flavour and crunchy texture combine well with red pepper and black beans.

2 tablespoons groundnut oil
375 g (12 oz) white radish,
  peeled, halved lengthways,
  then sliced diagonally
1 red pepper, cored, seeded
  and sliced
4 spring onions, sliced

1 clove garlic, crushed
1 tablespoon chopped fresh
  root ginger
1½ tablespoons salted black
  beans, soaked if packeted,
  or black bean sauce
1 teaspoon sesame oil

1. Heat the groundnut oil in a wok, add the radish, red pepper, spring onions, garlic and ginger and stir-fry for 2 minutes.
2. Stir in the black beans and trickle over the sesame oil. Toss well, transfer to a warmed serving dish and serve immediately.

Classic Spanish Gazpacho

Serves 4–6
Preparation time: 15 minutes, plus chilling
Freezing: Not recommended

3 small slices wholemeal	*4 tablespoons olive oil*
bread, cubed	*2 tablespoons red wine*
600 ml (1 pint) tomato juice	*vinegar*
1 green and 1 red pepper,	*1/2 teaspoon dried basil*
cored and seeded	*salt and pepper to taste*
1/2 cucumber	*TO SERVE:*
1 large onion	*croûtons*
750 g (11/2 lb) tomatoes,	*chopped onion, pepper, olives*
skinned and seeded	*and cucumber*
2 cloves garlic	

1. Place the bread in a bowl, pour over the tomato juice and leave for 5 minutes. Remove the bread, squeezing to extract the juice, and set aside. Reserve the tomato juice.
2. Place the bread, peppers, cucumber, onion, tomatoes and garlic in the food processor bowl and process, in batches if necessary, for about 20 seconds per batch, until smooth.
3. Add all the remaining ingredients and process, in batches, for 3–5 seconds per batch, to blend. Pour into a tureen and chill for at least 1 hour.
4. Serve with bowls of croûtons, and chopped onion, pepper, olives and cucumber, for sprinkling on the soup.

Stir-fried Bean Sprouts

Serves 4 *Cooking time: 6 minutes*
Preparation time: 15 minutes *Freezing: Not recommended*

This dish makes a lovely accompaniment to barbecued spare ribs. It can be easily varied according to the vegetables you have to hand.

1 tablespoon sesame oil	*500 g (1 lb) bean sprouts*
1 large onion, sliced	*2 tablespoons soy sauce*
2 celery sticks, sliced	*2 tablespoons dry sherry*
2 cloves garlic, crushed	*1/2 teaspoon 5-spice powder*
1 red pepper, cored, seeded	*(optional)*
and sliced	*1 tablespoon chopped parsley*
175 g (6 oz) mange tout	*salt and pepper to taste*
175 g (6 oz) button	
mushrooms, sliced	

1. Heat the oil in a wok, add the onion and celery and stir-fry for 2 minutes.
2. Add the garlic, red pepper and mangetouts and stir-fry for 2 minutes.
3. Add the remaining ingredients and stir-fry for 2 minutes, until heated through.

Pumpkin Purée

Serves 4–6
Preparation time: 10 minutes
Cooking time: 10 minutes
Freezing: Recommended

A rich, creamy tasting purée sprinkled with toasted pumpkin seeds. Greek-style yogurt or fromage frais replaces butter and cream for a healthier dish. Serve with roast turkey, or other roast or grilled meats.

750 g (1½ lb) pumpkin flesh,
cut into 3.5 cm (1½ inch)
pieces
4 tablespoons Greek-style yogurt
or natural fromage frais

¼ teaspoon grated nutmeg
salt and pepper to taste
2 tablespoons pumpkin seeds,
toasted, to serve.

1. Steam the pumpkin over boiling water for 10 minutes or until just soft.
2. Mash or purée the pumpkin with the yogurt or fromage frais, nutmeg, and salt and pepper. Transfer to a warmed serving dish and spinkle with the pumpkin seeds to serve.

Stir-Fried Jerusalem Artichokes

Serves 6
Preparation time: 10 minutes
Cooking time: 10 minutes
Freezing: Recommended

Stir-frying need not be confined to Chinese cooking. This tasty mixture of Jerusalem artichokes and tomatoes has a distinctly European flavour. Serve with cheese dishes and grilled or fried meats.

2 tablespoons olive oil
375 g (12 oz) Jerusalem
artichokes, scrubbed, then
cut into 1 cm (½ inch)
pieces
1 small onion, chopped finely

1 clove garlic, crushed
4 tomatoes, skinned and
chopped
1 tablespoon tomato purée
salt and pepper to taste
chopped parsley to garnish

1. Heat the oil in a wok or large frying pan, add the artichokes and onion and stir-fry for 8 minutes.
2. Add the garlic, tomatoes and tomato purée and cook for 2–3 minutes, until the artichokes are just cooked and the tomatoes are soft. Season with salt and pepper.
3. Transfer to a warmed serving dish and sprinkle with chopped parsley to serve.

Tomato Sauce

Makes 350 ml (12 fl oz)   *Cooking time: 20 minutes*
Preparation time: 15 minutes   *Freezing: Recommended*

A versatile sauce which enhances nut loaves, pasta and many other savoury dishes. If you cannot obtain fresh basil, use another fresh herb – such as parsley or chervil – instead.

1 tablespoon olive oil   *397 g (14 oz) can chopped*
1 onion, chopped   *tomatoes*
2 cloves garlic, crushed   *1 tablespoon tomato purée*
1 tablespoon plain wholemeal   *1 tablespoon chopped basil*
    flour   *salt and pepper to taste*
150 ml (¹/4 pint) water

1. Heat the oil in a pan, add the onion and fry until softened.
2. Add the garlic and mix in the flour, then stir in the water, tomatoes, tomato purée, and salt and pepper.
3. Bring to the boil, cover and simmer for 20 minutes, stirring occasionally.
4. Cool slightly, then place in a blender or food processor with the basil and work until smooth. Reheat when required.

Sprouted Mung Salad

Serves 4
Preparation time: 10 minutes, plus making dressing
Freezing: Not recommended

If you sprout mung beans at home you can use them at varying stages. If you use them when still quite short, they have a nutty flavour.

175 g (6 oz) sprouted mung   *2 celery sticks, chopped*
    beans   *6 spring onions, sliced thinly*
2 tomatoes, chopped   *4 tablespoons Soy Sauce*
2 tablespoons chopped parsley   *Dressing (page 9)*

1. Place the sprouted beans in a salad bowl with the tomato, parsley, celery and spring onions.
2. Pour over the dressing and toss thoroughly.

Fennel and Cress Salad

Serves 4
Preparation time: 15 minutes, plus marinating
Freezing: Not recommended

This fresh and tangy salad goes well with fish dishes.

2 bulbs fennel   *2 cartons mustard and cress*
2 tablespoons lemon juice   *salt and pepper to taste*
2 tablespoons olive oil

1. Trim the stalks, base and outer leaves from the fennel.
2. Cut the bulbs in half and shred finely. Place in a salad bowl with the lemon juice, oil, and salt and pepper. Toss thoroughly and leave to marinate for 2 hours.
3. Add the cress and toss again before serving.

Sweet Potato and Celeriac Bake

Serves 4
Preparation time: 30 minutes

Cooking time: 1 hour
Freezing: Not recommended

500 g (1 lb) sweet potatoes	grated finely
500 g (1 lb) celeriac, peeled	1 small onion, chopped finely
284 ml (10 fl oz) carton soured cream	3 spring onions, chopped
125 g (4 oz) Gruyere cheese, grated	25 g (1 oz) medium oatmeal
	15 g (1/2 oz) butter
25 g (1 oz) Parmesan cheese,	salt and pepper to taste

1. Cut the potatoes and celeriac into thin slices; cut the slices into halves or quarters if large. Parboil in salted water for 5 minutes, then drain.
2. Mix together the soured cream, cheeses, onion, spring onions, and salt and pepper.
3. Place half of the potatoes and celeriac in a buttered ovenproof dish. Spread with half of the cream mixture. Repeat the layers. Sprinkle with the oatmeal and dot with the butter.
4. Bake in a preheated oven, 180°C/350°F/Gas Mark 4, for 1 hour, until the vegetables are tender and the topping is golden brown. Serve with a green salad if you wish.

Winter Nut Crumble

Serves 4
Preparation time: 40 minutes

Cooking time: About 30 minutes
Freezing: Recommended

175 g (6 oz) carrots, chopped roughly	salt and pepper to taste
2 parsnips, diced	fresh herbs to garnish
1 small swede, diced	FOR THE TOPPING:
1 leek, sliced	25 g (1 oz) sunflower seeds
150 ml (1/4 pint) milk	25 g (1 oz) chopped nuts
300 ml (1/2 pint) vegetable stock	50 g (2 oz) wholemeal breadcrumbs
283 g can chestnuts, drained	50 g (2 oz) Lancashire cheese, grated
2 tablespoons cornflour, blended with 1 tablespoon water	

1. Place the vegetables in a pan with the milk and stock and bring to the boil. Partly cover and simmer for 15–20 minutes, until almost tender. Add the chestnuts, and salt and pepper, and stir well.
2. Stir in the blended cornflour and cook until thickened and smooth, stirring constantly.
3. Transfer the mixture to a warmed ovenproof dish.

Mix together the topping ingredients and sprinkle evenly over the top. Place under a preheated grill for 5 minutes, until the topping is crisp and golden brown. Serve immediately, garnished with fresh herbs.

Broccoli with Olives

Serves 4–6
Preparation time: 4 minutes

Cooking time: 7 minutes
Freezing: Recommended

A most delicious way to serve broccoli. Best with grilled meat or fish, and pasta dishes.

375 g (12 oz) broccoli
125 g (4 oz) black olives, pitted
3 tablespoons virgin olive oil

½ onion, chopped finely
pepper to taste

1. Trim the broccoli into florets with fairly short stalks. Place in a pan, just cover with boiling water, cover and cook for 4 minutes. Drain well.
2. Meanwhile, reserve about 8 olives; place the remainder in a food processor or blender with 2 tablespoons of the oil, and work to a paste.
3. Heat the remaining oil in a large frying pan, add the onion and fry gently for 3 minutes, until beginning to brown. Stir in the broccoli, olive paste and reserved olives, and heat through. Season with pepper to taste.

Courgettes with Lime and Rosemary

Serves 4–6
Preparation time: 5 minutes, plus marinating
Cooking time: 4 minutes
Freezing: Not recommended

Serve this unusual accompaniment with any grilled or barbecued food.

500 g (1 lb) courgettes, grated
grated rind and juice of 1 lime
2 teaspoons chopped rosemary
25 g (1 oz) butter

1 tablespoon olive oil
salt and pepper to taste
rosemary sprigs to garnish

1. Place the grated courgettes in a bowl and add the lime rind and juice, and rosemary. Stir well, cover the bowl with clingfilm and leave to marinate for at least 3 hours.
2. Drain the courgettes and squeeze out any excess liquid. Heat the butter and oil in a large frying pan, add the courgettes and sauté for 4 minutes, stirring, until hot.
3. Season with salt and pepper and serve immediately, garnished with rosemary sprigs.

Vegetable Kofta Curry

Serves 8
Preparation time:
35–45 minutes

Cooking time: 20 minutes
Freezing: Not recommended

250 g (8 oz) parsnips, chopped
   roughly
250 g (8 oz) carrots, chopped
   roughly
375 g (12 oz) potatoes, diced
2 large cloves garlic
large piece fresh root ginger
1 egg, beaten
6–8 tablespoons plain
   wholemeal flour
1 tablespoon cumin seeds
oil for shallow frying
FOR THE CURRY SAUCE:
2 tablespoons oil

25 g (1 oz) butter
2 onions, sliced
3 cloves garlic, sliced thinly
3.5 cm (1½ inch) piece fresh
   root ginger, chopped finely
1 green chilli, chopped finely
2 tablespoons garam masala
3 tablespoons tomato purée
600 ml (1 pint) water
250 g (8 oz) Greek-style yogurt
salt to taste
TO GARNISH:
lime twists

1. Cook the vegetables with the garlic, ginger and salt in boiling water until tender. Drain and remove the ginger.
2. Purée the vegetables in a food processor or blender. Add the egg and enough flour to make a smooth dropping consistency.
3. Fry the cumin seeds in a minimum of oil until they begin to spit. Add to the vegetable purée.
4. Heat some oil in a frying pan, and drop in spoonfuls of the purée. Fry on both sides until golden, drain on kitchen paper, place on a warmed serving dish and keep warm.
5. To make the sauce, heat the oil and butter in a pan, add the onions and fry gently until softened. Add the garlic, ginger and chilli and fry for 2 minutes. Stir in the garam masala, then add the tomato purée and blend in the water. Season with salt, bring to the boil, then simmer for 15 minutes.
6. Add the yogurt and bring back to the boil. Pour over the koftas and garnish with lime to serve.

Spinach Flans

Serves 6
Preparation time: 20 minutes, plus pastry making
Cooking time: 35–40 minutes
Freezing: Recommended

300 g (10 oz) Wholemeal	*2 eggs*
Pastry (page 118)	*¹/2 teaspoon grated nutmeg*
1 tablespoon oil	*175 g (6 oz) Ricotta or curd*
1 onion, chopped	*cheese*
2 cloves garlic, crushed	*2 tablespoons grated*
500 g (1 lb) frozen chopped	*Parmesan cheese*
spinach, thawed	*1 tablespoon sesame seeds*
4 tablespoons milk	*salt and pepper to taste*

1. Divide the pastry into 6 pieces. Roll out one piece on a floured surface and use to line a 10 cm (4 inch) fluted flan tin. Repeat with the remaining pastry. Chill in the refrigerator while making the filling.
2. Heat the oil in a pan, add the onion and fry until softened. Add the garlic and spinach and cook gently for 10 minutes, stirring occasionally.
3. Cool slightly, then beat in the milk, eggs, nutmeg, cheeses, and salt and pepper.
4. Divide the filling between the flan cases and sprinkle with the sesame seeds. Place on a baking sheet and bake in a preheated oven, 200°C/400°F/Gas Mark 6, for 35–40 minutes, until firm. Serve warm or cold.

Courgette Crumble

Serves 4	*Cooking time: 30 minutes*
Preparation time: 35 minutes	*Freezing: Not recommended*

2 tablespoons oil	*salt and pepper to taste*
2 onions, sliced	FOR THE CRUMBLE:
750 g (1¹/2 lb) courgettes,	*150 g (5 oz) plain wholemeal*
sliced	*flour*
2 cloves garlic, crushed	*25 g (1 oz) margarine*
397 g (14 oz) can chopped	*50 g (2 oz) Cheddar cheese,*
tomatoes	*grated finely*
1 teaspoon dried oregano	*25 g (1 oz) Parmesan cheese,*
1 tablespoon tomato purée	*grated*

1. Heat the oil in a pan, add the onions and courgettes and fry for 10 minutes, stirring occasionally.
2. Add the garlic, tomatoes, oregano, tomato purée, and salt and pepper. Cover and simmer for 10 minutes, then turn into a 1.5 litre (2¹/2 pint) ovenproof dish.
3. To make the crumble, put the flour into a mixing bowl and rub in the margarine until the mixture resembles breadcrumbs. Stir in the cheeses.
4. Sprinkle over the courgette mixture and bake in a pre-heated oven, 200°C/400°F/Gas Mark 6, for 30 minutes, until golden brown.

Vegetable Kebabs

Serves 4
Preparation time: 20 minutes,   Cooking time: About 5 minutes
plus marinating   Freezing: Not recommended

Marinating the vegetables improves their flavour.

12 baby onions
250 g (8 oz) aubergine
250 g (8 oz) courgettes
1 red pepper, cored, seeded
    and cut into squares
12 button mushrooms
salt and pepper to taste
FOR THE MARINADE:
8 tablespoons oil

2 tablespoons lemon juice
2 tablespoons chopped mixed
    herbs
2 cloves garlic, crushed
1 teaspoon ground cumin
1/2 teaspoon ground ginger
1/4 teaspoon turmeric
1/4 teaspoon chilli powder

1. Cook the onions in boiling water for 5 minutes; drain.
2. Cut the aubergine and courgettes into chunks.
3. Mix the marinade ingredients together in a large bowl, add all the vegetables and toss well. Leave for several hours, stirring occasionally.
4. Thread the vegetables onto 8 long skewers, season generously with salt and pepper and cook under a preheated moderate grill for about 5 minutes, turning once, until browned and tender. Serve immediately.

Fennel Goulash

Serves 4   Cooking time: About 30 minutes
Preparation time: 15 minutes   Freezing: Recommended

Goulash is a rich paprika and tomato based stew – here fennel is the main ingredient.

3 bulbs fennel, weighing about
    750 g (1 1/2 lb)
2 tablespoons oil
1 large onion, sliced
2 tablespoons paprika
1 large red pepper, cored,
    seeded and diced
500 g (1 lb) potatoes, cut into

2.5 cm (1 inch) cubes
125 g (4 oz) mushrooms, sliced
1 tablespoon plain flour
397 g (14 oz) can chopped
    tomatoes
300 ml (1/2 pint) vegetable stock
salt and pepper to taste
natural yogurt to serve

1. Cut the fennel stalks into 2.5 cm (1 inch) pieces, then quarter the bulbs.
2. Heat the oil in a pan, add the onion and paprika and fry gently until softened. Add the remaining ingredients, bring to the boil, then cover and simmer for about 30 minutes, until the vegetables are tender.
3. Serve with the yogurt and hot Garlic Bread (page 27).

Artichokes with Avocado Cream

Serves 4
Preparation time: 20 minutes, plus chilling
Cooking time: 40–50 minutes
Freezing: Not recommended

To eat an artichoke, work from the outside in, pulling off the leaves and dipping the fleshy base into the sauce. Eat the fleshy part, then discard the leaves. Eat the heart with a knife and fork. Do not prepare the avocado cream more than 30 minutes in advance.

4 globe artichokes	*3 tablespoons mayonnaise*
juice of 1 lemon	*2 spring onions, chopped*
1 large avocado, peeled,	*1 teaspoon Worcestershire*
halved and stoned	*sauce*
3 tablespoons soured cream or	*salt and pepper to taste*
natural yogurt	*chopped parsley to serve*

1. Remove the stalk from the artichokes and trim the leaf tops if you wish. Boil in plenty of salted water, with half of the lemon juice added, for 40–50 minutes, until the base leaves pull off easily. Drain upside down, cool and chill.
2. Part the leaves and remove the centre hairy choke with a teaspoon.
3. Blend the remaining ingredients together to make a smooth cream. Spoon into the centre of each artichoke and sprinkle with parsley to serve.

Autumn Loaf with Leek Julienne

Serves 6
Preparation time: 40 minutes
Cooking time: 25 minutes
Freezing: Recommended, at end of stage 4

This layered vegetable loaf with its almond filling is simple, though a little time-consuming, to prepare. Guests are sure to be impressed by a pretty slice served with their main course – best served as an accompaniment to crunchy-textured dishes.

375 g (12 oz) kohl rabi cut into 1 cm (1/2 inch) dice
375 g (12 oz) swede, cut into 1 cm (1/2 inch) dice
a little grated nutmeg
1 egg, separated
1 egg white
1/2 teaspoon Dijon mustard
175 g (6 oz) leeks, cut into fine julienne (matchstick pieces)
FOR THE FILLING:
25 g (1 oz) butter
175 g (6 oz) leeks, chopped very finely
75 g (3 oz) ground almonds
salt and pepper to taste

1. Cook the kohl rabi and swede separately in boiling water, or in a two-tiered steamer, for 8–10 minutes or until just soft.
2. Drain well and mash or purée separately, adding to each, nutmeg, salt and pepper, and 1 egg white; reserve the yolk. Stir the mustard into the kohl rabi purée. Set both purées aside.
3. To make the filling, melt the butter in a large frying pan, add the chopped leek and fry gently for 3–4 minutes, until soft and just beginning to brown. Remove from the heat and add the remaining filling ingredients with the reserved egg yolk, stirring well to bind.
4. Grease a 500 g (1 lb) loaf tin and spread the swede mixture over the base. Cover with the leek and almond filling, then spread the kohl rabi mixture on top. Press down firmly and cover with a sheet of buttered foil.
5. Cook in a preheated oven, 200°C/400°F/Gas Mark 6, for 25 minutes.
6. Just before the end of cooking time, blanch the leek julienne in boiling water for 1 minute.
7. Turn out the loaf onto a warmed serving plate. Slice and serve with the leek julienne.

Swede and Bacon Purée

Serves 4
Preparation time: 10 minutes
Cooking time: 8 minutes
Freezing: Recommended

The swede absorbs the full bacon flavour, making this an interesting accompaniment to all meat dishes.

500 g (1 lb) swede, cut into 1 cm (1/2 inch) dice
125 g (4 oz) Tendersweet back bacon, derinded
pepper to taste
1 teaspoon chopped parsley to garnish

1. Add the swede to boiling water, cover and cook for 8 minutes or until soft.
2. Meanwhile, grill the bacon until crisp. Leave to cool slightly, then crumble roughly; set aside 2 teaspoons.
3. Drain the swede well and return to the heat for a few seconds to dry off. Using a food processor or blender, work the swede and bacon together until smooth. Season with pepper and transfer to a warmed serving dish.
4. Sprinkle with the parsley and reserved bacon to serve.

2. Add the cider, vinegar, herbs and sultanas. Season liberally with salt and pepper. Cook for 10 minutes, stirring occasionally.

3. Add the aubergine and okra, cover and cook for 10 minutes. Add the apple and check the seasoning.

4. Transfer to an ovenproof dish and top with the potatoes, neatly overlapping. Sprinkle with salt and pepper and dot with low fat spread.

5. Cover and cook in a preheated oven, 190°C/375°F/Gas Mark 5, for 35–40 minutes. Place under a preheated hot grill for about 3 minutes to brown the potatoes.

6. Sprinkle with the chives to serve.

Vegetable Moussaka

Serves 4	Cooking time: 45 minutes
Preparation time: 30 minutes	Freezing: Recommended

1 large aubergine, sliced	4–5 tablespoons skimmed milk
oil for brushing	3–4 tomatoes, sliced
1 onion, chopped	50 g (2 oz) wholemeal
1 clove garlic, crushed	breadcrumbs
175 g (6 oz) mushrooms	25 g (1 oz) Parmesan cheese,
250 g (8 oz) leeks, sliced	grated
3 celery sticks, sliced	25 g (1 oz) peanuts, chopped
150 g (5 oz) low fat cream	salt and pepper to taste, plus
cheese with herbs and garlic	extra salt for sprinkling

1. Place the aubergine slices on a plate or dish. Sprinkle well with salt, cover and leave for about 10 minutes.

2. Brush a small non-stick pan with oil, add the onion and garlic and fry gently until translucent. Chop the mushrooms, add them to the pan and cook gently until softened, then cook rapidly for about 5 minutes to evaporate most of the liquid.

3. Blanch the leeks and celery in boiling, salted water for 2 minutes; drain well.

4. Drain the aubergines, rinse in cold water and dry on kitchen paper.

5. Blend together the cream cheese and milk until smooth.

6. Place half of the aubergines in an ovenproof dish, cover with the onion and mushrooms, then half of the tomatoes and finally the leeks and celery. Top with the remaining aubergine and tomato. Pour over the cheese sauce, then sprinkle with the breadcrumbs and grated cheese.

7. Cook in a preheated oven, 200°C/400°F/Gas Mark 6, for about 45 minutes. Place under a preheated hot grill for 2 minutes to brown, if you wish. Sprinkle with the peanuts and serve immediately.

Red Cabbage Hotpot

This rich winter mixture of ingredients is very high in fibre. It can be varied according to your own choice of vegetables or to those in season.

Serves 6	Cooking time: 40 minutes
Preparation time: 50 minutes	Freezing: Not recommended

oil for brushing	250 g (8 oz) okra, topped and
2 onions, sliced	tailed
500 g (1 lb) red cabbage,	2 apples, cored and chopped
shredded	250 g (8 oz) potatoes, par-
300 ml (½ pint) cider	boiled and sliced
2 tablespoons cider vinegar	15 g (½ oz) low fat spread
2 tablespoons chopped mixed	salt and pepper to taste
herbs	1 tablespoon snipped chives to
50 g (2 oz) sultanas	garnish
1 large aubergine, chopped	

1. Brush a large non-stick pan with oil, add the onion and fry until translucent. Add the cabbage and cook over a high heat for 5 minutes, stirring.

Minestrone Casserole with Pesto

Serves 4
Preparation time: 30 minutes
Cooking time: 25–30 minutes

Freezing: Recommended, at end of stage 3

2 tablespoons olive oil
1 large onion, sliced thinly
1 aubergine, diced
500 g (1 lb) tomatoes, skinned and chopped
75 g (3 oz) small pasta shapes
125 g (4 oz) cabbage, shredded
432 g (15¼ oz) can red kidney beans, drained

125 g (4 oz) French beans, cut into 2.5 cm (1 inch) lengths
2 courgettes, sliced
150 ml (¼ pint) vegetable stock
2 tablespoons pesto
salt and pepper to taste
TO SERVE:
25-50 g (1–2 oz) Parmesan cheese, grated
garlic bread (see below)

1. Heat the oil in a large pan, add the onion and fry until softened. Add the aubergine and tomatoes and cook gently for 10 minutes.
2. Meanwhile, cook the pasta shapes in boiling salted water for 5 minutes; drain well.
3. Add to the pan with the cabbage, beans, courgettes, stock, and salt and pepper. Bring back to the boil, then cover and simmer for 15–20 minutes, until the vegetables are tender.
4. Just before serving, add the pesto. Sprinkle each portion with Parmesan cheese, and serve with garlic bread.

GARLIC BREAD

Cut a small plain or wholemeal French stick into thick slices, without cutting right through. Mix 125 g (4 oz) softened butter with 3 crushed cloves garlic. Spread over the cut surfaces, wrap tightly in foil and bake in a preheated oven, 200°C/400°F/Gas Mark 6, for about 15 minutes, until the butter has melted and the bread is crisp.

Aubergine and Cheese Bake

Serves 4
Preparation time: 30 minutes

Cooking time: 40–45 minutes
Freezing: Not recommended

2 aubergines, sliced
1 egg, beaten
75 g (3 oz) wholemeal breadcrumbs
6 tablespoons olive oil
397 g (14 oz) can chopped tomatoes
1 teaspoon chopped oregano
1 clove garlic, crushed
1 tablespoon tomato purée

1 teaspoon clear honey
150 ml (¼ pint) red wine
175 g (6 oz) Mozzarella cheese, sliced
50 g (2 oz) Parmesan cheese, grated
salt and pepper to taste
garlic bread to serve (see above)

1. Coat the aubergine slices in the egg and breadcrumbs. Heat half of the oil in a large pan, add half of the aubergine slices and fry on both sides until lightly browned. Drain on kitchen paper. Repeat with the remaining aubergines and oil.
2. Place the tomatoes, oregano, garlic, tomato purée, honey, wine, and salt and pepper in a saucepan. Bring to the boil, stirring, then simmer for 5 minutes.
3. Arrange half of the aubergines in an oiled ovenproof dish and cover with half of the Mozzarella cheese. Repeat the layers. Pour over the tomato sauce and sprinkle with the Parmesan cheese.
4. Cook in a preheated oven, 190°C/375°F/Gas Mark 5, for 40–45 minutes, until the aubergines are tender and the topping is golden brown. Serve with the garlic bread.

Stuffed Marrow with Hazelnuts

Serves 4
Preparation time: 40 minutes   Freezing: Not recommended
Cooking time: 20 minutes

Marrows are only usually available from July to October, so make the most of their short season.

*1 small marrow, halved
  lengthways
oil for brushing
1 large onion, chopped
10 lambs' kidneys, halved and
  cored
3 tomatoes, skinned and
  quartered
150 ml (¼ pint) beef stock*

*1-2 tablespoons dry sherry
1 teaspoon Worcestershire
  sauce
75 g (3 oz) hazelnuts, halved
3 tablespoons wholemeal
  breadcrumbs
1 teaspoon chopped parsley
salt and pepper to taste*

1. Trim off the ends of the marrow halves, scoop out the centre seeds and cut the bases so they lay flat.
2. Cook in boiling salted water for 4–5 minutes; drain well on kitchen paper. Place in an ovenproof dish.
3. Brush a non-stick pan with oil, add the onion and cook gently. Add the kidneys and cook for 1 minute, stirring.
4. Add the tomatoes, stock, sherry and Worcestershire sauce and cook for about 10 minutes, stirring frequently, until the kidneys are just tender.
5. Add 50 g (2 oz) of the hazelnuts, and salt and pepper.
6. Fill the marrow halves with the kidney mixture, then sprinkle with the breadcrumbs. Press down well and cook in a preheated oven, 190°C/375°F/Gas Mark 5, for about 20 minutes or until the top is crisp and lightly golden.
7. Sprinkle with the parsley and remaining nuts to serve.

Right: Three Bean Cassoulet (page 90)

Aubergine Medley

Serves 4   *Cooking time: 40 minutes*
Preparation time: 15 minutes   Freezing: Recommended

*2 aubergines
oil for brushing
198 g (7 oz) can tuna in brine
4 tablespoons peas, cooked
4 tablespoons sweetcorn
  kernels, cooked
1 shallot, chopped finely*

*1 tablespoon lemon juice
25 g (1 oz) breadcrumbs
2 teaspoons sesame seeds
salt and pepper to taste
onion rings and bay leaves to
  garnish*

1. Cut the aubergines in half lengthways. Rub the cut surfaces with a little oil and sprinkle with salt. Place on a baking sheet and cook in a preheated oven, 200°C/400°F/Gas Mark 6, for 20 minutes.
2. Scoop out the centres, leaving a 1 cm (½ inch) thick shell, and chop the flesh into a mixing bowl.
3. Drain off most of the liquid from the tuna. Mix the fish with the chopped aubergine, peas, sweetcorn, shallot, lemon juice, and salt and pepper. Spoon into the aubergine shells and place in an ovenproof dish.
4. Top with breadcrumbs and sesame seeds. Return to the oven for 20 minutes. Garnish with onion and bay leaves and serve with tomato sauce if you wish (see page 18).

Spinach and Courgette Tian

Serves 4 *Cooking time: 35–40 minutes*
Preparation time: 30 minutes *Freezing: Not recommended*

This is a deliciously light dish best made in the summer with tiny sweet courgettes and young spinach leaves.

25 g (1 oz) butter	*2 eggs, beaten*
1 tablespoon oil	*284 ml (10 fl oz) carton single*
1 clove garlic, crushed	*cream*
750 g (1½ lb) courgettes,	*25 g (1 oz) Parmesan cheese,*
grated	*grated finely*
500 g (1 lb) spinach, chopped	*salt, pepper and nutmeg to*
roughly	*taste*

1. Heat the butter and oil in a pan, add the garlic and fry for 1 minute. Add the courgettes and spinach and stir to coat in the oil. Cover and cook gently for 5 minutes, until the spinach has wilted. Transfer to a buttered ovenproof dish.
2. Beat together the eggs, cream, and salt, pepper and nutmeg and add to the dish. Sprinkle with the cheese.
3. Place the dish on a baking sheet and cook in a pre-heated oven, 180°C/350°F/Gas Mark 4, for 35–40 minutes, until the mixture has set lightly and the top is golden.
4. Serve with sesame bread and a tomato and basil salad.

Potatoes Pesto

Serves 4–6 *Cooking time: 10–12 minutes*
Preparation time: 10 minutes *Freezing: Not recommended*

Pesto – the classic Italian sauce – served here with new potatoes, makes a wonderful accompaniment to fish and seafood, cheese dishes and all grilled meats. Use only fresh basil as dried is really not comparable.

750 g (1½ lb) new potatoes	*1 clove garlic, crushed*
FOR THE PESTO:	*3 tablespoons virgin olive oil*
15 g (½ oz) basil leaves	*pepper to taste*
40 g (1½ oz) pine kernels	

1. Cut the potatoes into even-size pieces, or leave whole if small, add to a pan of boiling water, cover and cook for 10–12 minutes or until just tender.
2. Meanwhile prepare the pesto, using either a pestle and mortar, or a food processor or blender. If using a pestle and mortar, chop the basil finely, then grind together with the pine kernels and garlic. Alternatively, work these 3 ingredients together in a food processor or blender.
3. Add the olive oil to the basil mixture and season generously with pepper.
4. Drain the potatoes, then return to the pan. Pour over the pesto, toss gently to coat and serve immediately.

Spinach with Pine Kernels

Serves 4   *Cooking time: 4–6 minutes*
Preparation time: 7 minutes   *Freezing: Not recommended*

This recipe goes well with Italian or Indian-style recipes, or more simply with eggs and fish.

40 g (1½ oz) pine kernels   *500 g (1 lb) spinach, stalks*
1 clove garlic, halved   *removed, shredded*
50 g (2 oz) butter   *salt and pepper to taste*

1. Place the pine kernels and garlic in a large non-stick frying pan and cook, stirring continuously, for 2–3 minutes or until the pine kernels are golden brown. Transfer the pine kernels to a plate and set aside. Discard the garlic.
2. Melt the butter in the same pan and stir in the spinach. Cook, stirring, for 2–3 minutes. Stir in the pine kernels, season with salt and pepper and serve immediately.

Asparagus with Dill Sauce

Serves 4   *Cooking time: 5–7 minutes*
Preparation time: 10 minutes   *Freezing: Not recommended*

Irresistible asparagus spears served with a delicious mock-hollandaise sauce flavoured with dill. Serve with eggs, white meats and fish – especially salmon – or alone as a perfect starter.

12 asparagus spears, total   *¼ teaspoon finely grated*
weight approximately 500 g   *lemon rind*
(1 lb)   *1 tablespoon chopped dill*
FOR THE SAUCE: *pepper to taste*
4 tablespoons mayonnaise   TO GARNISH:
40 g (1½ oz) butter   *dill sprigs (optional)*

1. Break off and discard the woody ends of the asparagus spears. Using a potato peeler, thinly peel the stems. Steam for 5–7 minutes, until just tender.
2. Meanwhile, prepare the sauce. Gently warm the mayonnaise in a small saucepan. Remove from the heat and add the butter, lemon rind and chopped dill. Stir well until the butter has melted, season with pepper and keep just warm.
3. Drain the asparagus and serve immediately, with the sauce poured over. Garnish with dill sprigs, if you wish.

Green Beans with Lemon Sauce

Serves 6
Preparation time: 8 minutes
Cooking time: 4–5 minutes
Freezing: Not recommended

Pretty bundles of beans and a light lemon sauce make a simple and attractive accompaniment – especially good with grilled meat and fish.

250 g (8 oz) dwarf beans
1 courgette or carrot, cut into 5 mm (¼ inch) slices
pepper to taste
FOR THE SAUCE:
1 shallot or ½ small onion, chopped finely

grated rind and juice of ½ lemon
¼ teaspoon celery seeds
5 tablespoons natural set or Greek-style yogurt
salt and pepper to taste
TO GARNISH:
celery seeds

1. Top and tail the beans, trimming to the same length.
2. Using an apple corer, cut out the centre of each courgette or carrot slice to form small rings.
3. Bundle together 6 or 7 beans into each courgette or carrot ring. Arrange the bundles in a steamer and sprinkle with pepper. Steam over boiling water for 4–5 minutes, until just tender.
4. Meanwhile, prepare the sauce. Place the shallot or onion, lemon rind and juice in a small pan. Add 2 tablespoons water, bring to the boil, then lower the heat and stir in the celery seeds and yogurt. Heat gently to warm through but do not boil. Season with salt and pepper.
5. Arrange the bundles of beans with the sauce on warmed serving plates and sprinkle with celery seeds.

Barbecued Aubergine 'Steaks'

Serves 4–6
Preparation time: 20 minutes, plus standing time
Cooking time: 6–8 minutes
Freezing: Not recommended

Thick slices of aubergine, marinated and barbecue grilled, served with a light yogurt sauce flavoured with orange and herbs. Vegetarians especially will love this tasty dish!

2 aubergines, each weighing approximately 250 g (8 oz)
2 teaspoons salt
FOR THE SAUCE:
150 g (5.3 oz) carton natural yogurt
1 teaspoon finely grated orange rind
2 tablespoons orange juice

2 tablespoons chopped mixed herbs
pepper to taste
FOR THE MARINADE:
3 tablespoons olive oil
3 tablespoons clear honey
1 clove garlic, crushed
TO GARNISH:
herb sprigs (optional)

1. Cut the aubergines into 1 cm (½ inch) slices and place in a colander or sieve. Rinse and sprinkle with salt. Leave to stand for 25–30 minutes.
2. To prepare the sauce, mix all the ingredients together in a small bowl and chill until required.
3. To prepare the marinade, mix all the ingredients together in a small bowl.
4. Rinse the aubergines thoroughly to remove the salt and drain well. Place in a bowl, pour over the marinade and leave to stand for at least 20 minutes.
5. Lift the aubergine slices from the marinade and arrange in a single layer on a rack over hot coals or on a grill. Baste liberally with the marinade and cook for 3–4 minutes on each side, basting frequently until well browned.
6. Serve the aubergine 'steaks' hot with the chilled yogurt sauce; garnish with herbs, if you wish.

Vegetable Hotpot with Stilton Croûtons

Serves 4
Preparation time: 45 minutes

Cooking time: 20 minutes
Freezing: Not Recommended

250 g (8 oz) swede, diced	*2 teaspoons Dijon mustard*
1 parsnip, diced	*2 tablespoons chopped parsley*
375 g (12 oz) potatoes, diced	*salt and pepper to taste*
4 celery sticks, chopped	*celery leaves to garnish*
4 leeks, sliced	*FOR THE CROÛTONS:*
40 g (1½ oz) butter or margarine	*75 g (3 oz) Stilton cheese, crumbled*
25 g (1 oz) plain flour	*25 g (1 oz) butter, softened*
150 g (5 oz) carton natural yogurt	*3 slices wholemeal bread, toasted*
50 g (2 oz) walnut halves	*paprika*

1. Place the swede and parsnip in a saucepan with salted water to cover. Bring to the boil, then cover and simmer for 5 minutes. Add the potatoes and celery and cook for 10 minutes, then add the leeks and cook for about 5 minutes, until all the vegetables are tender. Strain, reserving the liquid, and set aside.
2. Melt the butter or margarine in the saucepan, add the flour and cook for 1 minute. Gradually add 300 ml (½ pint) of the reserved vegetable liquid, making up with water if necessary, and cook, stirring, until thickened and smooth. Add the yogurt, walnuts, mustard, and salt and pepper and simmer for 2 minutes. Stir in the vegetables and parsley and mix well. Transfer to a 1.75 litre (3 pint) ovenproof dish and spread evenly.
3. To make the croûtons, beat together the Stilton and butter until smooth. Spread thickly over the bread, then cut into small cubes, about 12 from each slice.
4. Arrange the bread, cheese side up, over the vegetables, to cover them completely. Sprinkle with paprika and bake in a preheated oven, 200°C/400°F/ Gas Mark 6, for 20 minutes, until the topping is crisp and golden. Garnish wtih celery leaves and serve with a mixed salad.
Pictured on page 93

Tomato and Orange Soup

Serves 4–6
Preparation time: 10 minutes
Cooking time: 15–20 minutes

Freezing: Recommended, at end of stage 2

The combination of oranges and tomato is mouth-watering. Make this soup in the summer when tomatoes are plentiful, and serve chilled if you prefer.

1 kg (2 lb) ripe tomatoes, chopped roughly	*1 teaspoon caster sugar*
2 shallots, chopped	*900 ml (1½ pints) chicken stock*
1 carrot, grated	*250 g (8 oz) Greek-style yogurt*
2 tablespoons chopped basil	*¼ teaspoon grated nutmeg*
2 tablespoons grated orange rind	*salt and pepper to taste*
4 tablespoons freshly squeezed orange juice	*1 tablespoon snipped chives to garnish*

1. Place all the ingredients, except the yogurt, nutmeg and chives, in a saucepan. Bring to the boil, then simmer for 15–20 minutes, until the tomatoes are tender.
2. Purée in a food processor or blender, then sieve.
3. Return to the pan, stir in the yogurt and nutmeg and heat gently; do not boil.
4. Pour into individual soup dishes and sprinkle with the chives. Serve with savoury crackers.

Green and White Floret Gratin

Serves 4
Preparation time: 15 minutes

Cooking time: 15 minutes
Freezing: Recommended

A sophisticated variation of one of the most popular vegetable dishes ever known!

1 cauliflower, cut into florets
250 g (8 oz) broccoli, cut into florets
25 g (1 oz) butter
25 g (1 oz) plain flour
1 teaspoon coarse-grain mustard

300 ml (¹/2 pint) milk
175 g (6 oz) matured Cheddar cheese, or half Cheddar and half Gruyère, grated
25 g (1 oz) walnut pieces
1 tablespoon sesame seeds
salt and pepper to taste

1. Cook the cauliflower and broccoli in boiling water for 5 minutes. Drain, reserving 150 ml (¼ pint) of the cooking liquid, and keep warm.
2. Melt the butter in a small saucepan, stir in the flour and cook, stirring, for 1–2 minutes. Stir in the mustard and milk and bring to the boil, stirring constantly, until smooth.
3. Stir in three quarters of the cheese and the reserved liquid to give the sauce a coating consistency. Season with salt and pepper.
4. Arrange the vegetables in a heatproof serving dish, pour over the sauce, then sprinkle with the reserved cheese, walnuts and sesame seeds. Place under a pre-heated hot grill until golden brown. Serve with creamed or jacket potatoes.

Parsnip and Potato Cakes

Serves 4
Preparation time: 30 minutes
Cooking time: 10–15 minutes per batch
Freezing: Recommended

500 g (1 lb) parsnips, chopped roughly
500 g (1 lb) potatoes, chopped roughly
1 tablespoon oil, plus extra for shallow-frying
1 small onion, chopped finely
2 tablespoons chopped parsley
¹/2 teaspoon grated nutmeg
squeeze of lemon juice
salt and pepper to taste

FOR THE COATING:
50 g (2 oz) hazelnuts, shredded
25 g (1 oz) porridge oats
2 tablespoons chopped parsley
FOR THE SAUCE (OPTIONAL):
125 g (4 oz) redcurrants
125 ml (¹/4 pint) vegetable stock
1 teaspoon arrowroot
3 tablespoons light brown soft sugar

1. Cook the parsnips and potatoes together in a minimum of boiling salted water for about 15 minutes, until tender.

Drain well, then mash.
2. Heat the oil in a pan, add the onion and fry gently until golden, then add to the parsnip mixture with the remaining ingredients. Mix well, then shape into 16 'cakes'.
3. Combine the coating ingredients and use to coat the 'cakes', pressing on firmly.
4. Heat a little oil in a frying pan and fry the 'cakes' in batches until golden on both sides. Place on a warmed serving dish and keep warm.
5. To make the sauce, if required, place all the ingredients in a small pan. Heat gently, stirring, until thickened, then simmer for 1–2 minutes. Season with salt and pepper.
6. Serve the parsnip and potato cakes with the sauce, mange tout or peas and carrot sticks.

Bottom: Brazil and Bulgar Wheat Burgers (page 102)

Celery, Gruyère and Almond Bake

Serves 4
Preparation time: 20 minutes

Cooking time: About 1 hour
Freezing: Not recommended

This can be made more substantial by baking in a pastry crust, if you wish.

1 large head celery, sliced into 2.5 cm (1 inch) lengths
300 ml (1/2 pint) vegetable stock
3 eggs
450 ml (3/4 pint) milk
50 g (2 oz) ground almonds
25 g (1 oz) fresh wholemeal breadcrumbs

175 g (6 oz) Gruyère cheese, grated
good pinch of mustard powder
1 teaspoon paprika
25 g (1 oz) flaked almonds
salt and pepper to taste

1. Cook the celery in the stock for about 15 minutes, until just tender. Drain thoroughly. (Discard the stock, or use it for something else.)
2. Beat together the eggs and milk, then stir in the remaining ingredients, except the flaked almonds. Transfer to a buttered ovenproof dish and sprinkle with the almonds.
3. Place the dish in a roasting tin and pour in boiling water to come about halfway up the sides of the dish. Cook in a preheated oven, 160°C/325°F/Gas Mark 3, for about 1 hour, until set and golden. Serve with new potatoes and baked tomatoes.

Cashew Nut Curry

Serves 4
Preparation time: 25 minutes

Cooking time: 30 minutes
Freezing: Not recommended

50 g (2 oz) desiccated coconut
1 teaspoon coriander seeds
1 teaspoon poppy seeds
1 teaspoon ground cumin
1/2 teaspoon turmeric
1/4 teaspoon chilli powder
2 tablespoons oil
6 celery sticks, sliced
2 onions, sliced
250 g (8 oz) unsalted cashew nuts, broken
300 ml (1/2 pint) vegetable stock

4 tomatoes, skinned and chopped
salt and pepper to taste
FOR THE MANGO RAITA:
1 large ripe mango
150 g (5 oz) carton natural set yogurt
1 spring onion, sliced
1 teaspoon cumin seeds, roasted
TO GARNISH:
shredded coriander leaves

1. Grind the coconut, coriander and poppy seeds, cumin, turmeric and chilli powder together in a coffee grinder. Alternatively, use an electric blender, adding 1 tablespoon of the oil.
2. Heat the oil in a pan, add the celery and onions and fry gently for 5 minutes, until lightly coloured. Add the ground spices and cashews and cook for 5 minutes, stirring frequently. Add the stock and bring to the boil. Add the tomatoes, cover and simmer for 30 minutes. Season with salt and pepper.
3. Meanwhile, prepare the mango raita. Cut the mango either side of the stone, scoop out all the flesh and chop. Mix with the remaining ingredients.
4. Sprinkle the curry with shredded coriander and serve with the raita.

Pictured on page 7

Mediterranean Vegetable Stew

Serves 4
Preparation time: 45 minutes

Cooking time: 45 minutes
Freezing: Recommended

Ratatouille is traditionally made with a lot of oil. This is a lighter version which uses just a little oil and stews the vegetables in tomato sauce.

375 g (12 oz) aubergine, cut into large cubes
2 tablespoons olive oil
1 Spanish onion, chopped
2 cloves garlic, crushed
1 each red, yellow and green pepper, cored, seeded and cut into 2.5 cm (1 inch) squares

550 g (1.2 lb) jar passata
6 basil leaves, chopped roughly
1 teaspoon chopped oregano
250 g (8 oz) courgettes, sliced thickly
175 g (6 oz) mushrooms
salt and pepper to taste
cheese bread to serve (see below)

1. Place the aubergine in a colander, sprinkle with salt, place a plate on top and leave to drain for 30 minutes. Rinse and dry with kitchen paper.
2. Heat the oil in a heavy-based saucepan, add the onion and garlic and fry until softened. Add the peppers and fry for 5 minutes.
3. Add the aubergine, passata, herbs, and salt and pepper, bring to the boil, then cover and simmer for 20 minutes.
4. Add the courgettes and mushrooms and cook for 25 minutes, until the vegetables are tender. Serve with hot cheese bread.
To make cheese bread: Cut a small plain or wholemeal French stick into thick slices, without cutting right through. Grate 50 g (2 oz) matured Cheddar cheese and mix into 125 g (4 oz) softened butter. Spread over the cut surfaces, wrap tightly in foil and bake in a preheated oven, 200°C/ 400°F/Gas Mark 6, for about 15 minutes, until the butter has melted and the bread is crisp.
Pictured on page 111

Avocado and Watercress Salad

Serves 6
Preparation time: 15 minutes, plus making dressing
Freezing: Not recommended

This is a 'last-minute' salad, so allow yourself a few minutes to prepare the avocado and toss the salad.

2 bunches watercress
3 avocados
3 tablespoons chopped thyme
1 teaspoon grated lemon rind
1 quantity French Dressing (page 9)

FOR THE CROÛTONS:
6 slices bread
4 tablespoons oil
6 cloves garlic, sliced thickly
2 tablespoons chopped parsley

1. First, make the croûtons. Cut the bread into 1 cm (¹/₂ inch) squares.
2. Heat the oil in a small pan, add the garlic slices and cook until browned; discard with a slotted spoon. Add the bread to the pan and fry for 1–2 minutes, until golden brown. Drain on kitchen paper, then sprinkle with the parsley.
3. Place the watercress on a plate. Peel, stone and slice the avocados widthways and arrange on top.
4. Add the thyme and lemon rind to the dressing and shake well to blend. Spoon over the salad and sprinkle with the croûtons. Serve immediately.

Pasta and Rice Dishes

Wholewheat pasta and brown rice are two of the most popular and accessible wholefoods. Higher in dietary fibre – with all its benefits for health – than their refined counterparts, both these foods have delicious nutty tastes and add wonderful textures to dishes in which they are included.

This chapter contains a delicious selection of recipes for a wide range of accompaniments and main courses using pasta and rice. Most can be made either with wholewheat pasta and brown rice or with other kinds. Some are suitable as vegetarian meals, others include meat or fish, showing how easy it is to follow a wholefood diet that contains a wide range of foods yet conforms to the latest nutritional advice.

Right (clockwise from top left): Tagliatelle with Olive Sauce, Prawn Pilaf, Brown Rice and Bean Salad (page 39), Chicken Liver Pan Pasta (page 48)

Prawn Pilaf

Serves 4	Cooking time: 40–45 minutes
Preparation time: 15 minutes	Freezing: Not recommended

2 tablespoons oil	50 g (2 oz) cashew nuts
1 onion, chopped	1 clove garlic, crushed
2 celery sticks, sliced	125 g (4 oz) button
250 g (8 oz) brown rice	mushrooms, sliced
600 ml (1 pint) water	375 g (12 oz) peeled prawns
(approximately)	2 tablespoons chopped dill
1 red pepper, cored, seeded	salt and pepper to taste, plus
and diced	1 teaspoon salt

1. Heat 1 tablespoon of the oil in a pan, add the onion and celery and fry until softened.
2. Add the rice and cook for 2 minutes, stirring to coat it in the oil. Add the water and 1 teaspoon salt and bring to the boil.
3. Cover and simmer for 35–40 minutes, adding more water if necessary.
4. Meanwhile, heat the remaining oil in a pan, add the red pepper and cashew nuts, and fry for 3 minutes, stirring occasionally.
5. Add the garlic and mushrooms and fry for 3 minutes, stirring occasionally.
6. Add to the rice with the prawns, dill, and salt and pepper and heat through. Serve immediately.

Tagliatelle with Olive Sauce

Serves 4	
Preparation time: 10 minutes	
Cooking time: 10 minutes	
Freezing: Recommended for sauce only	

500 g (1 lb) wholewheat	397 g (14 oz) can chopped
tagliatelle or spaghetti	tomatoes
FOR THE SAUCE:	1/2 teaspoon dried oregano
1 tablespoon olive oil	50 g (2 oz) olives, stoned
1 onion, sliced	salt and pepper to taste
1 red pepper, cored, seeded	TO SERVE:
and sliced	grated Parmesan cheese
2 cloves garlic, crushed	

1. First, prepare the sauce. Heat the oil in a pan, add the onion and red pepper and cook gently for 5 minutes, stirring occasionally. Add the remaining ingredients and cook for 5 minutes.
2. Cook the tagliatelle or spaghetti according to packet directions, drain well, then turn into a warmed serving dish.
3. Pour over the sauce and sprinkle with Parmesan cheese, or hand it separately, to serve.

Brown Rice Salad with Chicory

Serves 4
Preparation time: 20 minutes, plus cooking rice
Freezing: Not recommended

250 g (8 oz) brown rice,	FOR THE DRESSING:
cooked and hot	*4 tablespoons olive or*
7.5 cm (3 inch) piece cucumber	*sunflower oil*
1 head chicory	*2 tablespoons wine vinegar*
2 hard-boiled eggs, chopped	*1 tablespoon freshly squeezed*
1 large carrot, grated	*orange juice*
4 spring onions, chopped	*1 teaspoon clear honey*
8–12 black olives, pitted	*1 teaspoon coarse-grain*
salt and pepper to taste	*mustard*

1. Mix together the dressing ingredients, then toss into the hot rice. Leave to cool.
2. Quarter the cucumber lengthways, discard the seeds, then slice thinly.
3. Cut off the tips halfway down the chicory head and set aside for garnish. Slice the stem into rings.
4. Add the cucumber, chicory and remaining ingredients to the rice and toss well. Check the seasoning.
5. Line the edge of a shallow dish with the chicory tips and pile the salad into the centre to serve.

Indonesian Hot Rice Salad

Serves 6
Preparation time: 15 minutes, plus cooking rice
Freezing: Not recommended

4 tablespoons sesame oil	*250 g (8 oz) bean sprouts*
juice of 2 limes or 1 lemon	*2 celery sticks, sliced*
1 clove garlic, crushed	*50 g (2 oz) raisins*
2 dried red chillies, seeded and	*50 g (2 oz) unsalted peanuts*
crushed	*50 g (2 oz) cashew nuts,*
2 tablespoons soy sauce	*toasted (optional)*
1–2 teaspoons clear honey	*2 tablespoons sesame seeds,*
2 tablespoons wine vinegar	*toasted*
375 g (12 oz) brown rice,	*1 small red pepper, cored,*
cooked and hot	*seeded and sliced*
3 spring onions, sliced thinly	*salt and pepper to taste*
227 g (8 oz) can pineapple	
pieces in natural juice	

1. Place the oil, lime or lemon juice, garlic, chillies, soy sauce, honey, vinegar, and salt and pepper in a large bowl and mix well.
2. Add the hot rice and remaining ingredients and mix well. Check the seasoning. Serve hot or cold.

Nutty Fish Risotto

Serves 4
Preparation time: 15 minutes

Cooking time: 40 minutes
Freezing: Recommended

2 onions, sliced
250 g (8 oz) brown rice
1 vegetable or chicken stock cube
900 ml (1½ pints) water
1 tablespoon chopped parsley
1 tablespoon lemon juice

500 g (1 lb) white fish,
    skinned, boned and flaked
50 g (2 oz) flaked almonds,
    toasted
125 g (4 oz) Gouda cheese, grated
pepper to taste
lemon wedges, to garnish

1. Place the onions, rice, stock cube and water in a large saucepan. Bring to the boil, cover and simmer for about 30 minutes, stirring occasionally.
2. Add the parsley, lemon juice, fish and lots of pepper. Cook over a high heat for about 10 minutes, until the fish is cooked and any remaining water has evaporated.
3. Add the almonds and cheese and check the seasoning. Serve garnished with lemon wedges.

Brown Rice and Bean Salad

Serves 6–8
Preparation time: 25–30 minutes,
plus making dressing

Cooking time: 30 minutes
Freezing: Not recommended

250 g (8 oz) brown rice
208 g (7 oz) can red kidney beans,
    drained
432 g (14 oz) can flageolets,
    drained
25 g (1 oz) butter
2 shallots, chopped finely
3 spring onions, chopped
2 celery sticks, chopped
50 g (2 oz) button mushrooms,
    sliced

1 each small red and green pepper,
    cored, seeded and sliced
2 tablespoons chopped marjoram
1 quantity French Dressing
    (page 9)
salt and pepper to taste, plus 1
    teaspoon salt
50 g (2 oz) roasted peanuts, to
    serve

1. Rinse the rice and beans separately under running cold water; drain well.
2. Melt the butter, add the shallots and fry gently for 5 minutes, stirring occasionally. Stir in the rice.
3. Cover with boiling water, add 1 teaspoon salt, cover and simmer for 25–30 minutes, until just tender. Drain well and cool under running cold water; drain again.
4. Place in a large bowl and add the beans, spring onions, celery, mushrooms, peppers, and salt and pepper. Mix well.
5. Add the marjoram to the dressing and shake well to blend. Pour over the salad and toss well.
6. Spoon into a serving dish and sprinkle with nuts.
Pictured on page 36

Bottom: Mackerel in Cider (page 75)

Macaroni and Vegetable Pie

Serves 4
Preparation time: 25 minutes, plus cooking beans and pasta
Cooking time: 30–35 minutes
Freezing: Recommended

25 g (1 oz) margarine	125 g (4 oz) red or white
2 leeks, sliced	kidney beans, cooked
2 carrots, sliced	250 g (8 oz) wholewheat
1 clove garlic, crushed	macaroni, cooked
2 × 397 g (14 oz) cans plum	175 g (6 oz) Cheddar cheese,
tomatoes	grated
2 oregano sprigs or 1 teaspoon	2 eggs, beaten
dried oregano	4 tablespoons fresh wholemeal
1 thyme sprig or 1/2 teaspoon	breadcrumbs
dried thyme	salt and pepper to taste

1. Melt the margarine in a pan, add the leeks, carrots and garlic, cover and cook gently until softened.
2. Add the tomatoes with their juice, herbs, and salt and pepper, and bring to the boil. Add the beans and simmer for 5 minutes.
3. Mix the vegetables with the pasta, add two thirds of the cheese and cool slightly. Stir in the eggs, then transfer to a large ovenproof dish.
4. Mix the remaining cheese with the breadcrumbs and sprinkle on top. Bake in a preheated oven, 190°C/375°F/Gas Mark 5, for 30–35 minutes, until crisp and golden. Leave to stand for a few minutes before serving.

Spaghetti Soufflé

Serves 3–4

Preparation time: 25 minutes, plus cooking pasta	Cooking time: 40 minutes
	Freezing: Not recommended

50 g (2 oz) butter	3 eggs, separated
40 g (1 1/2 oz) plain flour	75 g (3 oz) wholewheat
1/4 teaspoon mustard powder	spaghetti, cooked and
300 ml (1/2 pint) hot milk	chopped roughly
75 g (3 oz) matured Cheddar	3 tablespoons dried
or Gruyère cheese, grated	wholemeal breadcumbs
50 g (2 oz) Parmesan cheese,	salt and pepper to taste
grated	

1. Melt the butter in a pan, add the flour and mustard and cook, stirring, for 1 minute. Gradually stir in the milk until smooth. Simmer for 2 minutes.
2. Remove from the heat and stir in the cheeses, reserving 1 tablespoon Parmesan. Cool slightly, then beat in the egg yolks, spaghetti, and salt and pepper.
3. Brush the inside of a 1.2 litre (2 pint) soufflé dish with oil, then coat with the breadcrumbs.
4. Whisk the egg whites until stiff. Stir 1 tablespoon into the sauce to lighten, then fold in the rest. Spoon into the dish, sprinkle with the reserved Parmesan and bake in a preheated oven, 180°C/350°F/Gas Mark 4, for about 40 minutes, until risen and golden. Serve immediately.

Pasta with Carrots and Thyme

Serves 4–6
Preparation time: 10 minutes

Cooking time: About 10 minutes
Freezing: Not recommended

250 g (8 oz) pasta shapes	1 teaspoon clear honey
500 g (1 lb) carrots, cut into chunks or sticks	3 thyme sprigs or 1 teaspoon dried thyme
25 g (1 oz) butter	2 tablespoons chopped parsley
4 spring onions, chopped	juice of 1/2 lemon
150 ml (1/4 pint) vegetable stock or water	salt and pepper to taste chopped parsley to garnish
150 ml (1/4 pint) dry cider	

1. Cook the pasta according to packet instructions. Meanwhile, place all the remaining ingredients in a saucepan, cover and cook for 5–10 minutes, until the carrots are tender.
2. Drain the pasta, toss into the carrot mixture and serve hot, sprinkled with parsley.

Pasta with Ratatouille

Serves 4–6
Preparation time: 25 minutes

Cooking time: 10 minutes
Freezing: Recommended

This can be served as an accompaniment to meat, fish or other vegetables, or as a light meal in itself topped with grated cheese or served with poached eggs. It is particularly nice made with wholewheat pasta.

1 small aubergine	1 red or green pepper, cored, seeded and sliced
1 large courgette	
250 g (8 oz) pasta shapes	397 g (14 oz) can chopped tomatoes
3 tablespoons olive oil	
1 onion, sliced	1 teaspoon Herbes de Provence or mixed dried herbs
1 clove garlic, crushed	
	salt and pepper to taste

1. Cut the aubergine and courgette into fingers about 1 cm (1/2 inch) thick. Place the aubergine in a colander and sprinkle lightly with salt. Leave to drain for about 20 minutes, then rinse well and pat dry with kitchen paper.
2. Cook the pasta according to packet instructions.
3. Meanwhile, heat 2 tablespoons of the oil in a pan, add the onion and garlic and fry gently for about 3 minutes. Add the pepper, courgette and aubergine, cover and cook for 3 minutes.
4. Add the tomatoes, herbs, and salt and pepper. Cover and cook for 3 minutes.
5. Drain the pasta, toss in the remaining oil, then add to the ratatouille. Serve hot or cold.

Right: Chicken and Corn Pancakes (page 86)

1. Place the rice and stock in a pan, cover and simmer gently for 30 minutes. Add the butter.
2. Meanwhile, break the broccoli into small pieces and slice the stalks if necessary.
3. Towards the end of the rice cooking time, heat the oil and garlic in a pan, add the vegetables and stir-fry for about 5 minutes. Add the soy sauce or ketchup, and salt and pepper.
4. Stir into the rice and garnish with the nuts, if you wish.

Chunky Chicken Rice

Serves 2	*Cooking time: 45 minutes*
Preparation time: 25 minutes	*Freezing: Recommended*

Chicken joints could be used instead of cooked chicken. Add to the rice with the apple juice and stock. This is a good supper for children.

2 tablespoons oil	*175 ml (6 fl oz) passata or*
1 large onion, chopped	*creamed tomatoes*
1 clove garlic, crushed	*125 g (4 oz) frozen peas*
2 celery sticks, chopped	*250 g (8 oz) cooked chicken,*
125 g (4 oz) brown rice	*chopped*
150 ml (¼ pint) apple juice	*2 tablespoons chopped parsley*
300 ml (½ pint) chicken stock	*salt and pepper to taste*
or water	

1. Heat the oil in a large flameproof casserole, add the onion, garlic and celery and fry gently for about 10 minutes, stirring occasionally.
2. Add the rice and stir until coated with oil, then fry for 1 minute. Add the apple juice, stock or water, and salt and pepper and bring to the boil. Cover and cook in a pre-heated oven, 190°C/375°F/Gas Mark 5, for 30 minutes.
3. Add the passata, peas and chicken, stir thoroughly and return to the oven for 15 minutes.
4. Stir in the parsley and serve with a salad.

Brown Rice with Broccoli, Celery and Nuts

Serves 4	*Cooking time: 30 minutes*
Preparation time: 15 minutes	*Freezing: Recommended*

250 g (8 oz) brown rice	*4 spring onions, sliced*
750 ml (1¼ pints) light stock	*diagonally*
15 g (½ oz) butter	*2 tablespoons soy sauce or*
250 g (8 oz) broccoli florets	*mushroom ketchup*
3 tablespoons sunflower oil	*salt and pepper to taste*
1 clove garlic, crushed	*25 g (1 oz) hazelnuts or flaked*
2 celery sticks, sliced	*almonds, toasted, to*
diagonally	*garnish (optional)*

Saffron and Ginger Pilaf

Serves 4–6   Cooking time: 25 minutes
Preparation time: 30 minutes   Freezing: Recommended

An aromatic special rice, with an unusual crunch of fried vermicelli – ideal for entertaining.

pinch of saffron threads
1 tablespoon oil
25 g (1 oz) butter
1 onion, chopped
1 clove garlic, crushed
2.5 cm (1 inch) piece fresh root ginger, chopped

250 g (8 oz) long-grain rice, preferably Basmati
600 ml (1 pint) vegetable stock or water
25 g (1 oz) vermicelli
salt and pepper to taste

1. Soak the saffron in a little boiling water for 30 minutes.
2. Heat the oil and half of the butter in a large pan, add the onion, garlic, and ginger and fry for about 3 minutes, until softened.
3. Add the rice, fry for 7 minutes, stirring occasionally, then add the stock, saffron and liquid, salt and pepper. Bring to the boil, cover and simmer for 15 minutes.
4. Meanwhile, break up the vermicelli and fry in the remaining butter until brown, but not burnt.
5. Fork up the cooked rice and gently stir in the vermicelli or sprinkle it over the top to serve.

Fried Rice

Serves 4
Preparation time: 5 minutes, plus cooking rice
Cooking time: 5 minutes
Freezing: Not recommended

Fried rice is made with ready-cooked rice, unlike pilaf in which the rice is fried before cooking. This makes it ideal for using up leftovers. Note that you will need to double the quantity of rice if weighing it after cooking. Add any of the ingredients listed opposite.

2 tablespoons oil
1 clove garlic, crushed
3 spring onions, chopped
125 g (4 oz) long-grain rice, cooked
1 tablespoon soy sauce

1 tablespoon mushroom ketchup
salt and pepper to taste
TO SERVE:
1 teaspoon sesame oil
shredded spring onion

1. Heat the oil in a large frying pan or wok, add the garlic and spring onion and stir-fry for about 30 seconds. Add the rice and stir-fry until coated in the oil.
2. Stir in the soy sauce, mushroom ketchup, and salt and pepper. Heat through for a few minutes, until very hot. Serve sprinkled with sesame oil and spring onion.

VARIATIONS
Add 2 or 3 of the following to the fried rice, up to a total weight of 250 g (8 oz) so that they remain in proportion to the rice: chopped cooked chicken, pork or ham; prawns; mushrooms; cashew nuts or almonds; peas; sliced mange tout; sliced waterchestnuts; bean sprouts; firm scrambled egg; broccoli, cabbage or beans.
Include 1 teaspoon chopped fresh root ginger, a pinch of 5-spice powder, or 1–2 tablespoons dry sherry if you wish.

Curried Chicken Pasta Salad

Serves 1
Preparation time: 5 minutes
Freezing: Not recommended

As a change from curry flavour, omit the curry powder and blend in 1 teaspoon tomato purée instead. This is excellent for packed lunches.

3 tablespoons mayonnaise
2 tablespoons natural yogurt
1/2 teaspoon curry powder
1/2 teaspoon clear honey
125 g (4 oz) cooked chicken, cubed

1/2 red pepper, cored, seeded and sliced thinly
2 pineapple slices, cut into pieces
2 spring onions, sliced
25 g (1 oz) wholewheat pasta shapes, cooked

1. Mix the mayonnaise, yogurt, curry powder and honey together in a bowl.
2. Add the remaining ingredients and mix well until coated.

Breakfast Kedgeree

Serves 4
Preparation time: 15 minutes, plus cooking rice

Cooking time: 5 minutes
Freezing: Not recommended

A really tasty breakfast. Cook the rice the night before then it will only take you a few minutes to assemble and heat through. Finnan haddock is free from artificial colouring and has an excellent flavour.

125 g (4 oz) brown rice, cooked
2 hard-boiled eggs, chopped
1 tablespoon chopped parsley

250 g (8 oz) Finnan haddock, poached and flaked
2 tablespoons smetana
salt and pepper to taste

1. Place the rice, eggs, parsley, fish, and salt and pepper in a pan. Mix together, then heat through gently, stirring.
2. Stir in the smetana and serve immediately.

Cardamom Rice

Serves 4–6
Cooking time: 40 minutes
Preparation time: 15 minutes
Freezing: Recommended

Cardamom is a popular rice spice in the East. It is something of an acquired taste, so try it in small amounts at first. Leave the pods whole if you want a subtle flavour, or break them open and crush the seeds with a rolling pin if you want a stronger flavour.

25 g (1 oz) butter
1 tablespoon oil
1 small onion, chopped
1 clove garlic, crushed
250 g (8 oz) brown rice
1 teaspoon mild curry powder
1/4 teaspoon cinnamon
1/4 teaspoon ground cumin
600 ml (1 pint) vegetable stock
  or water
2 tablespoons lemon juice

1 bay leaf
3 cardamom pods
50 g (2 oz) raisins
1 tablespoon blanched
  almonds, halved
2 tablespoons natural roasted
  peanuts
1 tablespoon cashew nuts
salt and pepper to taste
coriander leaves or parsley
  sprigs to garnish

1. Heat the butter and oil in a large pan, add the onion and garlic and fry for about 3 minutes. Add the rice and fry, stirring occasionally, until opaque.
2. Add the curry, cinnamon and cumin and fry for 1 minute, then pour in the stock or water, and lemon juice. Add the bay leaf, cardamom, raisins, salt and pepper. Bring to the boil, then cover and simmer for about 35 minutes.
3. Meanwhile, spread the nuts in a grill pan and toast until golden, stirring occasionally.
4. Remove the bay leaf and cardamom pods, if used whole, and stir in the nuts. Garnish with coriander or parsley and serve hot as an accompaniment to grilled meats, fish or kebabs.

Bottom: Bulgar Wheat and Lentil Pilaf (page 102)

Tomato and Rice Soup

Serves 4–6
Cooking time: 35 minutes
Preparation time: 10 minutes
Freezing: Recommended

2 tablespoons oil
1 onion, chopped
1 clove garlic, crushed
1 small red pepper, cored,
  seeded and chopped
397 g (14 oz) can chopped
  tomatoes
1 teaspoon chopped marjoram

1.25 litres (2 1/4 pints) stock
1–2 tablespoons
  Worcestershire sauce
2 × 25 g (1 oz) peperami
  sausages, chopped
40 g (1 1/2 oz) long-grain rice
salt and pepper to taste
chopped parsley to garnish

1. Heat the oil in a large pan, add the onion, garlic and red pepper and fry gently for about 3 minutes.
2. Add the tomatoes, marjoram, stock, Worcestershire sauce to taste, and salt and pepper. Bring to the boil, cover and simmer for about 15 minutes.
3. Add the peperami and rice, bring back to the boil, cover and simmer for 15 minutes.
4. Pour into warmed individual bowls and sprinkle with parsley to serve.
Pictured on page 91

Brown Rice Biryani

Serves 4	Cooking time: 45 minutes
Preparation time: 25 minutes	Freezing: Not recommended

Serve puppodums and 1 or 2 Indian salads with this dish: try a mixture of yogurt, chopped cucumber and ground cumin; or try chopped onion and tomato, sprinkled with lemon juice.

2 tablespoons oil	5 cardamom pods, bruised
1 onion, chopped	1/2 teaspoon turmeric
1 cm (1/2 inch) piece fresh root ginger, peeled and chopped finely	1/2 teaspoon salt
	150 g (5 oz) carton natural yogurt
1 clove garlic, crushed	125 g (4 oz) cashew nuts
1/2 teaspoon each cumin and fenugreek seeds	50 g (2 oz) sultanas
	1 teaspoon garam masala
250 g (8 oz) long-grain brown rice	50 g (2 oz) button mushrooms, sliced
600 ml (1 pint) vegetable stock	
2.5 cm (1 inch) piece cinnamon stick	TO SERVE:
	2 hard-boiled eggs, chopped
4 cloves	25 g (1 oz) shelled pistachio nuts, skinned
2 bay leaves	

1. Heat the oil in a large pan with a tightly fitting lid. Add the onion, ginger, garlic, and cumin and fenugreek seeds and fry until the onion is lightly browned.
2. Stir in the rice and cook, stirring, until coated in oil. Add the stock, cinnamon, cloves, bay leaves, cardamom pods and turmeric, bring to the boil, then add the salt. Cover and cook gently for 30 minutes, until all the liquid is absorbed; add a little more stock if the pan becomes too dry.
3. Stir in the yogurt, cashew nuts, sultanas, garam masala and mushrooms, cover and cook gently for 15 minutes.
4. Turn the biryani into a warmed serving dish and sprinkle the egg and pistachio nuts over the top.

Tuna and Pasta Casserole

Serves 2	Cooking time: 20 minutes
Preparation time: 15 minutes	Freezing: recommended

This dish is also very good made with cooked smoked haddock or chicken.

2 carrots, sliced	300 ml (1/2 pint) milk (approximately)
2 celery sticks, sliced	
125 g (4 oz) frozen peas	198 g (7 oz) can tuna, drained and flaked
175 g (6 oz) dried wholewheat pasta	
	125 g (4 oz) Cheddar cheese, grated
2 tablespoons oil	
1 onion, chopped	3 tablespoons wholemeal breadcrumbs
2 tablespoons plain wholemeal flour	

1. Place the carrots and celery in a pan, cover with cold water and bring to the boil. Cover and cook for 15 minutes, adding the peas for the last 5 minutes. Drain, reserving the liquid, and set aside. Meanwhile, cook the pasta according to pack instructions; drain and set aside.
2. Heat the oil in a pan, add the onion and cook until softened. Remove from the heat and stir in the flour.
3. Make up the reserved liquid to 450 ml (3/4 pint) with the milk. Gradually add to the pan, stirring constantly until blended. Bring to the boil and cook for 3 minutes, until thickened.
4. Add the vegetables, pasta, tuna and half of the cheese. Turn into a shallow ovenproof dish and sprinkle with the remaining cheese and breadcrumbs.
5. Cook under a preheated hot grill for 3–4 minutes, until golden brown and bubbling. Serve immediately.

Stuffed Cabbage

Serves 4–6

Preparation time: 45 minutes, plus cooking rice

Cooking time: 45 minutes

Freezing: Not recommended

A whole stuffed cabbage makes an impressive centre-piece as a main meatless meal. It is best made with a close-textured filling which will cut into wedges to serve.

1 primo or Savoy cabbage	125 g (4 oz) brown rice, cooked
25 g (1 oz) butter	2 tablespoons pine kernels, toasted
1 onion, chopped	75 g (3 oz) hard cheese, grated (optional)
1 clove garlic, crushed	
125 g (4 oz) red lentils	1 egg, beaten
600 ml (1 pint) vegetable stock	salt and pepper to taste
1/2 teaspoon ground coriander	
2 tablespoons each chopped parsley and dill	

1. Remove any large loose outer leaves from the cabbage. Cut off the top of the cabbage, then remove the inside leaves, leaving about 2 cm (3/4 inch) thickness all round. (Use the inner leaves for another dish.)
2. Steam or blanch the cabbage shell and its top for 5–10 minutes or until just softened but still firm. Cook and drain upside down.
3. Melt the butter in a pan, add the onion and garlic and fry gently for 5 minutes. Add the lentils, stock, coriander, herbs, and salt and pepper. Bring to the boil, then cover and simmer for about 15 minutes, until the liquid has been absorbed and the lentils are cooked.
4. Stir in the rice, pine kernels, reserving a few for garnish, and cheese, if using. Leave to cool for 5 minutes, then add the egg. Check the seasoning.
5. Spoon into the cabbage shell. Peel some leaves from the blanched top and place over the filling to enclose. Stand the cabbage on a large sheet of greased foil and wrap to enclose completely.
6. Steam for about 45 minutes, or until tender. Leave to stand for about 5 minutes, then unwrap and sprinkle with the remaining nuts. Serve with a sauce such as cheese or lemon or Tomato Sauce (page 18).
Pictured on page 106

Rice and Almond Salad

Serves 8

Preparation time: 15 minutes, plus cooking rice and sweetcorn and making dressing

Freezing: Not recommended

A filling salad, particularly useful to serve at buffet parties. The choice of vegetables you can use is endless – vary according to what is in season.

175 g (6 oz) brown rice, cooked	2 celery sticks, chopped
6 spring onions, chopped	175 g (6 oz) sweetcorn kernels, cooked
1 red pepper, cored, seeded and chopped	2 tablespoons chopped parsley
50 g (2 oz) sultanas	6 tablespoons French Dressing (page 9)
50 g (2 oz) flaked almonds, browned	

1. Place all the ingredients in a bowl and toss thoroughly. Transfer to a serving dish.

Pasta with Mussels and Prawns

Serves 4
Preparation time: 10 minutes

Cooking time: About 12 minutes
Freezing: Not recommended

250 g (8 oz) dried pasta shapes
2 tablespoons olive oil
1 red or green chilli, seeded
  and sliced
1 clove garlic, crushed
250 g (8 oz) can mussels in
  brine
150 ml (1/4 pint) dry white
  wine or cider

397 g (14 oz) can chopped
  tomatoes
1 tablespoon chopped
  marjoram or 1 teaspoon
  dried
125 g (4 oz) peeled prawns
salt and pepper to taste
chopped parsley to garnish

1. Cook the pasta according to pack instructions.
2. Meanwhile, heat the oil in a pan, add the chilli and garlic and sauté gently. Strain the liquor from the mussels into the pan, then add the wine or cider. Simmer for about 5 minutes, until reduced by half.
3. Add the tomatoes and marjoram and cook for about 3 minutes, then add the mussels and prawns. Cook for about 2 minutes, until thoroughly heated. Season with salt and pepper.
4. Drain the pasta, add to the sauce and toss well. Serve immediately, sprinkled with parsley.

Chicken Liver Pan Pasta

Serves 4
Preparation time: 10 minutes

Cooking time: About 12 minutes
Freezing: Not recommended

200 g (7 oz) dried pasta
  shapes
25 g (1 oz) butter
250 g (8 oz) frozen chicken
  livers, thawed and sliced
  thinly
50 g (2 oz) bacon, derinded
  and chopped
2 courgettes, sliced
2 leeks, sliced

125 g (4 oz) button
  mushrooms, sliced
150 ml (1/4 pint) dry cider or
  stock
2 tablespoons dry vermouth
1/2 teaspoon dried sage
4 tablespoons natural yogurt
  or single cream
salt and pepper to taste

1. Cook the pasta according to pack instructions.
2. Meanwhile, melt the butter in a pan, add the liver and bacon and fry for 2 minutes. Add the courgettes, leeks and mushrooms and stir-fry for 5 minutes.
3. Add the cider or stock, vermouth, sage, and salt and pepper. Cover and simmer for 5 minutes.
4. Drain the pasta, add to the sauce with the yogurt or cream and toss gently. Serve immediately.

VARIATION
Use lambs' or calves' liver in place of the chicken livers. Add carrots or red pepper strips for colour.

Risi e Bisi

Serves 4
Preparation time: 10 minutes

Cooking time: 20 minutes
Freezing: Not recommended

This deliciously simple Venetian risotto-soup makes an ideal light lunch.

50 g (2 oz) butter
1 onion, chopped
3 rashers streaky bacon, derinded and chopped
250 g (8 oz) Italian risotto rice
1.25 litres (2¼ pints) chicken stock

½ chicken stock cube
pinch of sugar
500 g (1 lb) frozen peas
50 g (2 oz) Parmesan cheese, grated
2 tablespoons chopped parsley
salt and pepper to taste

1. Melt half of the butter in a pan, add the onion and bacon and fry gently for about 5 minutes, until softened. Add the rice and fry for 1 minute.
2. Pour in the stock, add the stock cube half, sugar, salt and pepper. Bring to the boil, stir, then cover and simmer for about 12 minutes.
3. Add the peas and cook for 3 minutes.
4. Stir in the remaining butter, the Parmesan cheese and parsley. The mixture should be like a very thick soup; add a little extra stock or water if it is too dry.
5. Serve in individual warmed bowls with crusty bread and salad.

Spiced Rice with Prawns

Serves 4
Preparation time: 10 minutes

Cooking time: 25 minutes
Freezing: Not recommended

A quick, spicy supper or light lunch dish. For best results, use Basmati rice.

2 tablespoons oil
1 onion, chopped
1 clove garlic, crushed
1 cm (½ inch) piece fresh root ginger, grated
250 g (8 oz) long-grain rice
1 teaspoon mild curry powder
25 g (1 oz) creamed coconut, in pieces
600 ml (1 pint) chicken stock

250 g (8 oz) peeled prawns
2 tablespoons chopped coriander leaves
4 tablespoons natural yogurt (optional)
25 g (1 oz) flaked almonds, toasted
salt and pepper to taste
lemon slices and coriander leaves to garnish

1. Heat the oil in a large pan, add the onion, garlic and ginger and fry for about 5 minutes.
2. Add the rice and fry for about 2 minutes, until opaque, then sprinkle in the curry powder and fry for 1 minute. Add the creamed coconut, stirring until dissolved.
3. Add the stock, and salt and pepper. Bring to the boil, cover and simmer for about 15 minutes. until the rice is tender and the liquid absorbed.
4. Stir in the prawns and coriander and heat well. If using, stir in the yogurt. Sprinkle with the almonds and garnish with lemon and coriander to serve.

Cashew Nut and Sesame Pilaf

Serves 4	Cooking time: 45 minutes
Preparation time: 35 minutes	Freezing: Not recommended

2 tablespoons oil	750 ml (1¼ pints) vegetable
25 g (1 oz) butter	stock
1 onion, chopped	2 teaspoons soy sauce
1 red pepper, cored, seeded	2 carrots, grated
and chopped	2 courgettes, grated
250 g (8 oz) brown rice	125 g (4 oz) cashew nuts
25 g (1 oz) sesame seeds	4 spring onions, chopped
5 tablespoons white wine	salt and pepper to taste

1. Heat the oil and butter in a heavy-based pan, add the onion and fry until softened. Add the red pepper, rice and sesame seeds and stir well, until all the rice grains are coated in oil.
2. Stir in the wine, stock and soy sauce and bring to the boil, then cover and cook gently for 35 minutes, until almost all of the liquid is absorbed.
3. Stir in the remaining ingredients, cover and cook for 10 minutes, until the rice is tender. Serve hot.

Calabrian Pasta

Serves 4	Cooking time: 10 minutes
Preparation time: 15 minutes	Freezing: Not recommended

375 g (12 oz) broccoli	397 g (14 oz) can chopped
2 tablespoons oil	tomatoes with herbs
2 cloves garlic, sliced thinly	375 g (12 oz) pasta shapes
4 tablespoons pine kernels	salt and pepper to taste
4 tablespoons raisins	

1. Peel the coarse skin from the broccoli stalks. Dice the stalks and cut the broccoli into small florets.
2. Heat the oil in a pan, add the garlic and fry gently until golden. Add the pine kernels, raisins and tomatoes, bring to the boil, then simmer for 10 minutes.
3. Meanwhile, cook the pasta in boiling salted water according to packet instructions, until just tender.
4. At the same time cook the broccoli in a minimum of boiling water for 5 minutes, until just tender. Drain well.
5. Drain the pasta and combine with the tomato sauce and broccoli. Stir well, and season with salt and pepper. Heat through gently and serve immediately.

Tikka Kebabs with Fried Rice

Serves 3–4
Preparation time: 15 minutes,   *Cooking time: 8 minutes*
plus cooking rice   *Freezing: Not recommended*

These kebabs have a slightly spicy flavour. They can also be barbecued very successfully.

1 tablespoon oil   *2 small onions, each cut into 8*
1 clove garlic   *pieces*
1 teaspoon tandoori spice mix   FOR THE FRIED RICE:
4 tablespoons natural yogurt   *1 tablespoon oil*
1 tablespoon lemon juice   *1 onion, chopped*
375 g (12 oz) lean lamb, cut   *375 g (12 oz) cooked brown*
into 2.5 cm (1 inch) cubes   *rice*
1 red pepper, cored, seeded   *198 g (7 oz) can sweetcorn*
and cut into squares   *kernels, drained*
     1 tablespoon chopped parsley

1. Mix together the oil, garlic, spice, yogurt and lemon juice. Add the meat and stir until well coated.
2. Thread alternate pieces of lamb, red pepper and onion onto 4 large or 8 small skewers. Cook under a medium grill for 8 minutes, turning frequently.
3. Meanwhile, make the fried rice: heat the oil in a non-stick pan, add the onion and fry until softened. Add the remaining ingredients and stir constantly until heated through. Serve the kebabs with the rice.

Kashmiri Chicken Pilau

Serves 6   *Cooking time: 1 hour*
Preparation time: 30 minutes   *Freezing: Not recommended*

500 g (1 lb) Basmati rice   *4 tablespoons chopped mint*
4 tablespoons oil   *1 teaspoon curry powder*
2 onions, chopped   *2.5 cm (1 inch) piece*
2 cloves garlic, crushed   *cinnamon stick*
2.5 cm (1 inch) piece fresh root   *125 g (4 oz) frozen peas*
ginger, peeled and chopped   *250 g (8 oz) tomatoes, skinned*
2 teaspoons cumin seeds   *and chopped*
750 g (1½ lb) boneless chicken   *50 g (2 oz) sultanas*
breast, cubed   *salt and taste*
1 teaspoon saffron strands   *50 g (2 oz) blanched almonds,*
300 ml (½ pint) boiling water   *toasted, to garnish*
6 cardamom pods, bruised

1. Rinse the rice several times in cold water, then drain and leave to dry.

2. Heat half the oil in a large heavy-based pan, add half of the onion, the garlic, ginger and cumin seeds and fry for 5 minutes.
3. Add the chicken and cook, stirring, until browned all over. Add the saffron, water, cardamom pods, mint, curry powder and cinnamon stick. Bring to the boil, then cover and simmer for 25 minutes, until the chicken is tender. Transfer to a bowl and rinse out the pan.
4. Heat the remaining oil in the pan, add the remaining onion and fry until lightly coloured. Stir in the rice and cook gently for 2–3 minutes, until it becomes opaque.
5. Add the chicken mixture, peas, tomatoes, sultanas and salt. Stir gently, then shake the pan to level the ingredients. Add sufficient boiling water to come 2 cm (³/4 inch) above the top of the rice. Cover the pan tightly and cook gently for 20–25 minutes, until the rice is tender and all the liquid is absorbed. Discard the cinnamon stick.
6. Transfer to a warmed serving dish and sprinkle with the almonds. Serve with mango chutney, puppodums, and chilled yogurt mixed with chopped cucumber.
Pictured on page 65

Spiced Rice Salad

Serves 4
Preparation time: 40 minutes
Freezing: Recommended

250 g (8 oz) brown rice	*125 g (4 oz) peas, cooked*
1 teaspoon each ground	*1 onion, chopped*
turmeric, cumin, curry	*2 carrots, grated*
powder and coriander	*75 g (3 oz) sultanas*
600 ml (1 pint) water	*75 g (3 oz) unsalted peanut*
2 tablespoons wine vinegar	*kernels, lightly roasted*
4 tablespoons sunflower oil	*salt to taste*

1. Place the rice, spices and water in a pan, bring to the boil, then cover and simmer for 30–35 minutes, until the water is absorbed and the rice is tender.
2. Turn into a bowl and stir in the vinegar, oil and salt. Leave until cold.
3. Fluff up the rice gently with a fork, then stir in the peas, onion, carrot, sultanas and peanuts.
4. Transfer the rice salad to a large serving bowl or 4 individual ones. Serve with a crisp green salad or tomato salad.
Pictured on page 8

Lentil and Coriander Cannelloni

Serves 6
Preparation time: About 1 hour
Cooking time: 40–45 minutes
Freezing: Not recommended

The taste of fresh coriander is unmistakable. Parsley may be used instead, but the flavour will be quite different.

12 sheets lasagne	*50 g (2 oz) fresh wholemeal*
25 g (1 oz) Parmesan cheese,	*breadcrumbs*
grated	*1 egg, beaten*
FOR THE FILLING:	*3 tablespoons chopped*
125 g (4 oz) onion	*coriander leaves*
125 g (4 oz) carrot	*salt and pepper to taste*
2 celery sticks	*FOR THE TOMATO SAUCE:*
1 tablespoon oil	*800 g (1 lb 12 oz) can peeled*
2 cloves garlic, crushed	*tomatoes*
175 g (6 oz) red lentils	*1 teaspoon dried basil*
450 ml (³/4 pint) vegetable stock	*FOR THE WHITE SAUCE:*
1 teaspoon chopped thyme	*25 g (1 oz) butter*
150 g (5 oz) Mozzarella	*25 g (1 oz) plain flour*
cheese, diced	*300 ml (¹/2 pint) milk*
113 g (4 oz) carton cottage	*1 bay leaf*
cheese	*pinch of grated nutmeg*

1. For the filling, finely chop the vegetables. Heat the oil in a pan, add the vegetables and garlic and fry gently for 5 minutes. Add the lentils, stock and thyme, bring to the boil, then cover and simmer for about 20 minutes, until the lentils are soft. Leave to cool.
2. Add half of the Mozzarella and all of the remaining filling ingredients. Stir well, then set aside.
3. To make the tomato sauce, place the tomatoes with their juice, basil, and salt and pepper in a pan. Stir to break up the tomatoes, then simmer for 15 minutes, until thickened. Set aside.
4. For the white sauce, melt the butter in a pan, stir in the flour and cook for 1–2 minutes, stirring. Gradually stir in the milk, then add the bay leaf and nutmeg. Simmer, stirring, for 2 minutes. Remove the bay leaf and season with salt and pepper. Set aside.
5. Cook the lasagne according to packet instructions, drain and lay flat on a work surface. Divide the filling between the sheets, roll up and place in a greased ovenproof serving dish. Top with the tomato sauce, then the white sauce, then sprinkle with the reserved Mozzarella and the Parmesan.
6. Cook in a preheated oven, 200°C/400°F/Gas Mark 6, for 40–45 minutes, until golden. Serve with a green salad.
Pictured on page 9

Paella de Montana

Serves 4–6

Preparation time: 10 minutes

Cooking time: 35 minutes

Freezing: Recommended

pinch of saffron threads
3 tablespoons olive oil
4 rabbit portions
4 chicken portions
250 g (8 oz) pork fillet, sliced
2 cloves garlic, crushed

397 g (14 oz) can chopped
  tomatoes
6 tablespoons chopped parsley
250 g (8 oz) long-grain rice
400 ml (14 fl oz) water
175 ml (6 fl oz) dry white wine
salt and pepper to taste

1. Soak the saffron in 1 tablespoon warm water.
2. Heat the oil in a large pan, add the meats and fry for 10 minutes, until well browned. Remove and set aside.
3. Add the garlic, tomatoes, saffron with its water, 4 tablespoons of the parsley, and salt and pepper. Cook for about 10 minutes, until thick.
4. Add the rice, water, wine and meats. Bring to the boil, then simmer for about 15 minutes, shaking the pan occasionally. Sprinkle with the remaining parsley to serve.

Squid Provençale

Serves 4

Preparation time: 15 minutes

Cooking time: 15 minutes

Freezing: Not recommended

250 g (8 oz) long-grain rice
2 tablespoons olive oil
1 onion, sliced
2 cloves garlic, crushed
1 green pepper, cored, seeded
  and sliced
150 ml (1/4 pint) dry white wine
397 g (14 oz) can chopped
  tomatoes

4 tablespoons water
1 small rosemary sprig
500 g (1 lb) cleaned squid,
  sliced
2 tablespoons brandy
salt and pepper to taste
rosemary sprigs to garnish

1. Cook the rice.
2. Meanwhile, heat the oil in a pan, add the onion, garlic and green pepper and fry until softened. Add the wine and cook until reduced by half.
3. Add the remaining ingredients, except the brandy, and simmer for 10 minutes, stirring. Stir in the brandy and cook for another minute.
4. Garnish with rosemary and serve with the rice.

Pigeon and Brown Rice Casserole

Serves 4
Preparation time: 30 minutes, plus cooking chick peas
Cooking time: 1 hour
Freezing: Recommended if using fresh pigeons

3 tablespoons plain wholemeal flour	1 onion, studded with 8 cloves
1 teaspoon chilli powder	2 bay leaves
1/2 teaspoon salt	2 tablespoons tomato purée
4 wood pigeons	175 g (6 oz) brown rice
2 tablespoons olive oil	1/4 small white cabbage, shredded
75 g (3 oz) streaky bacon, derinded and diced	125 g (4 oz) chorizo sausage, chopped
2 carrots, sliced	125 g (4 oz) chick peas, cooked
1 litre (1³/4 pints) chicken stock	pepper to taste

1. Mix the flour, chilli, salt, and pepper to taste in a polythene bag, then toss the pigeons in it. Reserve any leftover seasoned flour.
2. Heat the oil in a pan, add the pigeons and brown well. Remove from the pan and set aside. Add the bacon to the pan and fry for about 2 minutes, then add the carrots and fry lightly for 5 minutes. Transfer to a large casserole and place the pigeons on top.
3. Sprinkle the seasoned flour into the pan and stir well. Pour in the stock and bring to the boil, stirring. Pour over the pigeons. Add the onion, bay leaves and tomato purée. Cover and cook in a preheated oven, 180°C/350°F/Gas Mark 4, for 30 minutes.
4. Add the rice, cabbage, sausage and chick peas, cover and return to the oven for 30–40 minutes. Serve immediately.

Bean Sprout and Rice Salad

Serves 4
Preparation time: 20 minutes, plus cooking rice
Freezing: Not recommended

	FOR THE DRESSING:
125 g (4 oz) brown rice, cooked and hot	3 tablespoons lemon juice
2 spring onions, chopped	1 teaspoon Dijon mustard
2 carrots, sliced thinly	1 teaspoon sugar
125 g (4 oz) bean sprouts	4 tablespoons olive oil
2 bunches watercress	2 tablespoons single cream
	salt and pepper to taste

1. Mix the dressing ingredients together, then toss into the hot rice. Leave to cool.
2. Add the spring onions, carrots and bean sprouts and mix well. Check the seasoning.
3. Arrange the watercress around the edge of a serving platter and spoon the salad into the centre.

Tomato and Nut Cannelloni

Serves 4
Preparation time: 35 minutes
Cooking time: 15–20 minutes
Freezing: Recommended, at end of stage 6

This cannelloni has a rich nutty filling which blends well with the creamy sauce. The filling also makes a good sauce to go with wholewheat tagliatelle if you add a little stock or tomato juice to thin it down.

8 sheets dried wholewheat lasagne	¹/₂ teaspoon dried oregano
FOR THE FILLING:	75 g (3 oz) hazelnuts, chopped finely
1 tablespoon sunflower oil	2 tablespoons chopped parsley
1 onion, chopped	salt and pepper to taste
1 celery stick, chopped	FOR THE SAUCE:
1 tablespoon wholemeal flour	2 tablespoons sunflower oil
1 clove garlic, crushed	2 tablespoons wholemeal flour
397 g (14 oz) can chopped tomatoes	300 ml (¹/₂ pint) milk
125 g (4 oz) mushrooms, sliced	pinch of grated nutmeg
1 tablespoon tomato purée	2 tablespoons grated Parmesan cheese
1 teaspoon soy sauce	TO GARNISH:
	sage or parsley sprigs

Right: Black Eye Beanburgers (page 100)

1. Cook the pasta according to packet instructions. Drain, spread on kitchen paper and pat dry.
2. For the filling, heat the oil in a pan, add the onion and celery and fry gently until softened.
3. Stir in the flour, then add the garlic, tomatoes, mushrooms, tomato purée, soy sauce, oregano, and salt and pepper.
4. Bring to the boil, lower the heat and simmer for 8–10 minutes. Stir in the hazelnuts and parsley.
5. Spread a rounded tablespoon of filling over each piece of pasta. Roll up loosely from the shorter side and place join side down in a greased ovenproof dish.
6. For the sauce, heat the oil in a pan, then stir in the flour. Remove from the heat and stir in the milk. Bring to the boil, stirring constantly, then add the nutmeg, and salt and pepper. Pour over the pasta and sprinkle with the cheese.
7. Bake in a preheated oven, 200°C/400°F/Gas Mark 6, for 15–20 minutes, until golden. Garnish with sage or parsley sprigs to serve.

VARIATION

Use ground walnuts or almonds in place of the hazelnuts. Chopped coriander can be used instead of the parsley.

2. Add the tomato, stock, thyme, and salt and pepper, bring to the boil, cover and simmer for 10 minutes.
3. Add the beans and a little extra stock or water if the mixture looks dry. Cover and cook for 25 minutes, or until the stock is absorbed and the rice just tender. Gradually stir in the creamed coconut until it has melted, then stir in the parsley or coriander. Serve hot.

Caribbean Pork and Rice

Serves 4–6
Preparation time: 20 minutes, plus cooking beans and marinating
Cooking time: 45–50 minutes
Freezing: Recommended

250 g (8 oz) diced pork	*2 tablespoons oil*
75 g (3 oz) salt pork or ham, diced	*375 g (12 oz) brown rice*
50 g (2 oz) bacon, derinded and diced	*397 g (14 oz) can chopped tomatoes*
1 onion, sliced	*900 ml (1½ pints) stock*
1 large chilli, seeded and sliced	*125 g (4 oz) kidney or pinto beans, cooked*
1 green pepper, cored, seeded and sliced	*2 tablespoons capers (optional)*
2 bay leaves	*salt and pepper to taste*
juice of 2 limes	*TO GARNISH:*
1 teaspoon ground allspice	*1 avocado*
½ teaspoon ground cinnamon	*6–8 radishes, sliced*
	coriander sprigs

1. Place the meats, onion, chilli, green pepper, bay leaves, lime juice, spices, and salt and pepper in a bowl, cover and chill overnight.
2. Heat the oil in a pan, add the marinated ingredients and marinade and fry for 5 minutes, stirring occasionally.
3. Add the rice and fry for about 2 minutes, then add the tomatoes, stock, and salt and pepper. Bring to the boil, cover and simmer for 35 minutes.
4. Add the beans and capers, if using, and cook for 5 minutes. Remove the bay leaves and transfer to warmed individual serving plates.
5. Peel and slice the avocado and arrange around the edge of the plates with the radishes and coriander.

Beans 'n' Rice

Serves 4
Preparation time: 10 minutes, plus cooking beans
Cooking time: About 45 minutes
Freezing: Recommended

Hoppin' John, Limpin' Susan, Moors and Christians – whatever the name, the combination of beans and rice appears in many American and West Indian cuisines. The beans can be black, red or white. The dish may be hot and spicy or mild – adapt it to your own taste.

1 tablespoon oil	*900 ml (1½ pints) stock*
250 g (8 oz) minced pork	*1 thyme sprig*
1 onion, chopped	*125 g (4 oz) beans (see above), cooked*
1 green chilli, seeded and chopped finely	*50 g (2 oz) creamed coconut*
375 g (12 oz) brown rice	*2 tablespoons chopped parsley or coriander*
1 extra-large tomato, skinned and sliced	*salt and pepper to taste*

1. Heat the oil in a pan, add the pork and onion and fry for about 5 minutes. Add the chilli and rice and fry for about 2 minutes, until the rice turns opaque.

Mild Curry Spice Pilaf

Serves 4
Preparation time: 10 minutes

Cooking time: 20 minutes
Freezing: Recommended

2 tablespoons oil
1 onion, chopped
250 g (8 oz) long-grain rice
1 teaspoon turmeric
1/2 teaspoon ground coriander
pinch of ground cloves

600 ml (1 pint) light stock or
   water
1 bay leaf
15 g (1/2 oz) butter
salt and pepper to taste
lemon slices and parsley to
   garnish

1. Heat the oil in a large pan, add the onion and fry until softened. Add the rice and fry for about 2 minutes, until it turns opaque.
2. Sprinkle in the spices and fry for 1 minute. Pour in the stock or water, add the bay leaf, and salt and pepper.
3. Bring to the boil, cover and simmer for 15 minutes or until the rice is tender. Fork through and stir in the butter. Garnish with lemon and parsley to serve.

Arroz Verde

Serves 4
Preparation time: 15 minutes
Cooking time: About 20 minutes
Freezing: Recommended, without the eggs

From Central America, this rice dish will be popular with those who enjoy the flavour of green peppers. Serve it with grilled meats or fish.

3 tablespoons oil
2 green peppers, cored, seeded
   and chopped
1 large green chilli, seeded
   and chopped
3 spring onions, chopped
1 clove garlic, crushed

6 tablespoons chopped parsley
250 g (8 oz) long-grain rice
600 ml (1 pint) vegetable stock
   or water
salt and pepper to taste
2 hard-boiled eggs quartered,
   to garnish

1. Heat the oil in a large pan, add the peppers, chilli, spring onion and garlic and fry until softened.
2. Add the remaining ingredients, bring to the boil, cover and simmer for 15 minutes or until the rice is tender.
3. Fork the rice through and pile into a warmed serving dish. Arrange the eggs on top to garnish.

1. Heat the oil and butter in a pan, add the minced beef, chicken livers and bacon and fry until browned, stirring occasionally.
2. Add the onion, garlic, carrot and celery and fry for about 3 minutes, until softened.
3. Pour in the wine and cook for 3–5 minutes, until reduced by about half.
4. Stir in the stock, tomato purée, bay leaf, and plenty of nutmeg, salt and pepper. Bring to the boil, cover and simmer for 25–30 minutes.
5. Meanwhile, cook the pasta. Drain and toss in a little olive oil and add a little grated nutmeg and pepper.
6. Serve the sauce mixed in with the pasta, or separately. Hand the cheese separately, to sprinkle on top.

Lasagne Verdi al Forno

Serves 6–8
Preparation time: 50 minutes, plus cooking ragù and pasta
Cooking time: About 40 minutes
Freezing: Recommended at end of stage 3

twice the quantity of Ragù (opposite)	BÉCHAMEL SAUCE
	50 g (2 oz) butter
8–10 sheets lasagne verdi, cooked	75 g (3 oz) plain flour
	1.2 litres (2 pints) hot milk
75 g (3 oz) Parmesan cheese, grated	1 bay leaf
	grated nutmeg, salt and pepper to taste

1. Make the ragù the day before required, if possible.
2. To make the sauce, melt the butter in a saucepan and stir in the flour. Cook for about 1 minute, then gradually stir in the hot milk, until smooth. Bring to the boil, stirring. Season well with nutmeg, salt and pepper, add the bay leaf and simmer for about 5 minutes. Remove the bay leaf.
3. Lightly grease a large shallow dish and fill with alternate layers of ragù, pasta and sauce, sprinkling each layer with grated Parmesan.
4. Bake in a preheated oven, 190°C/375°F/Gas Mark 5, for about 40 minutes, until the top is browned. Leave to stand for a few minutes before cutting.
VARIATION
For a simpler supper-style lasagne, omit the ragù and substitute about 500 g (1 lb) cooked diced chicken, 125 g (4 oz) sliced button mushrooms, 125 g (4 oz) chopped ham and 2 tablespoons dry sherry: add to the sauce and arrange in layers with the pasta as above.

Ragù alla Bolognese

Serves 4
Preparation time: 25 minutes
Cooking time: 25–30 minutes
Freezing: Recommended for sauce only

The most famous spaghetti sauce which, when cooked authentically, is a far cry from the usual mince cooked with a can of tomatoes. Serve it with any pasta or use in lasagne or cannelloni.

2 tablespoons olive oil	300 ml (1/2 pint) beef stock
25 g (1 oz) butter	4–6 tablespoons tomato purée
250 g (8 oz) minced beef	1 bay leaf
125 g (4 oz) chicken livers, chopped	grated nutmeg, salt and pepper to taste
125 g (4 oz) unsmoked bacon, derinded and chopped finely	TO SERVE:
1 onion, chopped	375 g (12 oz) dried spaghetti or tagliatelle
2 cloves garlic, crushed	a little olive oil
1 carrot, chopped	50 g (2 oz) Parmesan cheese, grated
1 celery stick, chopped	
150 ml (1/4 pint) dry white wine	

Pork Fried Rice in Lettuce

Serves 2, or 4 as a starter   *Cooking time: 10 minutes*
Preparation time: 10 minutes   *Freezing: Not recommended*

Light, tasty and colourful, these make a lovely quick lunch dish or starter. An ideal recipe for using leftover rice – you will need 200 g (7 oz) cooked weight.

4 large crisp curly lettuce leaves   *1 clove garlic, crushed*
2–3 tablespoons sunflower oil   *2.5 cm (1 inch) piece fresh root*
2 eggs, beaten   *ginger, grated*
6–8 tablespoons chicken stock   *4 spring onions, sliced*
2 tablespoons soy sauce   *125 g (4 oz) bean sprouts*
1 tablespoon dry sherry   *125 g (4 oz) brown rice,*
1 tablespoon cornflour   *cooked*
2 teaspoons sesame oil   *4 teaspoons hoisin or*
* (optional)*   *barbecue sauce*
125 g (4 oz) minced pork   *salt and pepper to taste*

1. Place the lettuce leaves on a large platter or individual plates.
2. Heat 1 tablespoon of the oil in a small saucepan, add the eggs, and salt and pepper and cook, stirring only occasionally, until they are scrambled firm but not overcooked. Immediately transfer to a bowl.
3. Place the stock, soy sauce, sherry, cornflour and sesame oil, if using, in a cup and stir until smooth.
4. Heat the remaining oil in a wok or large frying pan, add the pork, garlic and ginger and stir-fry for 2–3 minutes, until browned.
5. Add the spring onions and bean sprouts and stir-fry for 1 minute.
6. Stir in the stock mixture, season with salt and pepper, then add the rice and heat through.
7. Spoon into the centre of each lettuce leaf, then top with the egg. Trickle a teaspoon of hoisin or barbecue sauce over each serving.
8. To eat, fold over the lettuce leaves like envelopes and eat with fingers.

VARIATION

This is an ideal recipe for using up leftover cooked and minced chicken or spicy sausage. Omit the pork. Stir-fry the ginger, garlic, spring onions and bean sprouts as above. Stir in the stock mixture and seasoning. Add the chicken or spicy sausage, with the rice, and heat through.

Dolmades

Serves 4–6
(Makes about 30)
Preparation time: 45 minutes

Cooking time: 1 hour
Freezing: Not recommended

150 ml (¼ pint) olive oil
250 g (8 oz) onions, chopped
125 g (4 oz) brown rice
40 g (1½ oz) currants
1 tablespoon chopped dill
1 tablespoon chopped mint
* (optional)*
150 ml (¼ pint) water

1 tablespoon pine kernels
1 teaspoon salt
pepper to taste
227 g (8 oz) pack vine leaves
* in brine*
juice of ½ lemon
lemon wedges to garnish

1. Heat half of the oil in a large pan, add the onion and fry gently until softened. Add the rice, cover and cook gently for 10 minutes or until all the liquid is absorbed.
2. Add the currants, herbs, water, pine kernels, and salt and pepper. Bring to the boil, then cover and simmer gently for 5 minutes.
3. Meanwhile, drain and rinse the vine leaves carefully. Lay them out on a clean worktop, rib side upwards with the stalk pointing towards you.
4. Put 1 teaspoon of the rice mixture at the stalk end of each leaf. Fold the bottom edge up, then fold the sides in and roll up firmly, but not too tightly.
5. Place side by side in a large shallow pan with a lid. Pour over the remaining oil, the lemon juice and enough water just to cover the top of the rolls.
6. Place an old heatproof china or glass plate on top of the rolls to hold them down, bring very slowly to the boil, then cover and simmer for 1 hour on a very low heat. Leave to cool in the pan, then remove carefully and arrange on a serving dish.
7. Serve chilled, garnished with lemon wedges.

Top: Succotash (page 111)

Curried Pasta Salad

Serves 4
Preparation time: 30 minutes
Freezing: Not recommended

175 g (6 oz) wholewheat pasta
1 tablespoon mild curry powder
4 tablespoons natural set
*   yogurt*
1 tablespoon French Dressing
*   (page 9)*
1 tablespoon pure apple juice
1 clove garlic, crushed

1 large red dessert apple
a little lemon juice
4 celery sticks, chopped
250 g (8 oz) cooked chicken,
*   diced*
1/2 avocado
salt and pepper to taste
curry powder to sprinkle

1. Cook the pasta according to packet instructions; drain thoroughly.
2. Meanwhile, mix together the curry powder, yogurt, French dressing, apple juice, garlic, and salt and pepper.
3. Toss the pasta in the dressing while still warm; leave to cool.
4. Chop the apple and toss in lemon juice. Add to the pasta with the celery and chicken, mix thoroughly and place in a serving dish.
5. Just before serving, cut the avocado into slices and dip into the lemon juice.
6. Arrange the avocado neatly on top of the salad and sprinkle with a little curry powder.

Tagliatelle with Pesto

Serves 4, or 6, as a starter
Preparation time: 10 minutes

Cooking time: 3–5 minutes
Freezing: Not recommended

Use only fresh basil, fresh Parmesan and the best olive oil you can afford, for this superb pasta sauce.

fresh basil leaves to fill a 300
*   ml (1/2 pint) jug*
50 g (2 oz) pine kernels
125 g (4 oz) Parmesan cheese,
*   grated*
2 cloves garlic, crushed

6 tablespoons olive oil
500 g (1 lb) fresh green and
*   white tagliatelle*
knob of butter
pepper to taste
basil leaves to garnish

1. First make the sauce, either by pounding with a pestle and mortar, or in a blender or food processor: work the basil, pine kernels, cheese, garlic and plenty of pepper together until well mixed. Slowly add the oil, blending or pounding until incorporated. Set aside.
2. Cook the pasta according to packet instructions, drain and toss in the butter. Mix in the pesto. Serve immediately, garnished with basil.

Left: Chicken-stuffed Courgettes (page 86)

Meat and Fish

A wholefood diet does not necessarily have to be vegetarian, as these recipes demonstrate. Meat is an excellent source of protein, and provides some nutrients that aren't available from any other source. Fish is an exceptionally good-value food, as it is high in protein and white fish is low in fat. Both can be included in a well-balanced wholefood diet, in moderate quantities and choosing leaner cuts.

The recipes that follow show how to cook meat and fish in simple and wholesome ways, combining them with the best of fresh vegetables, pulses and grains. Ranging from starters, salads and light meals to substantial main courses, this selection shows the versatility of the wholefood approach to eating.

Some of the recipes are especially suitable for children, with such great colours and textures that they'll never notice that they're eating what's good for them! On the other hand, the selection also includes delicious recipes that would grace any adult dinner party table; a wholefood diet fits into all areas of your cooking.

Right (clockwise from top left): Chilli Chicken with Peanuts (page 65), Fruited Game Casserole (page 64), Prawns with Almonds, Spiced Beef with Beans

Prawns with Almonds

Serves 4

Preparation time: 8 minutes

Cooking time: 7 minutes

Freezing: Not recommended

An attractive stir-fry dish that only takes minutes to cook. Serve with brown rice or egg noodles.

1 tablespoon sesame oil	250 g (8 oz) mange tout
1 onion, sliced	375 g (12 oz) peeled prawns
75 g (3 oz) flaked almonds	2 tablespoons dry sherry
1 teaspoon chopped fresh root ginger	1 tablespoon soy sauce
	2 tablespoons water
1 clove garlic, crushed	salt and pepper to taste

1. Heat the oil in a wok, add the onion and almonds and stir-fry over a high heat for 1 minute.
2. Add the ginger, garlic and mange tout and stir-fry for 2 minutes.
3. Add the remaining ingredients and stir-fry for 3 minutes, then serve immediately.

Spiced Beef with Beans

Serves 6–8

Preparation time: 25 minutes

Cooking time: 1 hour 50 minutes

Freezing: Recommended, at end of stage 3

2 tablespoons oil	2 bay leaves
1.25 kg (2¹/₂ lb) braising steak, cubed	450 ml (³/₄ pint) beef stock
2 onions, chopped	1 each red and yellow pepper, cored, seeded and chopped
2 cloves garlic, crushed	432 g (15¹/₄ oz) can red kidney beans, drained
1 teaspoon chilli powder	
2 teaspoons ground cumin	250 g (8 oz) Greek-style yogurt
1 teaspoon chopped marjoram	salt and pepper to taste
4 tablespoons tomato purée	

1. Heat the oil in a large pan, add the beef and fry until lightly browned. Add the onions and garlic and cook for 5 minutes. Stir in the chilli, cumin and marjoram and cook for 1 minute.
2. Add the tomato purée, bay leaves, stock, and salt and pepper, bring to the boil, then cover and simmer for 1¹/₂ hours, until the beef is tender.
3. Stir in the peppers and beans and cook for 15 minutes.
4. Gradually stir in the yogurt and simmer for 5 minutes. Discard the bay leaves. Serve with rice mixed with grains.

Chilli and Chicken Tortillas

| Serves 4, or 8 as a snack | Cooking time: 15 minutes |
| Preparation time: 20 minutes | Freezing: Not recommended |

Tostados can be used instead of canned tortillas.

2 tablespoons oil	125 g (4 oz) cooked chicken,
1 onion, chopped	diced
230 g (8 oz) can tomatoes	12 stuffed green olives, sliced
2 tablespoons tomato purée	oil for shallow frying
1/2 × 113 g (3.99 oz) can green	8 canned tortillas, or tostados
chillies in brine, drained	salt and pepper to taste
and chopped	TO GARNISH:
432 g (15¼ oz) can borlotti	shredded lettuce
beans, drained	1 ripe avocado, sliced

1. Heat the oil in a pan, add the onion and fry for 5 minutes. Add the tomatoes with their juice, tomato purée and chillies and simmer for 5 minutes or until most of the liquid has reduced. Stir in the beans, chicken and olives and cook for 2 minutes. Season well with salt and pepper.
2. Heat a little oil in a small frying pan and fry the tortillas one at a time for about 5 seconds on each side. Remove with tongs and immediately press over an upturned ramekin dish covered with kitchen paper. Press into shape, then carefully remove and place upside down on a wire rack to drain. If using tostados, cook according to packet instructions.
3. Place shredded lettuce in the tortilla baskets or tostados, fill with the bean mixture and garnish with the avocado slices.

Fruited Game Casserole

| Serves 4 | Cooking time: 1¾–2¼ hours |
| Preparation time: 40 minutes | Freezing: Recommended |

Choose plump birds for this casserole. The long slow cooking will tenderize an older bird.

2 tablespoons oil	2 bay leaves
1 oven-ready pheasant	25 g (1 oz) butter, softened
2 pigeons	25 g (1 oz) plain wholemeal
2 onions, chopped	flour
2 carrots, chopped	4 tablespoons ruby port
3 celery sticks, chopped	75 g (3 oz) raisins
450 ml (¾ pint) red wine	salt and pepper to taste
150 ml (¼ pint) water	

1. Heat the oil in a flameproof casserole, add the pheasant and pigeons and fry until browned all over. Drain off any excess oil, then add the onions, carrots, celery, wine, water, bay leaves, and salt and pepper. Bring to the boil, then cover and simmer for 1½–2 hours, until the meat is tender.
2. Lift out the birds and strip the meat from the bones. Chop into large pieces and return to the pan.
3. Place the butter and flour in a small bowl and work together with a teaspoon until well mixed. Add the paste, in small pieces, to the liquid and simmer, until thickened and smooth.
4. Add the port and raisins and simmer for 15 minutes. Check the seasoning and remove the bay leaves. Serve from the dish, accompanied by broccoli and cauliflower florets and sauté potatoes.

Pictured on page 63

Coconut Marinade

| Makes 300 ml (½ pint) | Cooking time: 10 minutes |
| Preparation time: 8 minutes | Freezing: Not recommended |

Use this to marinate any white fish, such as cod, haddock, plaice. Do not use for oily fish, e.g. herrings or mackerel.

50 g (2 oz) creamed coconut	1/2 teaspoon chilli powder
175 ml (6 fl oz) water	2 spring onions, chopped
grated rind and juice of 2	2.5 cm (1 inch) piece fresh root
limes	ginger, crushed
1 clove garlic, crushed	

Put all the ingredients in a pan and cook gently for 10 minutes, stirring constantly, until the coconut has dissolved and the flavours have intermingled. Leave to cool, then use as required.

Coriander Curried Chicken

Serves 4   *plus standing time*
Preparation time: 40 minutes,   *Cooking time: 35–40 minutes*

50 g (2 oz) desiccated coconut	*¹/₂ teaspoon fennel seeds*
150 ml (¹/₄ pint) boiling water	*¹/₂ teaspoon cumin seeds*
2 teaspoons turmeric	*¹/₂ teaspoon ground coriander*
4 chicken quarters, halved	*¹/₂ teaspoon black pepper*
2 tablespoons oil	*2 green chillies, chopped finely*
1 onion, sliced	*strip of lemon rind*
1 tablespoon crunchy peanut	*1 tablespoon lemon juice*
butter	*coriander leaves to garnish*

1. Soak the coconut in the boiling water for 20 minutes, then strain and set aside the liquid; discard the coconut.
2. Rub the turmeric into the chicken pieces.
3. Heat the oil in a large saucepan, add the onion and fry until lightly browned. Stir in the peanut butter, fennel and cumin seeds, ground coriander, pepper and chillies. Cook for 1 minute, then add the chicken, turning in the mixture until evenly coated.
4. Add the coconut liquid and lemon rind, bring to the boil, then cover and simmer for 35–40 minutes, until the chicken is tender. Stir in the lemon juice. Garnish with coriander leaves and serve with rice flavoured with herbs and puppodums.

Chilli Chicken with Peanuts

Serves 3–6   *Cooking time: 6 minutes*
Preparation time: 12 minutes   *Freezing: Not recommended*

This is a hot dish, so reduce the chillies if you prefer a milder strength. Removing the seeds also helps.

1 egg white	*3–5 small dried red chillies,*
1 tablespoon light soy sauce	*sliced*
1 tablespoon dry sherry	*50 g (2 oz) unsalted peanuts*
1 tablespoon cornflour	FOR THE SAUCE:
375 g (12 oz) boneless chicken,	*1 tablespoon soy sauce*
diced	*1 teaspoon wine vinegar*
3 tablespoons groundnut oil	*1 teaspoon sugar*
4 spring onions, sliced	*1 teaspoon cornflour*
diagonally	*4–6 tablespoons light stock or*
1 clove garlic, crushed	*water*
¹/₂ red or green pepper, cored,	*salt and pepper to taste*
seeded and diced	

1. Whisk the egg white with the soy sauce, sherry and cornflour. Add the chicken and mix well.

Below: Kashmiri Chicken Pilau (page 51)

2. Mix the sauce ingredients together; set aside.
3. Heat the oil in a wok, add the chicken and stir-fry for about 3 minutes.
4. Add the spring onions, garlic, pepper and chillies and stir-fry for 2 minutes. Add the peanuts.
5. Pour in the sauce and cook, stirring, until thickened. Check the seasoning, transfer to a warmed serving dish and serve immediately.
Pictured on page 63

1. Heat the oil in a large frying pan, add the bacon and fry until it is slightly crispy. Add the onions and fry until softened. Remove from the heat.

2. Arrange half of the sliced potato in a greased 1.5 litre (3 pint) shallow ovenproof dish and cover with the bacon and onion mixture. Arrange the chicken and mushrooms on top and sprinkle with the parsley, and salt and pepper.

3. Cover the chicken with the remaining potato. Pour over the stock and sprinkle with salt and pepper.

4. Cook, uncovered, in a preheated oven, 190°C/375°F/Gas Mark 5, for 1 hour, until the potatoes are cooked and the top is golden brown. Serve garnished with parsley.

Chicken and Tarragon Braise

Serves 4–5	*Cooking time: 1¹/₂–1³/₄ hours*
Preparation time: 40 minutes	*Freezing: Not recommended*

1 large lemon	*2 celery sticks, chopped*
1 frozen chicken with giblets,	*4 teaspoons chopped tarragon*
weighing 1.5 kg(3¹/₂ lb),	*1 bay leaf*
defrosted	*300 ml (¹/₂ pint) water*
25 g (1 oz) butter	*2 tablespoons single cream or*
1 tablespoon oil	*natural yogurt*
1 onion, chopped	*salt and pepper to taste*
3 carrots, chopped	*tarragon sprigs to garnish*

1. Halve the lemon, cut a few slices from each half and set aside for garnish, then squeeze the juice. Rinse the chicken giblets and set aside. Place the squeezed lemon halves inside the chicken.

2. Heat the butter and oil in a saucepan or flameproof casserole large enough to hold the chicken snugly. Add the chicken and fry for about 10 minutes, until evenly browned all over. Remove and set aside.

3. Add the vegetables to the pan and fry for 5 minutes. Add the giblets, lemon juice, half of the tarragon, bay leaf, water, and salt and pepper. Bring to the boil, return the chicken to the pan, cover and simmer for 1¹/₄–1¹/₂ hours.

4. Remove the chicken, place on a warmed serving dish and keep warm. Discard the giblets and bay leaf.

5. Purée the vegetable mixture in a food processor or blender; add a little stock or milk if the sauce is too thick. Return to the pan and stir in the cream or yogurt and reserved tarragon. Reheat gently and check the seasoning.

6. Garnish the chicken with the reserved lemon slices and tarragon, and serve with the sauce. Serve green beans, cooked with tomatoes and garlic, and sauté potatoes as accompaniments.

Chicken Stovies with Parsley

Serves 4	*Cooking time: 1 hour*
Preparation time: 30 minutes	*Freezing: Not recommended*

Always use old potatoes for this dish as new ones do not cook well this way.

1 tablespoon oil	*125 g (4 oz) mushrooms,*
125 g (4 oz) streaky bacon,	*sliced*
derinded and chopped	*3 tablespoons chopped parsley*
2 onions, sliced	*300 ml (¹/₂ pint) chicken stock*
1 kg (2 lb) potatoes, sliced	*salt and pepper to taste*
thinly	*parsley sprigs to garnish*
375 g (12 oz) boneless chicken	
breast, cubed	

Braised Chicken Breasts

Serves 4
Preparation time: 35 minutes, plus chilling

Cooking time: 30–35 minutes
Freezing: Recommended

¹/₂ teaspoon dried rosemary	*3 carrots*
1 clove garlic, crushed	*3 celery sticks*
25 g (1 oz) butter, softened	*2 leeks*
2 tablespoons grated	*1 tablespoon oil*
Parmesan cheese	*25 g (1 oz) butter*
4 partly boned chicken breasts,	*150 ml (¹/₄ pint) chicken stock*
each weighing about	*2 tablespoons lemon juice*
175 g (6 oz)	*salt and pepper to taste*

1. Mix together the rosemary, garlic, butter, cheese, and salt and pepper. Loosen the skin from the chicken and spread a little mixture between the flesh and skin. Smooth the skin back over the stuffing. Chill for 30 minutes.
2. Cut the carrots, celery and leeks into matchstick pieces.
3. Heat the oil and butter in a large heavy-based casserole, add the chicken and fry quickly until lightly browned. Remove from the pan.
4. Add the vegetables to the pan and fry for 5 minutes, until slightly softened. Add the stock, lemon juice, and a little salt and pepper. Bring to the boil.
5. Place the chicken breasts skin side up on top of the vegetables, cover and cook gently for 30–35 minutes, until tender. Accompany with a green salad and French bread.

Braised Duck

Serves 4
Preparation time: 30 minutes

Cooking time: 45 minutes
Freezing: Not recommended

Duck breast joints include both breasts. They are a good buy as most of the meat on a duck is on the breast.

1 duck breast joint weighing	*3 tablespoons freshly squeezed*
1 kg (2 lb)	*orange juice*
1 tablespoon oil	*4 tablespoons natural fromage*
1 onion, chopped	*frais*
2 carrots, chopped	*1 teaspoon cornflour*
150 ml (¹/₄ pint) white wine	*salt and pepper to taste*
¹/₂ teaspoon grated orange	*orange slices and chervil*
rind	*sprigs to garnish*

1. Trim off any excess fat from the underside of the duck breast. Heat the oil in a flameproof casserole, add the duck, skin side down, and fry until well browned. Turn and fry the other side. Remove and drain on kitchen paper.
2. Add the onion and carrot to the pan and fry until slightly softened. Add the wine and stir well, scraping up any sediment from the base of the pan. Add the orange rind, juice, and salt and pepper and bring to the boil.
3. Return the duck to the pan, cover and cook gently for 45 minutes, until tender. Remove the duck and keep warm.
4. Skim off any excess fat from the sauce, then purée in a blender or food processor and return to the pan.
5. Blend the fromage frais with the cornflour, stir into the pan and cook until thickened. Check the seasoning.
6. Carefully remove the duck meat from the bone and slice thinly. Spoon a pool of sauce over each warm plate and arrange the duck on top. Garnish with halved orange slices and chervil and serve with tiny new potatoes and green beans or mange tout.

Chicken with Fennel Ragu

Serves 4	Cooking time: About 50 minutes
Preparation time: 15 minutes	Freezing: Recommended

4 chicken quarters	125 g (4 oz) baby button
wholemeal flour to coat	mushrooms
2 tablespoons olive oil	500 g (1 lb) carton creamed
25 g (1 oz) butter	tomatoes or passata
2 bulbs fennel, sliced	1 tablespoon chopped marjoram
4 leeks, sliced thinly	4 tablespoons chopped parsley
1 clove garlic, crushed	salt and pepper to taste
300 ml (1/2 pint) dry white	50 g (2 oz) flaked almonds,
wine or cider	toasted, and fennel sprigs, to
	garnish

1. Coat the chicken in the flour. Heat the oil in a pan, add the chicken and fry until evenly browned. Set aside.
2. Add the butter, fennel, leeks, garlic and 2 tablespoons water to the pan, cover and cook for 10–15 minutes.
3. Add the wine or cider and simmer, uncovered, until reduced by half, then add the mushrooms, tomatoes, herbs, and salt and pepper. Return the chicken to the pan, cover, and simmer gently for about 30 minutes until cooked.
4. Sprinkle with almonds, garnish with fennel sprigs and serve with rice or pasta.

Spicy Sausages

Serves 4–6	Cooking time: 8–10 minutes
Preparation time: 20 minutes	Freezing: Recommended

Sausages will always be a firm favourite with children. Try these healthy homemade ones – arranged whirligig fashion for younger children.

125 g (4 oz) wholemeal	2 tablespoons tomato purée
breadcrumbs	1 teaspoon paprika
4 tablespoons water	1 teaspoon ground coriander
250 g (8 oz) lean minced beef	plain wholemeal flour for
1 small onion, chopped finely	coating
1 clove garlic, crushed	salt and pepper to taste
1 egg yolk	

1. Place the breadcrumbs in a bowl, pour over the water and mix together. Add the remaining ingredients and mix thoroughly with your hand.
2. Divide the mixture into 12 portions and, with dampened hands, roll each portion into an 11 cm (4 1/2 inch) long thin sausage shape, then roll in the flour to coat evenly.
3. Cook under a preheated hot grill for 8–10 minutes, turning occasionally. Serve with Tomato Sauce (page 18), mashed potato and a vegetable accompaniment, or in wholemeal pitta bread with salad.

Huntsman's Rabbit Casserole

Serves 4
Preparation time: 20 minutes

Cooking time: 1 hour
Freezing: Recommended

This tasty rabbit dish comes from the traditional cuisine of rural Spain.

3 tablespoons olive oil
1 kg (2 lb) rabbit portions
1 onion, chopped
2 cloves garlic, chopped
175 ml (6 fl oz) white wine
4 tomatoes, skinned and chopped

50 g (2 oz) piece Parma ham, diced
1 bouquet garni
125 g (4 oz) mushrooms, sliced
2 tablespoons chopped parsley
salt and pepper to taste

1. Heat the oil in a flameproof casserole, add the rabbit pieces and brown all over. Remove from the pan and set aside.
2. Add the onion and garlic to the pan and cook until softened. Add the wine, tomatoes, ham, bouquet garni and salt and pepper, then return the rabbit to the pan.
3. Cover and cook in a preheated oven, 180°C/350°F/Gas Mark 4, for about 45 minutes.
4. Stir in the mushrooms and parsley and cook for 15 minutes. Discard the bouquet garni and transfer to a warmed serving dish.

Circassian Chicken

Serves 4–8
Preparation time: 20 minutes

Cooking time: About 1 hour
Freezing: Not recommended

Known as çerkez tavuğu in Turkey, this delicious dish of chicken in a walnut sauce can be served as a first course for 6–8, or as a main course with rice for 4.

1 chicken, weighing about 1.5 kg (3 lb)
1 onion, quartered
1 carrot, quartered
1 bouquet garni
50 g (2 oz) wholemeal bread, crusts removed

175 g (6 oz) shelled walnuts
1 clove garlic, crushed
salt and pepper to taste
TO GARNISH:
2 tablespoons walnut or olive oil
1 teaspoon paprika

1. Place the chicken, onion, carrot and bouquet garni in a large saucepan. Cover with water, bring to the boil, then cover and simmer gently for about 1 hour, until cooked.
2. Remove the chicken from the pan and leave until cool enough to handle. Remove the flesh from the bones, cut into pieces about 5 × 1 cm (2 × 1/2 inch) and keep warm. Strain the stock and reserve.
3. Place the bread and walnuts in a food processor and work together until the walnuts are ground. Add the garlic, 250 ml (8 fl oz) of the reserved stock, and salt and pepper. Blend until the mixture is smooth and about the consistency of cream. Pour into a saucepan to reheat, adding a little more stock and seasoning if necessary.
4. Arrange the chicken on a warmed serving dish or individual plates and pour over some sauce. Hand any remaining sauce separately.
5. Mix the walnut or olive oil and paprika together and drizzle over the surface to serve.

Turkey Fillets with Asparagus and Pernod Sauce

Serves 4   Cooking time: About 15 minutes
Preparation time: 20 minutes   Freezing: Not recommended

250 g (8 oz) asparagus   2 shallots, chopped
2 teaspoons plain flour   300 ml (1/2 pint) chicken stock
4 turkey fillets, each weighing   1 small potato, chopped finely
    about 125 g (4 oz)   1 tablespoon Pernod
25 g (1 oz) butter   salt and pepper to taste

1. Remove the asparagus tips and set aside. Peel the stalks and slice thinly.
2. Season the flour with salt and pepper and use to coat the turkey fillets.
3. Heat the butter in a large frying pan with a lid. Add the turkey fillets and fry quickly on both sides until browned. Remove from the pan.
4. Add the shallots to the pan and fry until softened. Add the asparagus stalks and fry for 2 minutes. Add the stock, potato, Pernod, and salt and pepper and bring to the boil.
5. Return the turkey fillets to the pan, cover and simmer for 10–12 minutes, until the potato and asparagus are cooked and the turkey is tender.
6. Meanwhile, cook the asparagus tips in lightly salted water for 5–6 minutes, until just tender; drain.
7. Transfer the turkey fillets to warmed serving plates with a slotted spoon. Purée the sauce in a blender or food processor and pour around the turkey. Garnish with the asparagus tips and serve with a green salad.

Locro

Serves 6
Preparation time: 35 minutes
Cooking time: 2 1/4–2 1/2 hours
Freezing: Recommended, at end of stage 3

This dish is popular in South America. If you can't get chorizo sausage, use kabanos instead

2 tablespoons oil   432 g (15 1/4 oz) can chick
2 large onions, sliced   peas, drained
750 g (1 1/2 lb) stewing beef,   125 g (4 oz) chorizo sausage,
    cubed   sliced
397 g (14 oz) can peeled   125 g (4 oz) frozen sweetcorn
    tomatoes   kernels
150 ml (1/4 pint) water   salt to taste
2 tablespoons paprika   50 g (2 oz) Mozzarella cheese,
1/2 teaspoon chilli powder   chopped, to serve

1. Heat the oil in a large saucepan, add the onion and fry until softened and lightly coloured. Add the meat and fry, stirring, for 5 minutes.
2. Stir in the tomatoes with their juice, water, paprika, chilli powder and salt. Bring to the boil, then cover and simmer for 1 3/4–2 hours, until the meat is almost tender.
3. Stir in the chick peas, chorizo and sweetcorn and simmer for 30 minutes.
4. Transfer to a warmed serving dish or individual soup plates and sprinkle with pieces of Mozzarella cheese.

Duck Breasts with Lemon Sauce

Serves 4
Preparation time: 10 minutes

Cooking time: 10–15 minutes
Freezing: Not recommended

4 duck breasts, each weighing 175 g (6 oz), skinned	1 large clove garlic, sliced
wholemeal flour for coating	juice of 1 lemon
1 tablespoon olive oil	2 teaspoons sugar
15 g (½ oz) butter	salt and pepper to taste
	lemon twists to garnish

1. Toss the duck breasts in flour to coat evenly.
2. Heat the oil and butter gently in a pan, add the garlic and fry slowly until it starts to brown; discard.
3. Increase the heat and add the duck breasts. Fry for about 5 minutes on each side or until cooked to your liking.
4. Pour in the lemon juice, sprinkle with sugar and season with salt and pepper.
5. Slice the breasts diagonally and garnish with twists of lemon.

Salmon and Ginger Steaks

Serves 4
Preparation time: 15 minutes

Cooking time: 20–25 minutes
Freezing: Not recommended

4 salmon steaks, each weighing 250 g (8 oz)	75 g (3 oz) each carrot and leek, cut into julienne strips
50 g (2 oz) butter, softened	2–3 tablespoons dry sherry (optional)
2 teaspoons grated fresh root ginger	salt and pepper to taste
75 g (3 oz) fennel, sliced thinly	

1. Place the salmon steaks in a shallow ovenproof dish and season with salt and pepper.
2. Mix the butter with the ginger and spread half on the salmon steaks.
3. Blanch the vegetables in boiling water for 2 minutes. Drain and place on the salmon.
4. Sprinkle with the sherry, if using, and top with the remaining butter. Season lightly with salt and pepper.
5. Cover and cook in a preheated oven, 190°C/375°F/ Gas Mark 5, for 20–25 minutes or until cooked.
6. Serve with new potatoes, green beans in tomato sauce and a crisp salad.

Prawn and Vegetable Stir-Fry

Serves 4   *Cooking time: 5 minutes*
Preparation time: 30 minutes   *Freezing: Not recommended*

To make spring onion tassels, trim the stalks and slice very thinly lengthways almost to the centre, from both ends. Place in iced water until the ends curl up.

125 g (4 oz) carrots
125 g (4 oz) broccoli
3 tablespoons soy sauce
3–4 tablespoons apple juice
1 tablespoon lemon juice
1 teaspoon dried dill
1 thin slice ham, diced finely
1 bunch spring onions
3–4 tablespoons vegetable oil
125 g (4 oz) frozen brussels sprouts, thawed and quartered

2.5 cm (1 inch) piece fresh root ginger, peeled and grated
125 g (4 oz) curly endive or frisée, shredded
1 red dessert apple, cored and diced
250 g (8 oz) peeled prawns
salt and pepper to taste
4 cooked shell-on prawns to garnish

1. Cut the carrots into matchstick-size pieces. Cook in boiling water for 5 minutes, then drain.
2. Divide the broccoli into small florets and cook in boiling water for 3 minutes; drain well.
3. Mix the soy sauce, apple and lemon juice, dill, ham, and salt and pepper together well. Set aside.
4. Set aside 4 spring onion stalks for garnish; chop the rest.
5. Heat the oil in a wok or large shallow frying pan, add the sprouts, broccoli and carrots and cook for 3 minutes.
6. Add the chopped spring onions, ginger, endive or frisé, apple and prawns and stir-fry for 1 minute.
7. Drain off any excess fat, then stir in the soy sauce mixture. Bring to the boil quickly, then transfer to a warmed serving dish.
8. Garnish with the reserved spring onions, made into tassels (see above), and whole prawns. Serve immediately.

Ocean Salad

Serves 4
Preparation time: 25 minutes, plus chilling
Freezing: Not recommended

250 g (8 oz) squid, sliced thinly
500 g (1 lb) mussels, cleaned
125 g (4 oz) peeled prawns
2 tomatoes, sliced
1 small onion, chopped finely
1 clove garlic, crushed

1 tablespoon each chopped parsley and chives
2 tablespoons white wine vinegar
2 tablespoons vegetable oil
3 tablespoons white wine
salt and pepper to taste

1. Cook the squid in a small pan of boiling salted water for 2–3 minutes; remove and drain well. Add the mussels to the pan, discarding any that have already opened. Cook, covered, for 4–5 minutes, until the shells open; discard any that do not. Drain.
2. Mix together the squid, mussels and remaining ingredients. Chill in the refrigerator for 1–2 hours. Toss well before serving.

Haddock and Watercress Tart

Serves 4–6
Preparation time: 45 minutes,   Cooking time: 25–30 minutes
plus chilling   Freezing: Recommended

175 g (6 oz) Wholemeal Pastry (page 118)	1 celery stick, chopped
FOR THE FILLING:	25 g (1 oz) plain flour
375 g (12 oz) smoked haddock fillet	1/2 bunch watercress, chopped finely
300 ml (1/2 pint) milk	2 eggs, beaten
40 g (11/2 oz) butter	1 tablespoon grated Parmesan cheese
1 shallot or small onion, chopped finely	salt and pepper to taste

1. Turn the pastry onto a lightly floured surface and knead briefly, then roll out and use to line a 20–23 cm (8–9 inch) deep flan tin. Chill for 15 minutes.
2. Line the pastry case with foil, fill with baking beans and bake blind in a preheated oven, 200°C/400°F/Gas Mark 6, for 15 minutes. Remove the beans and foil. Lower the temperature to 190°C/375°F/Gas Mark 5.
3. Meanwhile, place the haddock and milk in a pan and bring to the boil. Lower the heat, cover and cook for 8–10 minutes, until the fish flakes easily. Remove with a fish slice, skin and flake the fish and set aside; reserve the milk.
4. Heat the butter in a pan, add the shallot or onion and celery and fry until softened. Stir in the flour and cook for 1 minute. Gradually stir in the reserved milk and cook, stirring, until thickened. Remove from the heat. Stir in the fish, watercress, eggs, and salt and pepper.
5. Pour into the flan case, sprinkle with Parmesan and return to the oven for 25–30 minutes, until the filling is risen and golden brown. Serve warm or cold.

Mussel and Leek Tarts

Serves 4   Cooking time: 25 minutes
Preparation time: 30 minutes   Freezing: Not recommended

175 g (6 oz) Wholemeal Pastry (page 118)	2 leeks, sliced
600 ml (1 pint) fresh mussels, cleaned	pinch of turmeric
4 tablespoons dry white wine	3 tablespoons natural fromage frais
25 g (1 oz) butter	salt and pepper to taste
	pinch of paprika to garnish

1. Divide the pastry into 4 and roll out each piece to line a 10 cm (4 inch) tart tin. Line with foil and beans and bake blind in a preheated oven, 200°C/400°F/Gas Mark 6, for 15 minutes. Remove the paper and beans and return to the oven for 10 minutes.
2. Meanwhile, make the filling. Place the mussels and wine in a large pan, cover and cook over a high heat for about 5 minutes, until the shells open; discard any that do not. Drain, reserving the liquid, remove the mussels from their shells and set aside.
3. Melt the butter in a saucepan, add the leeks and cook until softened. Strain the reserved cooking liquid into the pan, add the turmeric and simmer for 5 minutes. Add the mussels and heat through.
4. Lower the heat, stir in the fromage frais and heat through without boiling. Taste and add pepper, and a little salt if necessary.
5. Fill the warm pastry cases with the mussel mixture. Sprinkle with paprika and serve warm.

Coconut Fish Steak Parcels

Serves 4
Preparation time: 20 minutes, plus marinade and marinating
Cooking time: 15 minutes
Freezing: Not recommended

4 cod steaks, each weighing 175 g (6 oz)	*2 tablespoons chopped coriander*
1 quantity Coconut Marinade (page 64)	*TO GARNISH: coriander leaves lime wedges or slices*

1. Place the cod steaks in a single layer in a shallow dish. Spoon over the marinade, then turn them over to coat the other side. Cover and chill for 1 hour.
2. Lift the fish from the marinade and place each one on a piece of foil large enough to enclose the fish and marinade. Spoon the marinade over and sprinkle with the coriander.
3. Wrap the foil around the fish and form into a parcel, sealing all the edges to ensure that it does not leak during cooking.
4. Place the parcels in a preheated oven, 180°C/350°F/Gas Mark 4, for 12–15 minutes, until tender.
5. Remove the fish from the foil, garnish with coriander and lime and serve immediately, with jacket potatoes and a green salad.

Trout and Cucumber Parcels

Serves 4	*Cooking time: 20 minutes*
Preparation time: 18 minutes	*Freezing: Not recommended*

4 trout, each weighing about 250-300 g (8–10 oz)	*125 g (4 oz) peeled prawns*
1 celery stick	*1 lemon, halved*
1/2 cucumber, peeled	*2 tablespoons chopped parsley*
	salt and pepper to taste

1. Cut a piece of foil for each trout, long enough and wide enough to enclose and seal. Grease lightly.
2. Sprinkle the trout with salt and pepper and place in the centre of each piece of foil.
3. Cut the celery and cucumber into matchstick pieces.
4. Mix together the prawns, cucumber, celery, 1 tablespoon lemon juice, half of the parsley, and salt and pepper. Stuff the trout with some of this mixture and sprinkle the rest on top.
5. Seal the foil parcels tightly and place on a baking sheet. Cook in a preheated oven, 200°C/400°F/Gas Mark 6, for 20 minutes.
6. Transfer to warmed serving plates, sprinkle with the remaining parsley and garnish with the remaining lemon, cut into slices.

Mackerel in Cider

Serves 4
Preparation time: 10 minutes

Cooking time: 30–40 minutes
Freezing: Not recommended

Mackerel is a good, economical source of protein, vitamins A, B, and D and many minerals. Cooked in this way you have a tangy, very tasty result.

2 teaspoons herb mustard
4 small or 2 large mackerel,
  cleaned
2 small dessert apples

1 small onion, chopped
300 ml (1/2 pint) dry cider
pepper to taste

1. Spread a little mustard inside the mackerel and place in a roasting tin or baking dish.
2. Chop 1 apple, mix with the onion and pack into the fish. Sprinkle with lots of pepper and pour on the cider.
3. Cover with foil or a lid and cook in a preheated oven, 190°C/375°F/Gas Mark 5, for 30–40 minutes, depending on the size of the fish.
4. Strain off the juice carefully. Slice and core the remaining apple and poach in the strained juice for 2–3 minutes. Remove with a slotted spoon. Boil the juice for a few minutes until reduced.
5. Serve the mackerel topped with the apple slices and some of the liquid.
Pictured on page 39

Indian Fishball Curry

Serves 4
Preparation time: 40 minutes

Cooking time: About 30 minutes
Freezing: Recommended

Sweet-tasting coconut tastes remarkably good in this fish dish, particularly combined with subtle spices. Serve the curry with saffron rice and traditional accompaniments. A tomato salad, topped with yogurt and paprika, goes well.

750 g (1 1/2 lb) cod fillet
150 ml (1/4 pint) each milk and
  water
75 g (3 oz) desiccated coconut
300 ml (1/2 pint) boiling water
1 egg, beaten
1 onion, grated
2 potatoes, boiled and mashed
2 green chillies, seeded and
  chopped finely

3 tablespoons oil
2 teaspoons each garam
  masala, ground coriander
  and cumin
1 teaspoon turmeric
3 tablespoons lemon juice
2 teaspoons tomato purée
salt to taste
mint sprigs to garnish

1. Place the cod in a shallow pan and add the milk and water. Bring to the boil, then cover and simmer for 10–12 minutes, until the fish flakes easily. Drain and flake the fish, discarding the skin and any bones.
2. Place the coconut in a bowl and pour over the boiling water. Leave to infuse for 20 minutes, then strain through a sieve, pressing out as much liquid as possible, and set aside. Reserve the coconut.
3. Mix the flaked fish in a bowl with the egg, onion, potato, chillies and salt. Form into 12–14 balls.
4. Heat the oil in a large frying pan, add the fish balls and fry carefully on all sides until lightly browned, then remove with a slotted spoon and drain on kitchen paper.
5. Add the spices to the pan and cook for 1 minute, stirring well. Add the lemon juice, coconut liquid and tomato purée and bring to the boil. Add 1 tablespoon of the reserved coconut and a little salt and simmer for 10 minutes, stirring occasionally.
6. Add the fishballs to the sauce, cover and simmer for 10 minutes, turning after 5 minutes.
7. Toast 1 tablespoon of the reserved coconut under a preheated moderate grill until lightly browned. Serve the fishballs in the sauce, sprinkled with the toasted coconut and garnished with mint.

Pork with Mung Beans

Serves 4   *Cooking time: 1¼–1½ hours*
Preparation time: 20 minutes   *Freezing: Recommended*

Mung beans are tiny little green dried beans most often used for sprouting. They do not require soaking.

375 g (12 oz) mung beans	*2 tablespoons chopped celery*
2 bay leaves	*leaves*
2 onions	*125 g (4 oz) mushrooms,*
2 cloves	*sliced*
450 ml (¾ pint) chicken or	*4 pork shoulder steaks*
vegetable stock	*1 teaspoon chopped marjoram*
2 carrots, sliced	*salt and pepper to taste*
2 celery sticks, sliced	

1. Place the beans in a pan with water to cover. Add the bay leaves and one onion stuck with the cloves. Bring to the boil, then cover and simmer for 40–45 minutes, until the beans are fairly tender. Drain, then discard the bay leaves and onion. Return the beans to the pan.
2. Chop the remaining onion and add to the pan with the stock, carrots, celery, celery leaves and mushrooms. Mix well and season with salt and pepper.
3. Sprinkle the pork with the marjoram and push into the beans. Bring to the boil, then cover and simmer for 35–40 minutes, until tender. Serve with wholemeal bread.

Scallops Napoletana

Serves 4   *Cooking time: 11 minutes*
Preparation time: 35 minutes   *Freezing: Not recommended*

175 g (6 oz) wholewheat	*3 tablespoons dry vermouth*
spaghetti	*375 g (12 oz) scallops*
oil for brushing	*250 g (8 oz) button*
1 onion, sliced	*mushrooms, sliced*
2 rashers back bacon,	*1 tablespoon chopped parsley*
derinded and chopped	*1 tablespoon grated Parmesan*
300 ml (½ pint) Tomato Sauce	*cheese*
(page 18)	*salt and pepper to taste*

1. Cook the spaghetti according to packet instructions; drain.
2. Meanwhile, brush a non-stick pan with oil, add the onion and bacon and cook for 3–4 minutes. Add the tomato sauce and vermouth and simmer for 2 minutes.
3. Cut the scallops into thin slices and add to the sauce with the mushrooms and parsley. Cook gently for 5 minutes. Season with salt and pepper.
4. Toss the hot spaghetti into a very little oil and sprinkle with pepper. Pile onto warmed serving plates and spoon the sauce into the centre. Sprinkle lightly with the Parmesan cheese to serve.

Paprika Fish Brochettes

Serves 1
Preparation time: 8 minutes

Cooking time: 10 minutes
Freezing: Not recommended

75 g (3 oz) monkfish, skinned and boned
oil for brushing
1 potato, boiled
5 cm (2 inch) piece cucumber
¼ teaspoon paprika
¼ teaspoon ground coriander

½ clove garlic
1 tablespoon Tomato Sauce (page 18)
1 tablespoon natural low fat yogurt
salt and pepper to taste

1. Cut the fish into 6 pieces, and the potato and cucumber into 4 pieces each. Arrange alternately on 2 small skewers and brush with oil.
2. Mix together the paprika, coriander, and a little salt and pepper and sprinkle over the kebabs.
3. Cook under a preheated moderate grill for about 5 minutes on each side, until the fish is just firm.
4. Rub the cut side of the garlic around the inside of a small pan, add the tomato sauce and yogurt and heat through gently.
5. Carefully push the food from the skewers onto a bed of cooked brown rice and spoon the sauce over to serve.

Mackerel with Rhubarb Sauce

Serves 1
Preparation time: 10 minutes

Cooking time: 10 minutes
Freezing: Not recommended

Mackerel and rhubarb sound a very strange combination but it works well – the rich fish flavour is offset by the tangy, fruity sauce. This is good hot or cold.

½ teaspoon Dijon mustard
1 small fresh mackerel, cleaned and gutted
lemon juice for sprinkling

125 g (4 oz) rhubarb
1 teaspoon brown sugar
salt and pepper to taste

1. Spread the mustard inside the fish. Sprinkle with lemon juice, and salt and pepper.
2. Cook under a preheated hot grill for about 5 minutes. Turn and cook for another 5 minutes.
3. Meanwhile, simmer the rhubarb with 1–2 tablespoons water and the sugar until very soft. Sieve thoroughly to give a thin purée; add a little extra water if you wish.
4. Serve the mackerel with the rhubarb sauce poured over.

Crispy Liver with Sage

Serves 1
Preparation time: 7 minutes

Cooking time: 6 minutes
Freezing: Not recommended

15 g (½ oz) fresh wholemeal breadcrumbs
1 teaspoon chopped sage

125 g (4 oz) lambs' liver, sliced thinly
salt and pepper to taste
sage leaves to garnish (optional)

1. Mix together the breadcrumbs, sage, and salt and pepper, and use to coat the liver.
2. Cook under a preheated fairly hot grill for 3 minutes on each side, or according to taste.
3. Garnish with the sage leaves to serve if wished.

1. For the kebabs, mix together the oil, lemon juice, soy sauce, garlic and rosemary, pour over the meat and leave to marinate for 2 hours, turning occasionally.
2. Thread alternate pieces of lamb, red pepper and onion onto 8 skewers, then baste with the marinade.
3. Cook under a preheated moderate grill for 8 minutes, turning and basting frequently.
4. For the pilaf, cook the bulgar wheat in boiling salted water for 10 minutes, or until tender; drain well.
5. Heat the oil in a pan, add the onion and red pepper and fry for 5 minutes. Add the mushrooms and cook for 2 minutes, stirring.
6. Stir in the bulgar wheat, parsley and soy sauce. Turn into a serving dish and arrange the kebabs on top.

Russian Fish Pie

Serves 4–6

Preparation time: 30 minutes, plus pastry making, and cooking rice and fish	*Cooking time: 30 minutes* *Freezing: Recommended*

1 tablespoon oil	*375 g (12 oz) Finnan haddock,*
1 onion, chopped	*cooked and flaked*
125 g (4 oz) mushrooms,	*375 g (12 oz) Wholemeal*
sliced	*Pastry (page 118)*
50 g (2 oz) brown rice, cooked	*beaten egg to glaze*
2 tablespoons chopped parsley	*salt and pepper to taste*

1. Heat the oil in a pan, add the onion and fry until softened. Add the mushrooms and fry, stirring, for 3–4 minutes.
2. Add to the rice with the parsley, haddock, and salt and pepper.
3. Divide the pastry in half and roll out one piece to form a rectangle 30 × 18 cm (12 × 7 inches).
4. Place on a baking sheet and cover with the filling, leaving a 2.5 cm (1 inch) border all the way round; dampen these edges.
5. Roll out the remaining pastry slightly larger than the first piece. Cover the filling and trim the edges to fit. Press together, pinch the edges to seal and make 2 holes in the top. Decorate with leaves cut from the trimmings.
6. Brush with beaten egg and bake in a preheated oven, 200°C/400°F/Gas Mark 6, for 30 minutes, until golden.

Kebabs with Bulgar Pilaf

Serves 4

Preparation time: 15 minutes, plus marinating	*Cooking time: 20 minutes* *Freezing: Not recommended*

Bulgar wheat takes far less time to cook than other grains because it is cracked and partly cooked already, so it is very useful when you are in a rush.

KEBABS:	*3 small onions, each cut into 8*
1 tablespoon olive oil	*pieces*
2 tablespoons lemon juice	*BULGAR PILAF:*
1 tablespoon soy sauce	*175 g (6 oz) bulgar wheat*
1 clove garlic, crushed	*1 tablespoon oil*
1 teaspoon chopped rosemary	*1 onion, chopped*
500 g (1 lb) lean lamb, boned and cut into 2.5 cm (1 inch) cubes	*1 red pepper, cored, seeded and diced*
1 large red pepper, cored, seeded and cut into 2.5 cm (1 inch) squares	*125 g (4 oz) mushrooms, sliced* *1 tablespoon chopped parsley* *1 tablespoon soy sauce*

Pigeons Niçoise

Serves 4
Preparation time: 20 minutes

Cooking time: About 1½ hours
Freezing: Recommended

An excellent method of cooking pigeons, which can sometimes be dry and tough. This dish is delicious served with flageolet beans.

2 tablespoons oil
2 plump pigeons
125 g (4 oz) piece streaky bacon, chopped
175 g (6 oz) small onions, blanched and peeled
1 tablespoon wholemeal flour
2 cloves garlic, crushed

4 tomatoes, skinned and chopped
1 bouquet garni
125 ml (4 fl oz) red wine
125 ml (4 fl oz) chicken stock
10 black olives, pitted
salt and pepper to taste
1 tablespoon chopped parsley to garnish

1. Heat the oil in a flameproof casserole, add the pigeons and brown on all sides. Remove from the pan and keep warm.
2. Add the bacon and onions to the pan and fry, stirring, until they begin to turn golden. Stir in the flour.
3. Add the remaining ingredients and bring to the boil. Return the pigeons to the casserole, cover and cook in a preheated oven, 160°C/325°F/Gas Mark 3, for about 1½ hours, until tender.
4. Split the pigeons in half, arrange on a warmed serving dish with the onions and keep warm.
5. Discard the bouquet garni and spoon off any excess fat from the sauce, then boil rapidly to reduce slightly. Pour over the pigeons and sprinkle with the parsley to serve.

Braised Quail with Olives

Serves 4
Preparation time: 25 minutes

Cooking time: About 25 minutes
Freezing: Recommended

Quail and other game birds are very popular in Spain and are everyday items on restaurant menus. Quail is full of flavour, but it is a tiny bird so you will need two per person.

8 quail
4 tablespoons olive oil
1 onion, chopped
2 cloves garlic, crushed
4 tomatoes, skinned and chopped
150 ml (¼ pint) white wine

2 tablespoons brandy
50 g (2 oz) green olives, pitted and halved
2 tablespoons chopped parsley
1 bay leaf
1 thyme sprig
thyme sprigs to garnish

1. Truss each quail by tucking the wing tips under the body. Cross the legs and place each in a slit made on either side of the cavity.
2. Heat half of the oil in a large flameproof casserole, add the quail and fry until browned all over. Remove from the pan and keep warm.
3. Add the remaining oil, onion and garlic to the casserole and fry until softened. Add the remaining ingredients and bring to the boil. Return the quail to the pan, cover and simmer gently for about 25 minutes, until tender.
4. Remove the bay leaf and thyme and transfer to a warmed serving dish. Garnish with thyme to serve.

3. Pour in the wine or cider and cook until reduced a little, then stir in the stock. Season with salt and pepper and simmer for about 10 minutes, then stir in the butter.
4. Sprinkle with parsley and serve with crusty wholemeal bread and salad.

Haddock and Bean Cassoulet

Serves 4
Preparation time: 50 minutes, plus cooking beans
Cooking time: 30–35 minutes
Freezing: Recommended, if using fresh fish

Cassoulets are usually mixed meat and bean stews, but this one uses firm fish with beans for a lighter, quicker meal.

750 g (1½ lb) Finnan haddock
250 g (8 oz) monkfish tail
1 litre (1¾ pints) fish stock or water
1 large bay leaf
25 g (1 oz) butter
1 onion, chopped
1 celery stick, sliced
1 carrot, chopped
1 clove garlic, crushed
50 g (2 oz) Tendersweet bacon, derinded and chopped
125 g (4 oz) salt pork or ham
4 tablespoons dry white wine or cider

175 g (6 oz) haricot beans, cooked
½ teaspoon ground mace
1 each thyme, rosemary and savory sprig, or ½ teaspoon each dried herb
pinch of saffron threads, soaked in 1 tablespoon warm water (optional)
4 tomatoes, skinned and quartered
salt and pepper to taste
FOR THE TOPPING:
3 tablespoons fresh wholemeal breadcrumbs
2 tablespoons chopped parsley

1. Place the fish, stock or water, bay leaf and black pepper in a saucepan and cook gently for 10–15 minutes, until the flesh just flakes. Drain, reserving about 600 ml (1 pint) of the liquor.
2. Skin, bone and flake the fish and set aside.
3. Melt the butter in a pan, add the onion, celery, carrot and garlic and fry gently for about 5 minutes. Add the bacon and salt pork or ham and cook for 3 minutes.
4. Pour in the reserved fish liquor and wine or cider. Add the beans, mace and herbs and cook for about 10 minutes, until the liquid has nearly all been reduced.
5. Add the saffron and its water, if using, fish and tomatoes. Check the seasoning, then transfer to a shallow casserole.
6. Mix the breadcrumbs and parsley together and sprinkle over the top. Bake in a preheated oven, 190°C/375°F/Gas Mark 5, for 30–35 minutes, until the top is crisp and golden. Serve hot.

Lamb Steaks with Beans

Serves 4
Preparation time: 5 minutes, plus cooking beans

Cooking time: 25 minutes
Freezing: Recommended

2 tablespoons olive oil
4 chump chops
1 rosemary sprig or ½ teaspoon dried
2 cloves garlic, crushed
125 g (4 oz) haricot, cannellini or flageolet beans, cooked

125 g (4 oz) small onions
4 tablespoons dry white wine or cider
300 ml (½ pint) stock
knob of butter
salt and pepper to taste
chopped parsley to garnish

1. Heat the oil in a frying pan, add the lamb and cook for 3–5 minutes on each side, according to taste. Season with salt and pepper while cooking and sprinkle with the rosemary. Remove and keep warm.
2. Add the garlic, beans and onions to the pan and cook for about 5 minutes.

Lamb and Lentil Curry

Serves 4
Preparation time: 30 minutes
Cooking time: 1 hour

Freezing: Recommended, at
end of stage 3

2 tablespoons oil	1 teaspoon each ground
2 onions, sliced thinly	cumin, coriander and
1 clove garlic, crushed	turmeric
2.5 cm (1 inch) piece fresh root	1/2 teaspoon chilli powder
ginger, peeled and grated	600 ml (1 pint) water
2 teaspoons cumin seeds	250 g (8 oz) red lentils
500 g (1 lb) boneless lamb, e.g.	2 tablespoons lemon juice
leg or fillet, cubed	1 teaspoon garam masala
250 g (8 oz) tomatoes, skinned	salt to taste
and chopped	

1. Heat 1 tablespoon of the oil in a saucepan, add the onion, garlic, ginger and half of the cumin seeds and fry until the onion is softened and lightly browned. Add the lamb and cook, stirring, until well browned.
2. Add the tomatoes, cumin, coriander, turmeric, chilli powder and salt and stir well. Add the water and bring to the boil, then cover and simmer for 30 minutes.
3. Add the lentils and cook for 30 minutes or until the lamb and lentils are tender.
4. Just before serving, stir in the lemon juice and garam masala. Transfer to a warmed serving dish and keep warm.
5. Heat the remaining oil in a pan, add the remaining cumin seeds and fry quickly until they start to spit. Pour over the curry. Serve with brown rice and curry accompaniments.

Lamb Muglai

Serves 6–8
Preparation time: 20 minutes
Cooking time: 1 hour

Freezing: Recommended, at
end of stage 4

If you bone the lamb yourself, allow about 500 g (1 lb) of the total weight for the bone when buying the joint.

1.25–1.5 kg (2 1/2–3 lb) boneless	2 onions, chopped
lamb, cut into 2.5 cm	1 tablespoon curry powder
(1 inch) cubes	2 teaspoons ground coriander
600 ml (1 pint) water	2 teaspoons garam masala
5 cm (2 inch) piece cinnamon	1/2 teaspoon hot chilli powder
stick	5 tablespoons tomato purée
2 bay leaves	750 g (1 1/2 lb) potatoes, cut
8 cloves	into 2.5 cm (1 inch) chunks
5 cardamom pods	450 g (1 lb) carton natural set
2 tablespoons oil	yogurt

1. Place the lamb in a saucepan with the water, cinnamon stick, bay leaves, cloves and cardamom pods. Bring to the boil, then cover and simmer for 30 minutes.
2. Remove the meat with a slotted spoon and set aside. Strain the liquid into a jug.
3. Heat the oil in a saucepan, add the onions and fry gently until softened and lightly browned.
4. Add the lamb and the strained liquid, the spices, tomato purée and potatoes. Bring to the boil, stirring well, then cover and simmer for 25–30 minutes, until the lamb is very tender and the potatoes are cooked.
5. Stir in the yogurt a tablespoon at a time, stirring well and heating after each addition; do not allow to boil.
6. Serve the muglai with saffron rice, warm pitta bread and a shredded lettuce, cucumber and onion salad.

1. Season the flour with salt and pepper and use to coat the lamb.
2. Heat the oil in a flameproof casserole, add the onion and fry until lightly browned. Add the lamb and remaining ingredients, bring to the boil, then simmer for 5 minutes.
3. Cover the casserole tightly and cook in a preheated oven, 180°C/350°F/Gas Mark 4, for 1 hour.
4. Meanwhile, cut each slice of bread into 16 pieces.
5. Place the butter and paprika in a pan and heat gently until melted. Brush this mixture over one side of each piece of bread.
6. Cover the casserole with the bread, buttered side up and overlapping the pieces. Return to the oven, uncovered, for 30 minutes, until the bread topping is crisp and brown at the edges. Serve with leeks or green beans.

Boston Bean Pot

Serves 6
Preparation time: 15 minutes,   Cooking time: 2–2¹/2 hours
plus soaking time   Freezing: Recommended

500 g (1 lb) haricot beans, soaked overnight	3 tablespoons molasses
2 onions, chopped	2 tablespoons wine vinegar
2 celery sticks, chopped	pinch of ground cloves
2 tablespoons Dijon mustard	1 tablespoon tomato purée
2 tablespoons light brown soft sugar	750 g (1¹/2 lb) piece streaky pork
	1/2 teaspoon salt (optional)

1. Drain the beans and cook in boiling water for 10 minutes. Drain, then place in a flameproof casserole with the onion and celery.
2. Mix together the mustard, sugar, molasses, vinegar, cloves and tomato purée, add to the pan and top up with water until the beans are just covered.
3. Bury the pork in the beans. Bring the mixture slowly to the boil, skimming off any scum. Stir the beans.
4. Cover tightly and cook in a preheated oven, 180°C/350°F/Gas Mark 4, for 2–2¹/2 hours, until the beans are very tender; add a little boiling water halfway through the cooking if the mixture seems dry. Add the salt if using, and stir well.
5. To serve, remove the pork from the pot and cut into large chunks or slices, then return to the beans. Serve with wholemeal rolls.

Lamb and Ale Stew with Paprika Bread

Serves 6
Preparation time: 20 minutes   Freezing: Recommended, at
Cooking time: 1¹/2 hours   end of stage 3

Use real ale if possible as it gives the best flavour.

1 tablespoon plain flour	1 teaspoon Worcestershire sauce
1 kg (2 lb) lamb fillet, cut into 2.5 cm (1 inch) cubes	2 teaspoons sugar
1 tablespoon oil	salt and pepper to taste
2 onions, chopped	FOR THE TOPPING:
3 carrots, sliced	2 large slices white bread, crusts removed
2 celery sticks, sliced	25 g (1 oz) butter
300 ml (¹/2 pint) beer	1 teaspoon paprika
1 teaspoon Dijon mustard	

Cassoulet Robert

Serves 8

Preparation time: 30 minutes,   *Cooking time: 4 hours*
plus soaking time   *Freezing: Recommended*

Cassoulet originates in South West France, where every town has its own version. This recipe may not be strictly authentic, but it is delicious.

500 (1 lb) haricot beans,
  soaked overnight
750 g (1½ lb) belly pork slices
half shoulder of lamb, weighing
  about 750 g (1½ lb), boned
2 leeks
2 large carrots
2 cloves
1 large onion
2 thyme sprigs

4 cloves garlic
500 g (1 lb) ripe tomatoes,
  skinned and quartered
1 tablespoon oil
500 g (1 lb) coarse spicy
  sausage, such as Cumberland
50 g (2 oz) fresh wholemeal
  breadcrumbs
salt and pepper to taste
thyme sprigs to garnish

1. Drain and rinse the beans and cook in boiling water for 10 minutes. Drain, then place in a very large pan with water to cover. Bury the pork and lamb in the beans.

2. Tie the leeks together. Halve the carrots lengthways. Stick the cloves into the onion. Place these vegetables in the pan with the thyme, 2 garlic cloves and plenty of black pepper.

3. Bring slowly to the boil, skimming off any scum that rises to the surface, then cover and simmer for about 1½ hours, skimming occasionally, until the beans are tender.

4. Remove the meat and strain the beans, reserving the stock. Remove the vegetables and thyme from the beans. Taste the stock and add salt if necessary.

5. Remove the rind from the pork. Cut the lamb into 2.5 cm (1 inch) chunks and cut the pork slices the same length.

6. Crush the remaining garlic and mix with the tomatoes.

7. Place half of the beans in a large casserole. Cover with the meat, then the tomatoes. Place the remaining beans on top. Pour over 600 ml (1 pint) of the reserved stock and cover tightly.

8. Cook in a preheated oven, 140°C/275°F/Gas Mark 1, for 1½ hours; add more stock if it becomes too dry.

9. Heat the oil in a pan, add the sausage and fry until well browned. Drain and cut into 5 cm (2 inch) lengths. Stir into the beans. Sprinkle the breadcrumbs over the top. Return to the oven, uncovered, for 1 hour, until the top is crusty and golden brown.

10. Serve garnished with thyme, with plenty of warm French bread to mop up the juices, and a green salad.

Right: Potato, Egg and Anchovy Salad (page 10)

Crisp Whisky Drumsticks

Serves 12
Preparation time: 15 minutes,
plus marinating

Cooking time: 35–40 minutes
Freezing: Recommended
Calories per portion: 170

12 chicken drumsticks, skinned
6 tablespoons whisky
3 tablespoons soy sauce
4 tablespoons fresh orange
*　juice*

1 tablespoon grated root
*　ginger*
125 g (4 oz) porridge oats
salt and pepper to taste
orange slices to garnish

1. Make several deep cuts in each drumstick and place in a shallow dish. Mix together the whisky, soy sauce, orange juice and ginger. Pour over the drumsticks, cover and leave to marinate in the refrigerator for 3–4 hours.
2. Drain off the marinade and set aside.
3. Place the oats in a bowl and season lightly with salt and pepper. Toss the chicken drumsticks in this to coat well.
4. Place on a greased baking sheet and cook in a preheated oven, 190°C/375°F/Gas Mark 5, for 35–40 minutes, until golden. Boil the marinade until reduced by half.
5. Garnish the chicken with orange and serve the marinade hot or cold as a sauce or dip.

Chilli Con Carne

Serves 4
Preparation time: 15 minutes,
plus soaking beans

Cooking time: 2 hours
Freezing: Recommended

This dish is best made the day before it is eaten.

2 tablespoons oil
500 g (1 lb) stewing beef, diced
1 onion, chopped
1–2 green chillies, chopped
2 cloves garlic, crushed
1 tablespoon paprika
1–2 teaspoons chilli powder
1 tablespoon ground cumin

2 tablespoons tomato purée
600 ml (1 pint) beef stock or
*　water*
2 teaspoons dried oregano
2 bay leaves
125 g (4 oz) red kidney or pinto
*　beans, soaked overnight*
salt and pepper to taste

1. Heat the oil in a large pan, add the beef and fry, stirring, for about 5 minutes, until browned. Set aside.
2. Add the onion, chilli and garlic to the pan, and fry gently for about 3 minutes, then add the spices and fry for 1 minute.
3. Add the tomato purée, stock or water, oregano, bay leaves, and salt and pepper, return the meat, cover and simmer for 1 hour.
4. Meanwhile, drain the beans and cook rapidly in boiling water for 10 minutes; drain. Add them to the chilli mixture and cook for a further hour, or until the beans are tender.
5. Serve with plain boiled brown rice.

Bacon and Apricot Olives

Serves 4
Preparation time: 35 minutes

Cooking time: 35 minutes
Freezing: Recommended

50 g (2 oz) dried apricots,
  chopped
25 g (1 oz) fresh brown
  breadcrumbs
1 onion, chopped finely
1 tablespoon chopped parsley
25 g (1 oz) butter, melted
4 thin gammon steaks, derinded
2 leeks, cut into strips

1 small head celeriac, cut into
  sticks
150 ml (1/4 pint) vegetable stock
salt and pepper to taste
FOR THE SAUCE:
150 ml (1/4 pint) red wine
2 tablespoons redcurrant jelly
grated rind and juice of 1
  orange and 1 lemon
1 teaspoon Dijon mustard

1. Mix together the apricots, breadcrumbs, onion, parsley and butter. Season lightly with salt and pepper.
2. Divide the mixture between the gammon steaks and roll up. Secure with fine string or cocktail sticks.
3. Place the leeks and celeriac in an ovenproof dish, arrange the bacon olives on top and add the stock. Cover and cook in a preheated oven, 180°C/350°F/Gas Mark 4, for 35 minutes, until the bacon and vegetables are tender.
4. Place all the sauce ingredients in a small pan and bring to the boil, stirring, then simmer for 5 minutes.
5. Arrange the vegetables and bacon olives on a warmed serving dish and serve with the sauce and courgettes.

Venison and Redcurrant Casserole

Serves 4–6
Preparation time: 30 minutes,
plus marinating

Cooking time: 2 1/4 hours
Freezing: Recommended

1 kg (2 lb) stewing venison, cut
  into 2.5 cm (1 inch) cubes
450 ml (3/4 pint) red wine
2 cloves garlic, bruised
2 strips lemon rind
2 tablespoons lemon juice
3 tablespoons olive oil
1 cinnamon stick
2 onions

250 g (8 oz) streaky bacon
  rashers, derinded and
  halved
1 tablespoon plain flour
150 ml (1/4 pint) beef stock
125 g (4 oz) redcurrants
4 tablespoons redcurrant jelly
salt and pepper to taste

1. Place the venison in a bowl and pour over the wine. Add the garlic, lemon rind and juice, 2 tablespoons of the oil and the cinnamon stick. Cover and leave to marinate in the refrigerator overnight.
2. Remove the venison with a slotted spoon and dry on kitchen paper; strain and reserve the marinade.
3. Cut each onion into 6 wedges. Stretch the bacon with the back of a knife, then roll up each piece.
4. Heat the remaining oil in a flameproof casserole, add the onion, and fry until lightly browned, then remove.
5. Add the bacon rolls to the casserole and fry gently until the fat runs and they are lightly coloured. Remove with a slotted spoon.
6. Add the venison to the pan and fry until browned all over. Sprinkle in the flour and cook for 1 minute. Gradually stir in the reserved marinade and the stock and bring to the boil. Return the onions and bacon to the pan and stir well. Season with pepper, then cover and simmer for 2 hours, until the venison is tender.
7. Add the redcurrant and jelly to the pan and simmer for 10 minutes, until the redcurrants are tender and the jelly dissolved. Taste and add salt if necessary.
8. Serve with braised fennel and baked potatoes, topped with soured cream and chives.

Chicken-stuffed Courgettes

Serves 4
Preparation time: 25 minutes
Cooking time: 40 minutes

Freezing: Recommended, at end of stage 6

oil for brushing	*25 g (1 oz) wholemeal*
1 small onion, chopped finely	*breadcrumbs*
1 clove garlic, crushed	*4 large or 8 small courgettes*
150 g (5 oz) raw chicken,	*50 g (2 oz) Edam cheese,*
minced	*grated*
1 teaspoon mixed dried herbs	*3 tablespoons natural yogurt*
1 small dessert apple, peeled	*salt and pepper to taste*
and chopped	*herb sprigs to garnish*

1. Brush a non-stick frying pan with oil, add the onion and garlic and fry gently, until tender.
2. Add the chicken, herbs, apple, breadcrumbs, and salt and pepper, and cook for 5 minutes.
3. Top and tail the courgettes, cut in half lengthways and hollow out the centres with a teaspoon.
4. Chop the courgette flesh, add to the chicken mixture and cook for 1 minute.
5. Cook the courgettes in a boiling water for 2 minutes. Drain on kitchen paper and place close together in a baking dish.
6. Fill the courgettes with the chicken mixture, cover with foil and bake in a preheated oven, 190°C/375°F/ Gas Mark 5, for about 35 minutes, until tender.
7. Blend the cheese and yogurt together and spoon over the top. Place under a preheated hot grill for 4–5 minutes, until lightly browned. Garnish with herbs to serve.
Pictured on page 61

Chicken and Corn Pancakes

Serves 2–4
Preparation time: 35 minutes

Cooking time: 15 minutes
Freezing: Recommended

Serve 2 pancake rolls per person for a light meal, or more for a main course.

8 Wholemeal Pancakes	*175 g (6 oz) cooked chicken, diced*
(page 118)	*198 g (7 oz) can sweetcorn*
FOR THE FILLING:	*kernels, drained*
1 tablespoon oil	*1 tablespoon chopped parsley*
1 onion, chopped	*salt and pepper to taste*
4 tablespoons plain wholemeal	*TO FINISH:*
flour	*75 g (3 oz) Cheddar cheese,*
300 ml (1/2 pint) milk	*grated*

1. First, make the filling: heat the oil in a pan, add the onion and cook until softened. Remove from the heat and stir in the flour, then gradually add the milk, stirring until blended. Bring back to the boil, stirring constantly, and cook for 3 minutes, until thickened. Add the remaining ingredients.
2. Divide the filling between the pancakes, roll up and place in a shallow ovenproof dish. Sprinkle with the cheese and cook in a preheated oven, 190°C/375°F/ Gas Mark 5, for 15 minutes. Serve immediately, with a salad.
Pictured on page 42

Pork and Red Cabbage Bake

Serves 4
Preparation time: 35 minutes

Cooking time: 45–50 minutes
Freezing: Recommended

Red cabbage cooked with apples and wine vinegar is a delicious foil for rich pork. A crunchy potato topping completes the dish. Serve it with crusty wholemeal bread.

2 tablespoons oil
500 g (1 lb) pork shoulder or tenderloin, cubed
1 teaspoon cumin seeds
1 onion, chopped finely
750 g (1½ lb) red cabbage, shredded
1 cooking apple, peeled, cored and chopped

1 tablespoon light brown soft sugar
1 tablespoon wine vinegar
25 g (1 oz) raisins
150 ml (¼ pint) chicken stock
750 g (1½ lb) potatoes, parboiled in their skins and cubed
salt and pepper to taste

1. Heat half of the oil in a large pan, add the pork and fry until lightly browned. Remove and set aside.
2. Add the cumin seeds and onion to the pan and fry for about 2 minutes, stirring. Add the cabbage, apple, sugar, vinegar, raisins, stock, and salt and pepper. Bring to the boil, then simmer for 3–4 minutes, until the cabbage has softened slightly.
3. Toss the potatoes in the remaining oil, and sprinkle with salt and pepper. Place half of the cabbage mixture in an ovenproof dish and spoon over the pork. Cover with the remaining cabbage, then top with the potatoes.
4. Cook in a preheated oven, 180°C/350°F/Gas Mark 4, for 45–50 minutes, until the topping is crisp and golden.

Rabbit with Prunes and Walnuts

Serves 6
Preparation time: 20 minutes

Cooking time: 35–40 minutes
Freezing: Recommended

1 tablespoon plain wholemeal flour
500 g (1 lb) diced boneless rabbit, defrosted
1 tablespoon oil
25 g (1 oz) butter
175 g (6 oz) streaky bacon, derinded and chopped
125 g (4 oz) small onions

3 celery sticks, chopped
1 bay leaf
1 blade mace
12 ready-to-eat prunes
150 ml (¼ pint) white wine
300 ml (½ pint) chicken stock
50 g (2 oz) walnut pieces
3 tablespoons single cream
salt and pepper to taste

1. Season the flour with salt and pepper and use to coat the rabbit.

2. Heat the oil and butter in a large saucepan or flameproof casserole, add the rabbit and fry until evenly browned. Remove from the pan and set aside.
3. Add the bacon and onions to the pan and fry until lightly coloured. Add the celery, bay leaf, mace, prunes, wine and stock, bring to the boil, then simmer for 5 minutes, stirring. Return the rabbit to the pan with the walnuts, and salt and pepper, cover and simmer for 35–40 minutes, until the rabbit is tender. Discard the bay leaf and mace.
4. Transfer the rabbit, bacon, onions, prunes and walnuts to a warmed serving dish with a slotted spoon. Keep warm.
5. Boil the sauce rapidly until reduced by a third. Check the seasoning and stir in the cream. Pour over the rabbit. Serve with steamed potatoes, green beans sprinkled with sesame seeds, and a mixed salad.

Pulses and Grains

At the heart of the wholefood diet are these wonderful wholesome foods. The tremendous variety of pulses and grains now available means that the fussiest eater can find something to his or her taste, and with recipes including a range of fascinating dishes from a variety of ethnic cuisines around the world, there is plenty of interest for the cook.

Pulses and grains are high in dietary fibre and are also excellent sources of low-fat protein. In this chapter you will find plenty of ideas for main course meals that are vegetarian, as well as ideas for combining pulses and grains with meat and fish for nutritionally balanced, varied eating.

Accompaniments and side dishes are not forgotten, and there are plenty of ideas for starters, snacks and soups too.

Right (clockwise from top left): Sweet and Sour Red Salad (page 93), Bean and Vegetable Stew with Herb Dumplings (page 107), Kibbeh, Muesli (page 93), Cabbage with Bulgar Wheat (page 91)

Kibbeh

Serves 6–8
Preparation time: 45 minutes, plus soaking time
Cooking time: About 4 minutes per batch
Freezing: Recommended

So popular are Kibbeh in the Middle East that nimble 'Kibbeh' fingers are a prime requisite for gaining a good husband. Kibbeh orginated in Syria and the Lebanon, but they are now found in various forms throughout the Eastern Mediterranean region. They all have certain ingredients in common – bulgar wheat, minced meat, nuts, herbs and spices – but their preparation, shape, size and method of cooking differ from country to country.

500 g (1 lb) bulgar wheat	*25 g (1 oz) pine kernels*
2 tablespoons olive oil	*4 tablespoons chopped parsley*
2 onions, chopped finely	*salt and pepper to taste*
375 g (12 oz) lamb fillet, cut	*oil for deep-frying*
into small pieces	*lime wedges to serve*
1 teaspoon ground allspice	

1. Place the bulgar wheat in a bowl, pour over 1.2 litres (2 pints) boiling water and leave to soak for about 40 minutes, until it is cool enough to handle.
2. Meanwhile, make the filling. Heat the oil in a pan, add the onions and fry until softened. Add the lamb and fry, stirring, for about 10 minutes, then add the allspice, pine kernels, parsley, salt and pepper, and cook for a few more minutes. Leave to cool.
3. Add salt and pepper to the soaked bulgar wheat, then knead it for about 5 minutes until it becomes sticky and will form into a ball.
4. Take a small piece and roll in the palms of your dampened hands to make an egg shape. Make a hole in the middle with your forefinger and form the wheat into a hollow pot shape with fairly thin walls.
5. Fill it with the meat mixture, then pinch the open ends together and make into a pointed oval shape. Repeat with the remaining mixture to make about 22.
6. Deep fry a few at a time in hot oil for about 4 minutes, until golden brown.
7. Drain on kitchen paper and serve with lime wedges.
NOTE: You may find you have a little bulgar mixture or filling left over, depending on how good you are at shaping the bulgar shells.

flour, chives, salt, garlic, suet and pepper. Add the water, mix to a soft dough and knead briefly. Using lightly floured hands, shape the mixture into 8 balls.

3. Drop the dumplings into the stew, cover tightly and simmer for 25 minutes, until they are light and puffy.

4. Serve in soup plates, sprinkled with snipped chives.

Three Bean Cassoulet

Serves 4	*Cooking time: 25 minutes*
Preparation time: 15 minutes	*Freezing: Not recommended*

Turn this dish into a more substantial meal for the family if you wish by adding grilled, chopped sausages.

1 onion, sliced
1 clove garlic, crushed
432 g (14¹/2 oz) can flageolet beans, drained
208 g (7¹/2 oz) can red kidney beans, drained
250 g (8 oz) cut green beans, cooked
230 g (8 oz) can peeled tomatoes

1 vegetable stock cube
150 ml (¹/4 pint) water
1 tablespoon chopped mixed herbs, or 1 teaspoon dried herbs
125 g (4 oz) Mozzarella cheese, sliced thinly
50 g (2 oz) sunflower seeds, toasted
salt and pepper to taste

1. Place the onion, garlic, all the beans, tomatoes with their juice, stock cube and water in a flameproof casserole and bring to the boil.

2. Add the herbs, and salt and pepper, cover and simmer for about 20 minutes, stirring occasionally.

3. Lay the cheese on top and heat through for about 5 minutes.

4. Sprinkle with the sunflower seeds to serve.

Pictured on page 28

Haricot Bean Stew

Serves 4–6	
Preparation time: 25 minutes, plus soaking time	*Cooking time: 1¹/2–1³/4 hours* *Freezing: Not recommended*

Vegetarian suet makes excellent light dumplings without a strong fatty taste.

250 g (8 oz) haricot beans, soaked overnight
900 ml (1¹/2 pints) water
500 g (1 lb) piece unsmoked bacon, derinded and cubed
2 onions, chopped
250 g (8 oz) carrots, cut into large pieces
4 celery sticks, cut into large pieces
2 cloves garlic, crushed
250 g (8 oz) tomatoes, skinned and chopped

2 bay leaves
3 thyme sprigs
snipped chives to garnish
FOR THE DUMPLINGS:
125 g (4 oz) self-raising flour, sifted
1 tablespoon snipped chives
1 teaspoon salt
1 clove garlic, crushed
50 g (2 oz) vegetarian suet
4–5 tablespoons water
pepper to taste

1. Drain the beans and cook in boiling water for 10 minutes, then drain and place in a large saucepan with the remaining ingredients. Bring slowly to the boil, skimming off any scum, then cover and simmer for 1–1¹/4 hours, until the bacon is tender, skimming occasionally.

2. Meanwhile, make the dumplings. Mix together the

Cabbage with Bulgar Wheat

Serves 4–6
Preparation time: 10 minutes

Cooking time: 25–30 minutes
Freezing: Not recommended

2 tablespoons sunflower oil
6 spring onions, chopped
2.5 cm (1 inch) piece fresh root
   ginger, chopped finely
175 g (6 oz) bulgar wheat
600 ml (1 pint) chicken stock
1½ teaspoons garam masala
2 teaspoons soy sauce

50 g (2 oz) roasted cashew nuts
50 g (2 oz) raisins
2 tomatoes, chopped finely
1 tablespoon chopped parsley
1 Savoy cabbage, cut into
   wedges or shredded
salt and pepper to taste

1. Heat the oil in a pan, add the spring onions and ginger and fry gently until soft.
2. Stir in the bulgar wheat until it is coated in the oil. Add half of the stock and the garam masala. Bring to the boil, then cover and simmer gently for 10 minutes.
3. Add the soy sauce, nuts, raisins, tomatoes, parsley, remaining stock, and salt and pepper and simmer for 10–15 minutes, until the bulgar wheat is light and separate.
4. Meanwhile, cook the cabbage in a little boiling salted water for 7–10 minutes, until just tender.
5. Place the bulgar wheat in the centre of a warmed serving dish and place the cabbage wedges around the edge.
Pictured on page 89

Black Bean and Cheese Soup

Serves 4–6
Preparation time: 20 minutes,
plus cooking beans

Cooking time: 25 minutes
Freezing: Recommended

2 tablespoons oil
1 leek, sliced
1 clove garlic, crushed
125 g (4 oz) black or red kidney
   beans, cooked
1.25 litres (2¼ pints) vegetable
   stock

1 tablespoon light brown soft
   sugar
2 sage leaves, chopped
2 slices bread
oil for shallow frying
50 g (2 oz) Cheddar cheese,
   grated
salt and pepper to taste

1. Heat the oil in a large pan, add the leek and garlic and fry until softened. Add the beans, stock, sugar, sage, and plenty of salt and pepper. Bring to the boil, cover and simmer for about 20 minutes.
2. Meanwhile, remove the crusts from the bread and cut into small cubes. Shallow-fry in the hot oil for 1–2 minutes, until golden and crisp. Drain.
3. Pour the soup into warmed individual bowls and sprinkle the cheese and croûtons.

Below: Tomato and Rice Soup (page 45)

Couscous with Spiced Lamb

Serves 4–6

Preparation time: 20 minutes, plus cooking chick peas	Cooking time: About 35 minutes
	Freezing: Recommended

500 g (1 lb) couscous	1/2 teaspoon ground cinnamon
25 g (1 oz) butter	1 teaspoon ground coriander
500 g (1 lb) boned shoulder of lamb, diced	1 litre (1³/4 pints) stock
2 onions, quartered	1 small bulb fennel, quartered
2 carrots, sliced	230 g (8 oz) can tomatoes
2.5 cm (1 inch) piece fresh root ginger	75 g (3 oz) raisins
	juice of 1 lemon
1/2 teaspoon turmeric	125 g (4 oz) chick peas, cooked salt and pepper to taste

1. Place the couscous in a bowl, cover with hot water and drain. Spread out on a clean tray and leave for about 20 minutes; sprinkle with a little water about every 5 minutes and work the grains with your hands to free them of any lumps.
2. Meanwhile, melt the butter in a pan, add the lamb and fry until well browned. Add the onions, carrots and ginger and fry for about 5 minutes, until softened.
3. Sprinkle in the spices and fry for 1 minute, then stir in the remaining ingredients and bring to the boil.
4. Put the couscous into a steamer and place on top of the stew. When the steam starts to rise, cover and simmer for about 30 minutes.
5. Serve the couscous topped with the spiced lamb.

Vegetable and Bean Couscous

Serves 4–6

Preparation time: 30 minutes, plus cooking beans	Cooking time: 20 minutes
	Freezing: Not recommended

500 g (1 lb) couscous	125 g (4 oz) button mushrooms
2 tablespoons olive oil	175 g (6 oz) French beans, halved
25 g (1 oz) butter	
1 large onion, sliced	4 tomatoes, skinned and quartered
1 clove garlic, crushed	
2 carrots, sliced	300 ml (1/2 pint) each vegetable stock and dry cider
250 g (8 oz) parsnips, diced	
1 teaspoon each turmeric and ground coriander	
125 g (4 oz) white beans, cooked	6 canned artichoke hearts, halved

1. Prepare the couscous according to packet instructions.
2. Heat the oil and butter in a pan, add the onion, garlic, carrot and parsnip and fry gently for 10 minutes, or until softened. Sprinkle in the spices and cook for 1 minute.
3. Add the remaining ingredients, except the couscous, and bring to the boil.
4. Put the couscous into a steamer that fits on top of the saucepan, cover and simmer for about 20 minutes.
5. Serve the couscous topped with vegetables.

Chilli Bean Pot

Serves 4–6
Preparation time: 20 minutes,
plus soaking time

Cooking time: 1¹/₂–1³/₄ hours
Freezing: Recommended, at
end of stage 3

The pulses suggested here give a good colour combination
and have similar cooking times, so they can be cooked
in the same pot.

250 g (8 oz) red kidney beans,
  soaked overnight
125 g (4 oz) each blackeye
  beans and chick peas,
  soaked overnight
2 tablespoons oil
2 onions, chopped
1 clove garlic, crushed
1–2 teaspoons hot chilli powder
2 × 397 g (14 oz) cans chopped
  tomatoes

¹/₂ teaspoon caraway seeds
150 ml (¹/₄ pint) vegetable
  stock
1 green pepper, cored, seeded
  and chopped
125 g (4 oz) mushrooms,
  chopped
salt and pepper to taste
TO SERVE:
4 tablespoons natural yogurt
paprika

1. Drain and rinse the beans and place in a large pan.
Cover with cold water, bring to the boil and boil hard for 10
minutes, then partly cover and simmer for about 45
minutes, until almost tender. Drain well and rinse the pan.
2. Heat the oil in the pan, add the onion and garlic and
fry until softened. Add the chilli powder, tomatoes,
caraway seeds, stock and green pepper and bring to the
boil. Add the beans and simmer for 25–30 minutes.
3. Stir in the mushrooms, and salt and pepper, and cook
for 10–20 minutes, until the beans are tender.
4. Top each portion with a little yogurt and paprika.

Right: Vegetable Hotpot with Stilton Croûtons (page 32)

Muesli

Makes 750 g (1¹/₂ lb)
Preparation time: 15 minutes

Freezing: Not recommended

Also try adding grated apple or other fresh fruits. Use
apple juice instead of milk, and add yogurt or smetana.

175 g (6 oz) porridge oats
125 g (4 oz) wheat flakes
125 g (4 oz) barley flakes
  (optional)
75 g (3 oz) hazelnuts, chopped
  and browned

75 g (3 oz) sultanas
75 g (3 oz) chopped dates
25 g (1 oz) dried apple rings,
  chopped
25 g (1 oz) Muscovado sugar

1. Mix all the ingredients together in a large bowl. Store
in an airtight container and use as required.
Pictured on page 89

Sweet and Sour Red Salad

Serves 6
Preparation time: 35 minutes   Freezing: Not recommended

A brightly-coloured salad with an oriental flavour.

250 g (8 oz) red cabbage,
  shredded
432 g (15¹/₄ oz) can red
  kidney beans, drained
125 g (4 oz) radishes, sliced
1 small red onion, sliced very
  thinly
1 red pepper, cored, seeded
  and diced

200 g (7 oz) beetroot, cut into
  strips
FOR THE DRESSING:
4 tablespoons red wine
  vinegar
4 tablespoons light brown soft
  sugar
2 tablespoons light soy sauce
2 teaspoons oil

1. Cover the cabbage with boiling water, leave for 5
minutes, then drain well.
2. Combine all the salad ingredients.
3. Combine all the dressing ingredients.
4. Mix the salad and dressing together.
Pictured on page 89

Bulgar Parcels

Serves 4
Preparation time: 30 minutes, plus soaking time

Bulgar has a wonderfully nutty texture and needs no cooking – just a quick soak before using. The parcels can be made up and chilled for several hours before serving.

175 g (6 oz) bulgar wheat	*3 tablespoons lemon juice*
1 onion, chopped finely	*3 tablespoons olive oil*
3 tablespoons each chopped	*8 large crisp lettuce leaves*
parsley and mint	*salt and pepper to taste*
50 g (2 oz) cooked sweetcorn	*mint sprigs or spinach leaves*
kernels	*to garnish*
2 tomatoes, skinned and	
chopped finely	

1. Place the bulgar in a bowl and pour over plenty of hot water. Leave to soak for 30 minutes; it will swell considerably. Drain well, pressing out as much liquid as possible.
2. Place the bulgar in a bowl with the onion, herbs, sweetcorn and tomatoes and stir thoroughly.
3. Drizzle over the lemon juice and olive oil, mixing well, and season with salt and pepper.
4. Place a heaped tablespoon of bulgar on each lettuce leaf, fold in the sides and roll up to enclose the filling.
5. Place the parcels in a shallow dish or on a large plate and garnish with mint or spinach leaves to serve.

Granola

Makes 550 g (1 lb 2 oz)   *Cooking time: 30–35 minutes*
Preparation time: 15 minutes   *Freezing: Not recommended*

A scrumptious cereal to serve at breakfast time with milk or natural yogurt and fruit. Alter the cereals, nuts and seeds according to what you have available. Coconut gives it an interesting flavour for a change.

Granola is particularly nice with apricot purée – made simply by cooking 150 g (5 oz) dried apricots in 300 ml (½ pint) water for 20 minutes, then working in a blender or food processor until smooth.

3 tablespoons sunflower oil	*75 g (3 oz) buckwheat flakes*
4 tablespoons malt extract	*(optional)*
1 tablespoon clear honey	*50 g (2 oz) hazelnuts, chopped*
75 g (3 oz) porridge oats	*25 g (1 oz) sunflower seeds*
75 g (3 oz) jumbo oats	*2 tablespoons sesame seeds*

1. Place the oil, malt extract and honey in a large saucepan and heat gently until the malt is runny.
2. Stir in the remaining ingredients and mix thoroughly.
3. Turn the mixture into a large roasting tin and bake in a preheated oven, 180°C/350°F/Gas Mark 4, for 30–35 minutes, stirring occcasionally so that it browns evenly.
4. Leave to cool, breaking up the granola to separate the pieces as it does so. Store in an airtight container.

VARIATION

Mix together 125 g (4 oz) granola, two 150 g (5 oz) cartons natural yogurt, and 1 sliced banana or 2 sliced peaches and divide between 4 individual bowls.

Spinach and Lentil Galette

Serves 4
Preparation time: 35 minutes

Cooking time: 1 hour
Freezing: Recommended

14 Wholemeal Pancakes (page 118)
oil for frying
FOR THE 1ST FILLING:
1 bulb fennel, sliced thinly
1 onion, chopped
175 g (6 oz) red lentils
3 tomatoes, skinned and chopped
450 ml (³/4 pint) vegetable stock
1 tablespoon chopped marjoram

FOR THE 2ND FILLING:
25 g (1 oz) butter
500 g (1 lb) spinach, shredded
1 onion, chopped
1 clove garlic, crushed
250 g (8 oz) Ricotta or curd cheese
salt, pepper and grated nutmeg to taste
TO FINISH:
50 g (2 oz) Parmesan cheese, grated

1. Place the ingredients for the first filling in a pan and simmer for 25 minutes, until pulpy. Add salt and pepper.
2. Meanwhile, make and cook the pancakes.
3. To make the second filling, melt the butter in a pan, add the spinach, onion and garlic and cook for about 5 minutes, until wilted and just tender. Season with salt, pepper and nutmeg and stir in the cheese.
4. Lightly grease a 20 cm (8 inch) round deep cake tin and line the base and side with pancakes, cutting to fit.
5. Cover the base with a layer of the first filling, top with a pancake, sprinkle lightly with Parmesan, then cover with a layer of the second filling. Repeat the layers, finishing with a pancake.
6. Cover with greased foil and steam for 1 hour.
7. Cut into wedges and serve with Tomato Sauce (page 18) and broccoli.

Mushroom and Barley Bake

Serves 4
Preparation time: 15 minutes,
plus soaking time

Cooking time: 30–45 minutes
Freezing: Recommended

175 g (6 oz) pearl or pot barley, washed thoroughly	1 vegetable stock cube, crumbled
25 g (1 oz) butter	1 tablespoon cornflour
1 onion, chopped	300 ml (1/2 pint) milk
6 celery sticks, sliced	4 tomatoes, sliced
250 g (8 oz) mushrooms, sliced	salt and pepper to taste
	chopped herbs to garnish

1. Place the barley in a measuring jug and add water to reach the 600 ml (1 pint) mark. Leave to soak in a cool place for at least 4 hours, or overnight.
2. Melt the butter in a pan, add the onion and celery and fry gently until the onion is transparent. Add the mushrooms and fry gently for 1–2 minutes. Add the barley with its liquid and the stock cube. Cover and simmer for 30–45 minutes, until tender.
3. Blend the cornflour with a little of the milk, then add to the barley with the remaining milk. Heat gently, stirring, until thickened and creamy. Season with salt and pepper.
4. Transfer to a heatproof serving dish. Arrange the tomatoes on top, then place under a preheated hot grill until lightly browned. Sprinkle with the herbs and serve with crisp green vegetables.

Mushroom Caps with Buckwheat

Serves 4
Preparation time: 30 minutes

Cooking time: 15–20 minutes
Freezing: Not recommended

If you cannot buy buckwheat, use bulgar wheat instead.

125 g (4 oz) buckwheat	3 tablespoons chopped parsley
1 egg, beaten	2 tablespoons dry sherry
300 ml (1/2 pint) vegetable stock	50 g (2 oz) Parmesan cheese, grated
2 cloves garlic, crushed	salt and pepper to taste
4 large flat mushrooms	

1. Mix the buckwheat with the beaten egg and fry without any fat until dry and golden. Add the stock and garlic, cover and bring to the boil, then simmer for 15 minutes, until the buckwheat is tender. Remove the lid and bubble rapidly until no free liquid remains.
2. Remove the mushroom stalks and chop finely. Add to the buckwheat with the remaining ingredients.
3. Pile the mixture in top of the mushroom caps and place in an ovenproof dish. Cover and cook in a preheated oven, 200°C/400°F/Gas Mark 6, for 15–20 minutes, until the mushrooms are tender. Serve with Greek yogurt.

Frijoles Refritos

Serves 4

Preparation time: 5 minutes, plus cooking beans

Cooking time: 10–15 minutes

Freezing: Recommended

Refried beans or *frijoles refritos* are something of a staple food in Mexico, served in many ways. The idea behind frying already-cooked beans is to further develop their flavour. This is the authentic method of refrying, using the bean cooking liquor; however you can substitute water. If you have any left over – no problem, simply refry them again. The flavour gets better still!

3–4 tablespoons oil

1 small onion, chopped

250 g (8 oz) red kidney, pinto or black beans, cooked until very soft

about 450 ml (¾ pint) cooking liquor from beans

salt and pepper to taste

1. Heat the oil in a large frying pan, add the onion and fry gently.
2. Add about a quarter of the beans and a little of the cooking liquor, mashing with a potato masher, and stirring occasionally as they cook. Gradually add the remaining beans and cooking liquor, mashing and stirring until you have a coarse purée. Season with salt and pepper.
3. When the purée has started to dry around the edge, it is ready. Serve with tomato coulis (see below) or Tomato Sauce (page 18) if you wish.

USES FOR REFRIED BEANS
1. Serve on fried tortillas or tostados, topped with a fried egg or tomato coulis and slices of avocado or grated cheese.
2. Mix with rice as a quick stuffing for green peppers or tomatoes and top with grated cheese.
3. Spoon onto pancakes, roll up, spoon over tomato coulis, sprinkle with grated cheese and reheat in the oven.
4. Mix with cream cheese, grated cheese and tomato purée for a quick dip.
5. Serve on toast or a hot crispy roll, topped with an egg or melted Cheddar cheese and crumbled grilled bacon.

TOMATO COULIS
Place 500 g (1 lb) chopped ripe tomatoes, ½ teaspoon sugar, 1 teaspoon salt, ½ teaspoon dried mixed herbs, 2 tablespoons French dressing and pepper to taste in a saucepan. Cover and simmer for 10 minutes, then rub through a sieve.

Lentils with Spicy Sausage

Serves 4

Preparation time: 10 minutes

Cooking time: 25–45 minutes, depending on lentils used

Freezing: Recommended

Lentils make wonderful quick stews, especially when mixed with cured and smoked meats or sausages. This stew will go nicely with crusty bread or potatoes, or it can be served as a sauce for spaghetti.

50 g (2 oz) smoked or Tendersweet bacon, derinded and chopped

1 onion, chopped

1 clove garlic, crushed

250 g (8 oz) lentils

397 g (14 oz) can tomatoes

250 g (8 oz) cured and cooked sausage, e.g. chorizo or Polish kabanos

750 ml (1¼ pints) water

1 teaspoon paprika

salt and pepper to taste

1. Fry the bacon in a large pan until the fat runs, add the onion and garlic and fry gently until softened.
2. Add the remaining ingredients, bring to the boil, cover and simmer for 20–25 minutes if using red lentils, 35–40 minutes if using green or brown. Serve hot.

1. Cook the dried beans until tender; drain.
2. Blanch the French beans for 2 minutes; drain.
3. Combine the dressing ingredients in a large salad bowl. Add the beans while still hot and toss gently. Mix in the fennel.
4. Heat the oil in a pan, add the bacon and fry until crisp. Remove with a slotted spoon and set aside.
5. Pour the vinegar into the pan and scrape up any sediment. Heat gently, then pour onto the beans, stirring to coat.
6. Sprinkle the nuts and bacon over the salad and serve immediately.

Taco Chilli Bean salad

Serves 4
Preparation time: 15 minutes, plus cooking beans
Cooking time: 35 minutes
Freezing: Recommended for meat mixture only

1 tablespoon oil	*1 small onion, sliced*
250 g (8 oz) ground beef or minced pork	*1 small green pepper, cored, seeded and sliced*
1 clove garlic, crushed	*75 g (3 oz) matured Cheddar cheese, grated (optional)*
125 g (4 oz) can green chillies in brine, drained and chopped	*50 g (2 oz) taco shells or tortilla chips, broken roughly*
397 g (14 oz) can chopped tomatoes	*salt and pepper to taste*
125 g (4 oz) red kidney beans, cooked	*1 tomato, cut into wedges, to garnish*
1 small Iceberg, crisp or Cos lettuce	

1. Heat the oil in a frying pan, add the meat and garlic and fry until browned.
2. Add the chillies, tomatoes, beans, and salt and pepper, cover and simmer for 15 minutes. Uncover and continue cooking for 15 minutes.
3. Meanwhile, prepare the salad. Tear the lettuce into small pieces and place in a bowl. Mix in the onion, green pepper, cheese if using, and taco or tortilla pieces.
4. Pile the hot meat mixture into the centre and serve immediately, or allow the meat to get cold and then add to the salad. Garnish with tomato to serve.

Three Bean and Nut Salad

Serves 4
Preparation time: 15 minutes, plus cooking beans
Freezing: Not recommended

75 g (3 oz) pinto, red kidney or borlotti beans	*raspberry vinegar*
75 g (3 oz) white cannellini beans	*50 g (2 oz) walnuts, almonds or cashew nuts*
125 g (4 oz) French beans, quartered	*FOR THE DRESSING:*
1 small bulb fennel, sliced thinly	*1 teaspoon coarse-grain mustard*
1 tablespoon oil	*3 tablespoons finely chopped onion*
75 g (3 oz) Tendersweet bacon, derinded and diced	*2 tablespoons red wine vinegar*
2 tablespoons red wine or	*2 tablespoons olive oil*
	1/2 teaspoon salt
	black pepper to taste

Creamy Beans in Mushroom Cups

Serves 4
Preparation time: 10 minutes,
  plus cooking beans

Cooking time: 10–15 minutes
Freezing: Not recommended

4 large flat mushrooms	50 g (2 oz) cream cheese or
oil for brushing	low-fat soft cheese
25 g (1 oz) butter	150 ml (¼ pint) milk
4 spring onions, chopped	125 g (4 oz) flageolet or
2 tablespoons chopped parsley	haricot beans, cooked
1 teaspoon chopped dill	salt and pepper to taste
	dill sprigs to garnish

1. Remove the stalks from the mushrooms, chop them finely and set aside.
2. Brush both sides of the mushroom cups with oil, place in a baking dish, and season with salt and pepper. Cover and cook in a preheated oven, 200°C/400°F/Gas Mark 6, for 10–15 minutes, until softened. Reserve any juices.
3. Meanwhile, melt the butter in a pan, add the spring onions and chopped mushrooms stalks and fry gently for about 5 minutes. Add any mushroom juices, the parsley, dill, and salt and pepper.
4. Add the cheese and milk and stir gently until melted and creamy. Stir in the beans and reheat.
5. Arrange the mushrooms on warmed individual plates and fill with the bean mixture. Garnish with dill to serve.

Aduki Bean Burgers

Makes 8
Preparation time: 25 minutes,
  plus cooking beans

Cooking time: 12 minutes
Freezing: Recommended

250 g (8 oz) aduki beans,	½ vegetable stock cube
cooked	75 g (3 oz) wholemeal
2 tablespoons oil	breadcrumbs
1 large onion, chopped	wholemeal flour for coating
2 cloves garlic, crushed	oil for shallow frying
1 teaspoon yeast extract	salt and pepper to taste

1. Mash half of the beans, then mix in the rest.
2. Heat the oil in a pan, add the onion and garlic and fry for 5 minutes. Stir in the yeast extract and stock cube. Mix into the beans with the breadcrumbs, and salt and pepper.
3. With wet hands, form the mixture into 8 patties. Coat with flour and fry in the hot oil for 3 minutes on each side.
4. Serve in pitta bread with salad and relishes.

Black Eye Beanburgers

Serves 4

Preparation time: 25 minutes,	*Cooking time: 6 minutes*
plus cooking beans	*Freezing: Recommended*

You can use any beans for this recipe. Serve with a sauce made from natural yogurt flavoured with garlic and coriander, salad and wholemeal bread.

250 g (8 oz) black eye beans,	*1 teaspoon turmeric*
cooked	*2 teaspoons ground coriander*
3 tablespoons oil	*2 tablespoons tomato purée*
1 onion, chopped	*25 g (1 oz) fresh wholemeal*
1 celery stick, chopped	*breadcrumbs*
2 cloves garlic, crushed	*salt and pepper to taste*

1. Purée the beans in a food processor.
2. Heat 1 tablespoon of the oil in a pan, add the onion and celery and fry until softened. Add the garlic and spices and fry for 1 minute.
3. Mix the beans with the fried vegetables and tomato purée, then season with salt and pepper.
4. Shape into 8 burgers and coat with the breadcrumbs.
5. Heat the remaining oil in a pan, add the burgers and fry for 3 minutes on each side, until golden.
Pictured on page 55

Paprika Bean Casserole

Serves 4

Preparation time: 30 minutes,	*Cooking time: 1 hour 40 minutes*
plus soaking time	*Freezing: Recommended*

250 g (8 oz) haricot beans,	*2 tablespoons paprika*
soaked overnight	*1 teaspoon clear honey*
3 tablespoons oil	*2 × 397 g (14 oz) cans*
1 clove garlic, crushed	*chopped tomatoes*
3 onions, sliced	*2 tablespoons tomato purée*
2 green peppers, cored, seeded	*salt and pepper to taste*
and sliced	*parsley sprigs to garnish*

1. Drain and rinse the beans and place in a pan. Cover with cold water, bring to the boil and boil for 10 minutes, then cover and simmer for about 1 hour, until tender. Drain well.
2. Heat the oil in a large pan, add the garlic and onion and fry until softened and lightly browned. Add the peppers and fry for 5 minutes.
3. Add the beans and remaining ingredients, bring to the boil, then cover and simmer for 25 minutes.
4. Garnish with parsley to serve.

Grilled Halloumi Cheese on Rye

Serves 4	*Cooking time: 10 minutes*
Preparation time: 3–5 minutes	*Freezing: Not recommended*

4 slices rye bread with	*1 tablespoon each chopped*
caraway, toasted and	*dill and mint*
buttered lightly	*1/2 small cucumber, cut into*
150 g (5 oz) halloumi cheese,	*sticks, to serve*
cut into 8 slices	

1. Cut the toast in half lengthways. Top with the cheese and return to the grill for 3–5 minutes, until golden.
2. Sprinkle with the herbs and serve immediately, accompanied by the cucumber.

Beans à la Grecque

Serves 4

Preparation time: 10 minutes,
plus cooking beans and chilling

Cooking time: 8–10 minutes,
plus cooking beans

Use any white bean for this recipe, although the white kidney or haricot beans look the nicest. Overnight chilling allows the flavours to mature.

300 ml (¹/2 pint) water
2 tablespoons tomato purée
2 tablespoons olive or
*   sunflower oil*
2 tablespoons vinegar
1 clove garlic, crushed
¹/2 teaspoon ground coriander
1 small onion, chopped

1 large courgette, sliced
125 g (4 oz) button
*   mushrooms, halved*
125 g (4 oz) white beans,
*   cooked*
3 tablespoons chopped parsley
salt and pepper to taste
chopped parsley to serve

1. Place the water, tomato purée, oil, vinegar, garlic, coriander, and salt and pepper in a large saucepan, bring to the boil, then simmer for about 5 mintues.
2. Add the onion, courgette and mushrooms and cook for 3–5 minutes, until just cooked but still quite crunchy. Stir in the beans and parsley and check the seasoning. Leave to cool, then chill overnight.
3. Sprinkle with parsley and serve with wholemeal bread.

Falafels with Tahina Cream

Makes 8

Preparation time: 15 minutes,
plus cooking chick peas

Cooking time: 6 minutes
Freezing: Not recommended

Falafels are little protein-packed patties eaten as street food in the Middle East, tucked into pittas with salad and served with tahini cream. The cream will keep for up to 7 days in a screw-topped jar in the refrigerator.

125 g (4 oz) chick peas, cooked
1 clove garlic, crushed
2 tablespoons chopped parsley
2 tablespoons chopped
*   coriander, or ¹/2 teaspoon*
*   ground*
¹/2 teaspoon ground cumin
1 tablespoon wholemeal flour
1 teaspoon salt
pepper to taste
oil for shallow frying

FOR THE TAHINA CREAM:
6 tablespoons tahina
150 ml (¹/4 pint) water
juice of ¹/2 lemon
1 clove garlic, crushed
TO SERVE:
4 wholemeal pitta breads,
*   halved*
2 tomatoes, sliced
few lettuce leaves
cucumber slices

1. Drain the chick peas. Place in a blender or food processor and work until smooth but thick. Add the remaining ingredients and work until well blended.
2. With wet hands, divide the mixture into 8 pieces and shape into flat patties. Shallow-fry in hot oil for about 6 minutes, turning once, until golden. Drain on kitchen paper.
3. To make the tahina cream, gradually mix the tahina and water together until smooth. Stir in the lemon juice, garlic, and salt and pepper to taste.
4. To serve, place a falafel in each pitta, with a portion of the salad ingredients and a spoonful of tahina cream. Serve hot or cold.

Brazil and Bulgar Wheat Burgers

Serves 4   *Cooking time: 15–20 minutes*
Preparation time: 20 minutes   *Freezing: Recommended*

Use any nuts to vary these protein-packed burgers.

2 tablespoons oil	*2 teaspoons dried mixed herbs*
125 g (4 oz) onion, chopped finely	*1 egg (size 1), beaten*
2 celery sticks, chopped finely	FOR THE ORANGE SAUCE:
2 cloves garlic, crushed	*25 g (1 oz) butter*
125 g (4 oz) bulgar wheat	*25 g (1 oz) onion or shallot, chopped finely*
250 g (8 oz) brazil nuts, ground coarsely	*1 tablespoon plain flour*
300 ml (1/2 pint) vegetable stock	*150 ml (1/4 pint) vegetable stock*
2 tablespoons tomato purée	*grated rind and juice of 1 large orange*
2 tablespoons chopped parsley	*salt and pepper to taste*

1. Heat the oil in a pan, add the onion, celery and garlic and fry gently until soft. Add the bulgar wheat and nuts and sauté for a few minutes, until lightly golden. Add the stock and simmer until the liquid is absorbed.
2. Stir in the tomato purée, parsley, herbs and beaten egg, season generously with salt and pepper, and leave until cool enough to handle.
3. Shape into 4 oval 'burgers', place on a greased baking sheet and cook in a preheated oven, 200°C/400°F/Gas Mark 6, for 15–20 minutes, until heated through.
4. Meanwhile, make the orange sauce. Melt the butter in a pan, add the onion or shallot and fry gently until golden. Add the flour and cook, stirring, for 1–2 minutes. Stir in the stock, orange rind and juice and simmer for 2–3 minutes. Season with salt and pepper.
5. Transfer the burgers to a warmed serving dish and accompany with the sauce and courgettes.

Pictured on page 34

Bulgar Wheat and Lentil Pilaf

Serves 4–6   *Cooking time: 35 minutes*
Preparation time: 10 minutes   *Freezing: Recommended*

250 g (8 oz) bulgar wheat	*2 carrots, chopped*
1.2 litres (2 pints) vegetable stock or water	*1/2 teaspoon each ground coriander and cumin*
2 tablespoons oil	*125 g (4 oz) green lentils*
1 onion, chopped	*2 bay leaves*
1 small green pepper, cored, seeded and chopped	*salt and pepper to taste*
2 celery sticks, chopped	*chopped parsley to garnish*

1. Place the bulgar wheat and half of the stock or water in a pan, bring to the boil, cover and simmer for 5 minutes, until the liquid is absorbed.
2. Spread out on a baking sheet and place in a preheated oven, 190°C/375°F/Gas Mark 5, for about 25 minutes, forking through twice to separate the grains.
3. Meanwhile, heat the oil in a pan, add the vegetables and fry for 5 minutes. Add the spices and cook for 1 minute.
4. Add the lentils, remaining stock or water, bay leaves, and salt and pepper. Bring to the boil, cover and simmer for 30 minutes, until the lentils are soft but still holding their shape. Remove the bay leaves.
5. Spoon the bulgar wheat onto a serving platter and top with the lentils. Sprinkle with parsley to serve.

Pictured on page 45

Pea, Tofu and Avocado Dip

Makes 300 ml (¹/₂ pint)
Preparation time: 10 minutes, plus cooking peas
Freezing: Recommended

Most pulses are good bases for creamy, low-fat dips. This one uses dried green peas, with added flavouring and creaminess from the avocado and tofu.

125 g (4 oz) dried green peas, cooked	*1 tablespoon chopped parsley*
75 g (3 oz) tofu	*¹/₂ teaspoon ground cumin*
¹/₂ ripe avocado, peeled	*1 teaspoon Worcestershire sauce*
1 clove garlic, crushed	*juice of ¹/₂ lemon*
2 spring onions, chopped	*salt and pepper to taste*

1. Place all the ingredients in a blender or food processor and work until smooth. Chill until required. Serve with crackers, tortilla chips or raw vegetables.

VARIATION
Add a little chilli powder or hot pepper sauce, and chopped green pepper, chopped tomato and stuffed olives.

Red Bean Chilli Dip

Makes about 450 ml (³/₄ pint)
Preparation time: 10 minutes, plus cooking beans
Cooking time: 5 minutes
Freezing: Recommended

A spicy Mexican-style dip. Use mild or hot chilli powder according to taste.

2 tablespoons oil	*125 g (4 oz) red kidney or pinto beans, cooked for 1¹/₂ hours*
1 small onion, chopped	
1 clove garlic, crushed	
1 teaspoon chilli powder	*113 g (4 oz) carton cream cheese or curd cheese*
1 teaspoon ground cumin	
1 tablespoon tomato purée	*50 g (2 oz) matured Cheddar cheese, grated*
1 tablespoon red wine vinegar	
	salt and pepper to taste

1. Heat the oil in a small pan, add the onion and garlic and fry gently for about 4 minutes. Add the spices and fry for 1 minute, then stir in the tomato purée and vinegar. Leave to cool.
2. Place the beans, cheeses and onion mixture in a blender or food processor and work until the consistency of thick mayonnaise; add a little water if necessary.
3. Check the seasoning. Chill until required. Serve with raw vegetables or tortilla chips.

Hummus

Makes about 300 ml (¹/₂ pint)
Preparation time: 5 minutes, plus cooking chick peas
Freezing: Recommended

This will keep in the refrigerator for about 3 days. Tahina is a paste made from ground sesame seeds, sold in jars.

100 g (3¹/₂ oz) chick peas, cooked for 1¹/₂ hours	*salt and pepper to taste*
	TO GARNISH:
4 tablespoons tahina	*chilli powder*
3 tablespoons lemon juice	*chopped parsley*
1 clove garlic, crushed	*olive oil (optional)*

1. Place all the ingredients in a blender or food processor and work together until smooth and creamy, adding a little water if necessary; hummus should have a soft spooning consistency, not too dry.
2. Check the seasoning, then spoon into a serving bowl. Sprinkle with a little chilli powder and parsley and trickle over a little olive oil, if you wish. Serve as a dip with vegetable crudités or pieces of pitta bread, or use as a sauce with kebabs, burgers or chops.

Fish Tabbouleh

Serves 4
Preparation time: 20 minutes

Cooking time: 8 minutes
Freezing: Recommended

75 g (3 oz) bulgar wheat
300-350 g (10–12 oz) white
*   fish*
75 g (3 oz) parsley, chopped
*   finely*
2 tablespoons chopped mint
3 tomatoes, chopped finely
1 onion, chopped finely

grated rind and juice of 1
*   lemon*
2 tablespoons oil
2 teaspoons coarse-grain
*   mustard*
salt and pepper to taste
tomato slices and mint sprigs
*   to garnish*

1. Soak the bulgar in hot water for 10–15 minutes.
2. Poach the fish in a little water for 8 minutes, until just tender. Cool, remove the skin and bones, then break into chunks or flakes.
3. Drain the bulgar well to remove excess water.
4. Mix the bulgar with the parsley, mint, tomato, onion, and salt and pepper.
5. Stir in the fish and spoon into a serving dish.
6. Mix together the lemon rind and juice, oil and mustard. Pour over the salad.
7. Garnish with tomato slices and mint to serve.

Middle-Eastern Tabbouleh

Serves 4
Preparation time: 10 minutes, plus soaking time
Freezing: Not recommended

Tabbouleh is a traditional Middle-Eastern salad made with bulgar wheat – cracked wheat which has been hulled and parboiled to give it a mild nutty flavour.

175 g (6 oz) fine bulgar wheat
6 spring onions, chopped
2 tablespoons chopped mint
4 tablespoons chopped parsley
3 tablespoons olive oil

4 tablespoons freshly squeezed
*   lemon juice*
salt and pepper to taste
TO SERVE:
1 small Cos lettuce

1. Place the bulgar wheat in a bowl, cover with cold water and leave to soak for 30 minutes. Squeeze out the water with your hands and place in a bowl.
2. Mix in the remaining ingredients.
3. Arrange the lettuce and tabbouleh in individual serving bowls. Use the lettuce leaves to scoop up the salad.

Cashew Nut Pâté

Serves 4–6
Preparation time: 15 minutes, plus cooking beans
Freezing: Recommended

1 tablespoon oil	handful parsley
50 g (2 oz) mushrooms, chopped	125 g (4 oz) cooked pinto beans
1 clove garlic, crushed	2 tablespoons natural yogurt
125 g (4 oz) cashew nuts, roasted	salt and pepper to taste
	radish slices to garnish

1. Heat the oil in a pan, add the mushrooms and garlic and fry for 2–3 minutes, stirring occasionally. Set aside.
2. Place the nuts and parsley in a food processor or blender and chop. Add the beans and yogurt and work until smooth.
3. Turn the mixture into a bowl, add the mushrooms, and salt and pepper and mix well.
4. Turn into a serving dish, garnish with radish slices and serve with Wholemeal Melba Toast (see below).

Mushroom and Bean Pâté

Serves 4

Preparation time: 15 minutes, plus cooking beans	Cooking time: 10 minutes
	Freezing: Recommended

1 tablespoon sunflower oil	125 g (4 oz) cooked butter beans
1 onion, chopped	2 tablespoons chopped parsley
175 g (6 oz) mushrooms, chopped	1/4 teaspoon chopped thyme
2 cloves garlic, crushed	salt and pepper to taste
	thyme sprigs to garnish

1. Heat the oil in a pan, add the onion and fry until softened.
2. Add the mushrooms and garlic and fry for 5 minutes, stirring occasionally.
3. Purée the beans and herbs in a food processor or blender.
4. Mix with the mushroom mixture and season with salt and pepper. Turn into a serving dish and garnish with thyme. Serve with Wholemeal Melba Toast (see below).

WHOLEMEAL MELBA TOAST
Simply toast a slice of wholemeal bread on both sides. Place on a flat surface, cut off the crusts and, holding your hand firmly on top, split the slice horizontally with a knife, using a sawing action. Place under a preheated moderate grill, cut sides up, until the toasts curl up and turn golden.

Mushroom and Wheat Berry Soup

Serves 4–6
Preparation time: 15 minutes, plus soaking time

Cooking time: About 45 minutes
Freezing: Recommended

If you have difficulty finding wheat berries, use green lentils instead, but don't soak them.

175 g (6 oz) wheat berries
50 g (2 oz) butter
1 large onion, chopped
2 cloves garlic, chopped finely
250 g (8 oz) mushrooms, chopped finely

1 tablespoon coarse-grain mustard
1 teaspoon dried dill
1 teaspoon dried thyme
2 vegetable stock cubes
yeast extract or vegetable extract to taste

1. Soak the wheat berries in 1.5 litres (2½ pints) boiling water for at least 2 hours or overnight.
2. Melt the butter in a pan, add the onion, garlic and mushrooms and fry gently for 10 minutes.
3. Add the wheat berries with their soaking water, and the remaining ingredients.
4. Bring to the boil, then cover and simmer for about 45 minutes, until the wheat is tender. Serve hot.

Mixed Grain Croquettes

Makes 16
Preparation time: 15 minutes

Cooking time: 20 minutes
Freezing: Not recommended

This is a good way of using up leftover cooked grains. If possible, try to use home-sprouted beans.

1 tablespoon oil
1 onion, chopped finely
1 clove garlic, crushed
½ teaspoon curry powder
175 g (6 oz) mixed cooked grains, e.g. rice, bulgar wheat, pearl barley
75 g (3 oz) bean sprouts, e.g. lentil, mung, aduki

75 g (3 oz) roasted peanuts, ground
50 g (2 oz) matured Cheddar cheese, grated
25 g (1 oz) self-raising wholemeal flour
2 eggs, beaten
4 tablespoons milk
oil for deep-frying
salt and pepper to taste

1. Heat the oil in a pan, add the onion and garlic and fry for 5 minutes, then add the curry powder and fry for 1 minute. Leave to cool.
2. Stir in the remaining ingredients.
3. Drop a few dessertspoonfuls of the batter into hot oil and deep-fry for about 1½ minutes, until golden and crisp. Drain on kitchen paper. Repeat with the remaining batter. Serve piping hot as a light meal.

Below: Stuffed cabbage (page 47)

Bean and Vegetable Stew with Herb Dumplings

Serves 4　　　　　*Cooking time: 40 minutes*
Preparation time: 40 minutes　*Freezing: Recommended*

2 tablespoons oil
2 cloves garlic, chopped
500 g (1 lb) leeks, sliced
1 large carrot, diced
250 g (8 oz) mushrooms,
　sliced
397 g (14 oz) can tomatoes
300 ml (1/2 pint) vegetable
　stock
1 tablespoon paprika
1 tablespoon soy sauce

432 g (15 1/4 oz) can red kidney
　beans, drained
salt and pepper to taste
FOR THE DUMPLINGS:
125 g (4 oz) wholemeal self-
　raising flour, sifted
50 g (2 oz) vegetable suet
3 tablespoons chopped mixed
　herbs
5 tablespoons cold water

1. Heat the oil in a pan, add the garlic, leeks, carrot, and mushrooms and sauté until just tender.
2. Add the tomatoes with their juice, stock, paprika and soy sauce. Bring to the boil, then cover and simmer for 20 minutes.
3. Meanwhile, make the dumplings. Mix all the ingredients together to give a firm dough, then shape into 12 balls.
4. Add the kidney beans, and salt and pepper to the stew. Arrange the dumplings on top, cover and simmer for 20 minutes, until the dumplings are light and fluffy. Serve as soon as possible.
Pictured on page 89

Chick Pea Casserole

Serves 4
Preparation time: 15 minutes, plus standing time and cooking chick peas
Cooking time: 30 minutes
Freezing: Recommended

If you sprinkle the diced aubergine with salt and leave for 30 minutes, it removes the bitter juices and reduces the amount of oil needed for frying. Serve with brown rice.

375 g (12 oz) chick peas,
　cooked
1 aubergine, diced
1 tablespoon olive oil
2 cloves garlic, crushed
1 teaspoon ground cumin

397 g (14 oz) can tomatoes
2 tablespoons tomato purée
2 tablespoons chopped
　coriander leaves
salt and pepper to taste

1. Drain the chick peas, reserving 300 ml (1/2 pint) of the liquid, and set aside.
2. Place the diced aubergine in a colander, sprinkle with salt and leave for 30 minutes. Rinse well and pat dry with kitchen paper.
3. Heat the oil in a pan, add the aubergine and fry until golden, turning occasionally. Add the garlic and cumin, fry for 1 minute, then add the tomatoes with their juice, tomato purée, coriander, chick peas and reserved liquid.
4. Season with salt and pepper, bring to the boil, cover and simmer for 30 minutes. Serve in a shallow dish.

Bean and Tomato Soup

Serves 6–8   *Cooking time: 2 hours*
Preparation time: 10 minutes   *Freezing: Recommended*

A hearty, warming soup. For a quicker soup, use two 400 g (14 oz) cans of drained white kidney beans instead of the dried beans; reduce the water to 900 ml (1¹/₂ pints) and the cooking time to 30 minutes.

2 tablespoons oil   *1 tablespoon tomato purée*
1 large onion, chopped   *397 g (14 oz) can chopped*
2 celery sticks, chopped   *tomatoes*
2 cloves garlic, crushed   *1.2 litres (2 pints) water*
250 g (8 oz) haricot beans,   *2 teaspoons lemon juice*
soaked overnight   *2 tablespoons chopped parsley*
1 bouquet garni   *salt and pepper to taste*

1. Heat the oil in a pan, add the onion and celery and fry until softened.
2. Add the garlic, drained beans, bouquet garni, tomato purée, tomatoes and water. Bring to the boil, cover and simmer for about 2 hours, until the beans are tender, adding salt and pepper towards the end of cooking time.
3. Remove the bouquet garni. Add the lemon juice and parsley, check the seasoning and pour into a warmed soup tureen.

Curried Lentil Soup

Serves 4–6   *Cooking time: 45 minutes*
Preparation time: 10 minutes   *Freezing: Recommended*

1 onion, chopped   *1 teaspoon curry powder*
1 celery stick, chopped   *1 teaspoon turmeric*
1 carrot, chopped   *salt and pepper to taste*
1 clove garlic, crushed   *1 tablespoon chopped parsley*
175 g (6 oz) red lentils   *to garnish*
900 ml (1¹/₂ pints) water

1. Place all the ingredients, except the salt and pepper, in a large saucepan. Bring to the boil, cover and simmer for 45 minutes, stirring occasionally.
2. Add salt and pepper, pour into a warmed soup tureen and sprinkle with the parsley to serve.

Stuffed Leaves with Lemon Sauce

Serves 4–6
Preparation time: 40 minutes
Cooking time: 30 minutes – 1 hour
Freezing: Recommended for cabbage rolls only

12 large chard or cabbage leaves	*100 g (3½ oz) bulgar wheat*
25 g (1 oz) butter	*227 g (8 oz) pack low fat soft cheese*
1 leek, chopped	*salt and pepper to taste*
1 carrot, chopped	*lemon slices to garnish*
125 g (4 oz) mushrooms, sliced thinly	FOR THE SAUCE:
600 ml (1 pint) vegetable stock	*3 tablespoons plain flour*
100 g (3½ oz) red lentils	*150 ml (¼ pint) water*
½ teaspoon dried thyme	*juice of 1 lemon*
	3 eggs, beaten

1. Remove the thick ribs from the chard or cabbage leaves, forming a 'V' shape. Blanch the leaves in about 1 litre (1¾ pints) lightly salted water for 2–6 minutes, until softened. Drain, reserving the water, cool and lay out on a worktop.

2. Melt the butter in a pan, add the leek and carrot and fry for about 5 minutes, until softened. Add the mushrooms and cook for about 3 minutes.

3. Pour in three quarters of the stock and add the lentils, thyme, and salt and pepper. Bring to the boil, cover and simmer for about 10 minutes.

4. Meanwhile, soak the bulgar wheat in the remaining stock for 5 minutes. Stir into the lentil mixture with the cheese. Check the seasoning.

5. Spoon the filling onto the stalk end of the leaves. Fold the stalk ends over, then fold in the sides and roll up. Place in a roasting tin, join side down.

6. Pour over the reserved cabbage water, adding extra stock or water if the rolls are not covered. Season with salt and pepper, and cover with foil.

7. Bake in a preheated oven, 190°C/375°F/Gas Mark 5, for about 30 minutes for chard leaves and up to 1 hour for cabbage. Remove with a slotted spoon to a serving dish and keep warm. Strain 600 ml (1 pint) of the stock.

8. To make the sauce, blend the flour and water in a pan. Whisk in the reserved stock and bring to the boil, whisking until smooth. Add the lemon juice and cool slightly.

9. Put the eggs in a bowl, pour on a little stock, then return to the pan. On the lowest possible heat, stir until the sauce thickens then remove immediately; sometimes it thickens on mixing and does not need reheating.

10. Check the seasoning and pour over the stuffed rolls. Garnish with lemon slices to serve.

1. Heat the oil in a large saucepan, add the onion, garlic, green pepper and celery and fry for about 10 minutes, until softened. Sprinkle in the chilli powder and cook for 1 minute. Season with salt and pepper.

2. Stir in the remaining ingredients, bring to the boil, then simmer for 5 minutes. Spoon into a greased 1.8 litre (3 pint) ovenproof pie dish.

3. Blend the cornmeal with the flour, salt and baking powder, then beat in the egg, milk and oil until smooth; the mixture should resemble a thick batter. Spoon over the bean mixture and sprinkle with the cheese.

4. Bake in a preheated oven, 220°C/425°F/Gas Mark 7, for 40–45 minutes, until golden and firm. Serve hot.

Courgette and Tomato Dhal

Serves 4	Cooking time: 25 minutes
Preparation time: 20 minutes	Freezing: Recommended

250 g (8 oz) yellow split peas	1/2 green pepper, chopped
600 ml (1 pint) stock	1 teaspoon turmeric
1 onion, chopped	1 teaspoon garam masala
2 tablespoons oil	1 large courgette, sliced
1 teaspoon mustard seeds	2 large tomatoes, skinned and
2.5 cm (1 inch) piece fresh root	chopped
ginger, chopped	juice of 1/2 lemon
1 clove garlic, crushed	salt and pepper to taste

1. Place the split peas, stock, half of the onion, and salt in a saucepan. Cover, bring to the boil, then simmer for about 25 minutes, until the peas are soft but still whole.

2. Meanwhile, heat the oil in another pan, add the mustard seeds, cover and fry until they stop popping. Add the remaining onion, the ginger, garlic and green pepper and fry gently for 5 minutes.

3. Add the turmeric and garam masala and cook for 1 minute, then add the courgette, tomatoes, lemon juice, about 2 tablespoons water, and salt and pepper. Cover and simmer for 5 minutes.

4. Carefully mix the vegetables and split peas together and transfer to a warmed serving dish. If serving as a main dish, serve with brown rice and halved hard-boiled eggs, or with naan bread or chapatis.

Tamale Pie

Serves 4	
Preparation time: 30 minutes,	Cooking time: 40–45 minutes
plus cooking beans	Freezing: Recommended

This Mexican-style recipe is a bean and chilli pot topped with cornbread.

2 tablespoons oil	2 tablespoons chopped parsley
1 onion, chopped	salt and pepper to taste
1 clove garlic, crushed	FOR THE CORNBREAD:
1/2 green pepper, chopped	125 g (4 oz) cornmeal
1 celery stick, chopped	1 tablespoon plain flour
1/2 teaspoon chilli powder	1/2 teaspoon salt
1 tablespoon tomato purée	2 teaspoons baking powder
397 g (14 oz) can chopped	1 egg, beaten
tomatoes	100 ml (3 1/2 fl oz) milk
12 pitted green olives, sliced	1 tablespoon oil
75 g (3 oz) sweetcorn kernels	50 g (2 oz) Cheddar cheese,
150 g (5 oz) red kidney beans,	grated
cooked	

Dhal Sambar

Serves 4
Preparation time: 20 minutes

Cooking time: 40 minutes
Freezing: Recommended

Don't be put off by the inclusion of whole chillies in this recipe it's not as hot as it may appear, as the lentils add a creamy taste to offset the fire!

250 g (8 oz) red lentils
600 ml (1 pint) water
1 teaspoon turmeric
3 green chillies, halved
    lengthways
1 tablespoon chopped
    coriander leaves
250 g (8 oz) aubergine, cut
    into strips
230 g (8 oz) can peeled tomatoes

2 tablespoons oil
2 onions, chopped
2 cloves garlic, crushed
1 cm (1/2 inch) piece fresh root
    ginger, peeled and chopped
    finely
1 teaspoon cumin seeds
1/2 teaspoon each fenugreek
    and mustard seeds
1/2 teaspoon salt

1. Place the lentils and water in a saucepan, bring to the boil, then simmer for 10 minutes. Stir in the turmeric, chillies, coriander, aubergine and tomatoes with their juice. Bring to the boil, then cover and simmer for 30 minutes, until the lentils are soft and pulpy.
2. Meanwhile, heat the oil in a frying pan, add the onion and fry until softened and golden brown. Add the garlic, ginger, cumin, fenugreek and mustard seeds and fry for 2 minutes.
3. Add to the lentils with the salt and stir well. Serve with spiced Basmati rice and puppodoms.

Succotash

Serves 4
Preparation time: 5 minutes,
plus cooking beans

Cooking time: 15 minutes
Freezing: Recommended

Succotash is an American-Indian name for a mixture of lima (butter) beans and corn. For a quickly prepared version, use canned beans and frozen corn. This is an ideal soup for vegetarians.

2 fresh sweetcorn cobs or
    375 g (12 oz) frozen
    sweetcorn kernels
25 g (1 oz) butter or
    margarine
2 cloves garlic, crushed
1 onion, chopped
2 celery sticks, sliced
125 g (4 oz) butter beans,
    cooked

1 thyme sprig, or 1/2 teaspoon
    dried thyme
1 savory sprig, or 2 sage
    leaves
1 teaspoon chopped basil
300 ml (1/2 pint) milk
300 ml (1/2 pint) vegetable
    stock
salt and pepper to taste
thyme sprigs to garnish

Right: Mediterranean Vegetable Stew (page 35)

1. If using fresh sweetcorn, stand the cobs upright and using a sharp knife strip the kernels by cutting downwards.
2. Melt the butter or margarine in a pan, add the garlic, onion and celery and fry gently for about 5 minutes, until softened.
3. Add the remaining ingredients, and season well with salt and pepper. Bring to the boil, then cover and simmer for 10 minutes.
4. Check seasoning and serve garnished with thyme.
Pictured on page 60

Hamburgers

Makes 4	*Cooking time: 8 minutes*
Preparation time: 15 minutes, plus soaking time	*Freezing: Recommended, at end of stage 1*

Bulgur wheat swells to about 4 times its dry size, bulking out the meat and making a healthier burger.

50 g (2 oz) bulgar wheat, soaked in boiling water for 20 minutes	*1 clove garlic*
	1 tablespoon soy sauce
	1 teaspoon Worcestershire sauce
250 g (8 oz) minced beef	
1 small carrot, grated	*salt and pepper to taste*
1/2 onion, chopped finely	*oil for brushing*

1. Drain the bulgar wheat in a sieve, pressing out the moisture. Turn into a bowl and mix with the remaining ingredients, using your hands. Form into 4 burgers.
2. Brush lightly with oil and cook under a preheated hot grill for about 4 minutes on each side.
3. Serve with salad or in wholemeal baps, with a spicy fruit sauce or Tomato Sauce (page 18).

Milligetti

Serves 4	*Cooking time: 35 minutes*
Preparation time: 15 minutes	*Freezing: Recommended*

Millet is used to cut down on the quantity of meat needed in this recipe – its texture is ideal.

1 tablespoon oil	*397 g (14 oz) can tomatoes*
1 onion, chopped	*1 tablespoon tomato purée*
1 clove garlic, crushed	*1 tablespoon soy sauce*
250 g (8 oz) minced beef	*300 ml (1/2 pint) vegetable stock*
1 tablespoon flour	
50 g (2 oz) millet or bulgar wheat	*salt and pepper to taste*
	grated cheese to serve

1. Heat the oil in a saucepan, add the onion and fry until softened. Add the garlic and beef and cook, stirring so that the meat is broken up as it seals. Remove from the heat, drain off any fat, then stir in the flour.
2. Add the remaining ingredients, bring to the boil, then cover and simmer for 35 minutes, until cooked.
3. Serve with cheese and wholewheat spaghetti.

Bean Koftas

Serves 4–6
Preparation time: 30 minutes, plus cooking beans and chilling
Cooking time: 20 minutes
Freezing: Not recommended

Koftas, or Keftas, are North African spicy meat patties moulded around kebab sticks and grilled; this is a vegetarian version. They can be made ahead and stored chilled until ready to cook, but should be eaten as soon as they come out of the pan.

125 g (4 oz) bulgar wheat or millet
300 ml (¹/₂ pint) vegetable stock
2 tablespoons oil
125 g (4 oz) mushrooms, chopped finely
1 onion, chopped finely
2 cloves garlic, crushed
¹/₂ teaspoon ground coriander
1 teaspoon ground cumin
2 teaspoons paprika
125 g (4 oz) aduki beans, cooked until soft
1 tablespoon chopped mint
3 tablespoons chopped parsley
1 tablespoon chopped coriander (optional)
1 egg, beaten
wholemeal flour for coating
oil for shallow frying
salt and pepper to taste
FOR THE RAITA:
¹/₄ cucumber, peeled, seeded and grated
2 spring onions, chopped
6 tablespoons natural yogurt
1 tablespoon chopped mint
TO GARNISH:
chicory leaves
watercress sprigs

1. Place the bulgar wheat or millet and stock in a pan, cover and cook for 5 minutes, until the liquid has been absorbed. Season well with salt and pepper. Set aside.
2. Heat the oil in a pan, add the mushrooms, onion and garlic, cover and cook gently for about 10 minutes, until soft. Add the spices and fry for 2 minutes.
3. Place in a blender or food processor with the beans, herbs, egg, and salt and pepper and work to a thick purée.
4. Mix with the bulgar wheat or millet in a bowl and chill for 1 hour.
5. Using wet hands, shape into small oval patties and toss in flour to coat. Heat the oil in a frying pan and shallow fry the patties in batches until crisp and golden on both sides, turning once or twice.
6. Meanwhile, mix together the ingredients for the raita and season with salt and pepper. Spoon into a small bowl.
7. Serve the koftas garnished with chicory and watercress, and accompanied by the raita.

Desserts and Baking

No one looking at these recipes for delicious puddings and sweet and savoury bakes could think that a wholefood diet was lacking in treats! If you have a sweet tooth, you will find all sorts of ideas in this chapter for indulgences that can be included as part of a healthy eating campaign. And because the sweetness in these recipes comes more from a range of dried and fresh fruit than from refined sugars, these recipes are mainly low in calories and high in dietary fibre.

There are a range of delicious desserts in this chapter, from substantial hot puddings to delicate chilled fruit desserts. In addition, you will find a range of baking ideas that includes both sweet and savoury recipes, making full use of the delicious taste and texture of wholemeal flour. Whether you want a coffee-time treat or something wholesome to round off a packed lunch you will find a healthy, tasty cake, biscuit or cookie here to fit the bill. Many of these recipes are popular with children, so you can indulge their taste for sweet things and encourage good eating habits at the same time.

Right (clockwise from top left): Honey Apple Cake, Summer Peaches (page 129), Spiced Crackers, Apricot Fool (page 129)

Spiced Crackers

Makes about 18	*Cooking time: About 20 minutes*
Preparation time: About 20 minutes	*Freezing: Recommended*

125 g (4 oz) Granary ® flour	*1 egg yolk*
pinch of salt	*1 tablespoon milk*
25 g (1 oz) cornflour	*(approximately)*
1/4 teaspoon ground coriander	*lightly beaten egg white to glaze*
1/2 teaspoon baking powder	*crushed sea or rock salt*
50 g (2 oz) margarine	

1. Place the flour, salt, cornflour, coriander and baking powder in a bowl and mix well. Rub in the margarine until the mixture resembles fine crumbs, then add the egg yolk and enough milk to mix to a pliable dough. Knead until smooth.
2. Roll out the dough to 2.5 mm (1/8 inch) thickness and cut into squares with a 5 cm (2 inch) fluted cutter. Transfer to 2 greased baking sheets, brush with egg white and prick 3 times with a fork. Sprinkle with salt.
3. Bake in a preheated oven, 190°C/375°F/Gas Mark 5, for about 20 minutes, until lightly browned. Cool on a wire rack.

Honey Apple Cake

Makes one 20 cm (8 inch) cake	*Cooking time: 1–1 1/4 hours*
Preparation time: 15 minutes	*Freezing: Recommended*

Use dessert apples for natural sweetness, and grate the skin for extra fibre and texture. This is nice with Greek yogurt and apple purée.

250 g (8 oz) plain wholemeal flour	*2 eggs*
2 teaspoons baking powder	*125 ml (4 fl oz) apple juice*
2 teaspoons ground mixed spice	*125 ml (4 fl oz) sunflower oil*
3 tablespoons clear honey	*250 g (8 oz) dessert apples, cored and grated*
250 g (8 oz) dried chopped dates	*2 tablespoons chopped hazelnuts*

1. Grease and line a 20 cm (8 inch) round deep cake tin.
2. Place the flour in a mixing bowl, then sift in the baking powder and spice. Make a well in the centre and add the remaining ingredients, except the hazelnuts. Beat together vigorously until thoroughly mixed.
3. Turn into the prepared tin and sprinkle with the nuts.
4. Bake in a preheated oven, 180°C/350°F/Gas Mark 4, for 1–1 1/4 hours, until the cake springs back when pressed in the centre. Turn onto a wire rack to cool.

Wholemeal Waffles

Makes 4	Cooking time: 8–12 minutes
Preparation time: 10 minutes	Freezing: Recommended

These waffles are light and airy, and delicious served with fruit purée or strawberries and yogurt. It is well worth investing in the special waffle iron needed to make them.

75 g (3 oz) plain wholemeal flour	1 egg, separated
	1 teaspoon clear honey
1 teaspoon cinnamon	1 tablespoon oil
1½ teaspoons baking powder	250 ml (8 fl oz) milk

1. Place the flour in a mixing bowl and sift in the cinnamon and baking powder. Make a well in the centre.
2. Add the egg yolk, honey, oil and milk and beat until completely smooth.
3. Whisk the egg white until fairly stiff, then fold carefully into the batter.
4. Spoon a quarter of the mixture into a heated and oiled non-stick waffle iron and cook for 2–3 minutes on each side, until crisp and golden. Remove and keep warm.
5. Cook the remaining batter in the same way.

Fruit with Hazelnut Sauce

Serves 4
Preparation time: 20–30 minutes
Freezing: Recommended for sauce only

A lovely breakfast to serve in the summer when there are so many fresh fruits available. Choose several types, thinking about their colour, so they will look attractive on the plate. Serve with wholemeal bread.

50 g (2 oz) hazelnuts, browned	175 g (6 oz) smetana (approximately)
25 g (1 oz) wholemeal breadcrumbs	selection of fresh fruits in season (e.g. pineapple,
1 tablespoon clear honey	watermelon, peaches,
1 tablespoon lemon juice	apples, oranges, pears)

1. Grind the hazelnuts finely in a food processor.
2. Add the remaining ingredients, except the fruit, and blend until smooth; add extra smetana to thin if necessary.
3. Prepare the chosen fruits as necessary, slice and arrange on individual plates, then spoon a little hazelnut sauce onto each plate.

Anzac Biscuits

Makes about 20   *Cooking time: 25–30 minutes*
Preparation time: About 10   *Freezing: Recommended*
minutes

175 g (6 oz) margarine, melted   *125 g (4 oz) porridge oats*
1 teaspoon bicarbonate of soda,   *175 g (6 oz) light brown soft*
*   dissolved in 2 tablespoons*   *   sugar*
*   boiling water*   *150 g (5 oz) raisins, chopped*
125 g (4 oz) plain wholemeal   *   roughly*
*   flour*   *50 g (2 oz) cut mixed peel*

1. Mix all the ingredients together to form a dough. Place teaspoons of the mixture in heaps well apart on greased baking sheets.
2. Bake in a preheated oven 150°C/300°F/Gas Mark 2, for 25–30 minutes, until golden and just firm. Cool on a wire rack.

Apricot and Nut Bites

Makes about 16   *Cooking time: About 20 minutes*
Preparation time: 20 minutes   *Freezing: Recommended*

These delicious little cookies can be made instantly in a food processor: chop the apricots and nuts, then add the remaining ingredients and work for a few seconds until combined.

75 g (3 oz) margarine   *50 g (2 oz) dried apricots,*
75 g (3 oz) light brown soft   *   chopped finely*
*   sugar*   *50 g (2 oz) walnut halves or*
1 egg yolk   *   Brazil kernels, chopped*
175 g (6 oz) plain wholemeal   *walnut halves or Brazil*
*   flour*   *   kernels, halved lengthways,*
grated rind of 1/2 lemon   *   to decorate*
2 teaspoons lemon juice

1. Cream the margarine and sugar together until light and fluffy, then beat in the egg yolk.
2. Gradually work in the remaining ingredients to give a pliable dough. Roll out to 5 mm (1/4 inch) thickness and cut into rounds with a 6 cm (2 1/2 inch) plain cutter. Transfer to 2 greased baking sheets and top with nuts.
3. Bake in a preheated oven, 180°C/350°F/Gas Mark 4, for about 20 minutes, until lightly browned. Cool on a wire rack.

Wholemeal Scone Shapes

Makes about 15   Cooking time: 12–15 minutes
Preparation time: 15 minutes   Freezing: Recommended

Most children won't be able to resist these novelty-shaped scones. They are so quick to make you could serve them fresh from the oven when they come home starving from school. Delicious with a sweet or savoury spread.

250 g (8 oz) self-raising   125 ml (4 fl oz) milk
   wholemeal flour   (approximately) plus extra
50 g (2 oz) margarine   to glaze
                                    1/4 teaspoon sesame seeds

1. Place the flour, margarine and milk in a mixing bowl and mix with a fork to form a soft dough; add a little more milk if necessary.
2. Turn onto a lightly floured surface, knead lightly and roll out to a 2 cm (3/4 inch) thickness. Using a 5 cm (2 inch) shaped cutter (e.g. star, animal) cut out about 15 scones.
3. Place on a floured baking sheet, brush with milk and sprinkle with the sesame seeds.
4. Bake in a preheated oven, 220°C/425°F/Gas Mark 7, for 12–15 minutes. Cool on a wire rack. Serve warm or cold.

Wholemeal Pancakes

Makes 12–14
Preparation time: 10 minutes,   Cooking time: 15 minutes
plus standing time   Freezing: Recommended

These pancakes have far more flavour than those made with white flour. You can also use buckwheat flour, which Bretons usually use in their crêpes.

1 egg   125 g (4 oz) plain wholemeal
300 ml (1/2 pint) milk   flour
                                    oil for greasing

1. Place the egg and milk in a blender or food processor, add the flour and work for 30 seconds until smooth. Leave to stand for 30 minutes, to thicken.
2. Grease a 15 cm (6 inch) omelette pan and place over a moderate heat. Pour in 1 tablespoon of the batter, tilting the pan to coat the bottom evenly.
3. Cook until the underside is brown, then turn over and cook for 10 seconds.
4. Turn onto a plate and repeat with the remaining batter to make about 12–14 pancakes. Stack them interleaved with greaseproof paper and keep warm.

Wholemeal Pastry

Makes a 250 g (8 oz) quantity
Preparation time: 8 minutes, plus chilling
Freezing: Recommended

A simple pastry to make and far less crumbly than the results achieved with the conventional method; therefore it can be rolled out more thinly.

50 g (2 oz) margarine   250 g (8 oz) plain wholemeal
50 g (2 oz) white vegetable fat   flour
3 tablespoons iced water

1. Place the fats, water and a quarter of the flour in a mixing bowl and mix with a fork until blended.
2. Add the remaining flour and mix to a firm dough.
3. Turn onto a floured surface and knead lightly until smooth, then chill for 20 minutes.
4. Roll the pastry out thinly and use as desired.
VARIATION
Wholemeal Cheese Pastry: Mix in 75 g (3 oz) finely grated matured Cheddar cheese and 1 teaspoon sifted dry mustard when adding the remaining flour.

Farmhouse Festival Loaf

Makes one 500 g (1 lb) loaf
Preparation time: 30 minutes,   *Cooking time: 15–30 minutes*
plus rising time   *Freezing: Recommended*

Homemade bread can become an everyday luxury, especially if you mix and knead the dough in the food processor, then leave it to prove slowly overnight in the refrigerator ready for baking the following morning.

15 g (¹/₂ oz) fresh yeast   *¹/₂ teaspoon salt*
¹/₂ teaspoon molasses   *1¹/₂ teaspoons sunflower oil*
225 ml (7 fl oz) warm water   *buckwheat, bulgar wheat,*
375 g (12 oz) plain wholemeal   *seeds or nuts to sprinkle*
*   flour*   *(optional)*

1. Cream the yeast and molasses with a third of the water. Leave in a warm place for about 5 minutes, until frothy.
2. Fit the metal chopping blade to the food processor. Place the flour, salt and oil in the processor bowl. With the motor running, add the yeast liquid and remaining water through the feed tube; process for 30 seconds, to blend and knead the dough.
3. Cover the processor bowl with clingfilm and leave to rise in a warm place for 1¹/₂–2 hours, until doubled in size.
4. Process for about 10–15 seconds, to knock back and knead the dough.
5. Flatten the dough out to an oblong about 2.5 cm (1 inch) thick. Fold into three, like an envelope, and tuck the 2 short ends over the seam to fit the tin. Place seam-side down in a greased 500 g (1 lb) loaf tin.
6. Cover with clingfilm and leave to rise in a warm place for 30 minutes to 1 hour, until almost doubled in size. Sprinkle with buckwheat, bulgar wheat, seeds or nuts, or a combination, if you wish.
7. Bake in a preheated oven, 220°C/425°F/Gas Mark 7, for 25–30 minutes, until the bread sounds hollow when tapped underneath. Turn out and cool on a wire rack.

VARIATIONS

Plait: Divide the dough into 3 equal pieces. Roll each into a long strand and plait them loosely together, starting in the centre and working to each end in turn. Dampen the ends and pinch together to seal. Place on a greased baking sheet and proceed as above.

Cloverleaf Rolls: Divide the dough into 6 equal portions, then divide each into 3 pieces. Shape each piece into a small ball. Place in groups of 3 on a greased baking sheet and proceed as above, cooking for 15–20 minutes.

Picnic Squares

Makes 24	Cooking time: 25–30 minutes
Preparation time: 10 minutes	Freezing: Recommended

These are as good as, or better than, a bowl of cereal for an instant breakfast, or make part of a healthy lunch. The crunchiness is very popular.

3 tablespoons malt extract	125 g (4 oz) porridge oats
2 tablespoons clear honey	25 g (1 oz) sunflower seeds
125 ml (4 fl oz) sunflower oil	25 g (1 oz) peanuts, chopped
125 g (4 oz) jumbo oats	finely

1. Place the malt, honey and oil in a pan and heat gently until combined. Remove from the heat, add the remaining ingredients and mix thoroughly.
2. Press into a greased 30 × 20 cm (12 × 8 inch) Swiss roll tin and smooth the top with a palette knife.
3. Bake in a preheated oven, 180°C/350°F/ Gas Mark 4, for 25–30 minutes.
4. Cool in the tin for 2 minutes, then cut into squares. Cool completely before removing from the tin.

Fruity Fingers

Makes 20	Cooking time: 1–1¼ hours
Preparation time: 30 minutes	Freezing: Recommended

200 g (7 oz) plain wholemeal flour	4 eggs
	250 g (8 oz) currants
1 teaspoon each ground mixed spice and cinnamon	250 g (8 oz) sultanas
	175 g (6 oz) raisins
175 g (6 oz) margarine	1 tablespoon orange juice
150 g (5 oz) muscovado sugar	3 tablespoons chopped walnuts
2 tablespoons malt extract	

1. Grease and line a 28 × 18 cm (11 × 7 inch) baking tin.
2. Place the flour in a bowl and sift in the spices.
3. Cream the margarine with the sugar and malt extract until fluffy. Beat in the eggs one at a time, adding a tablespoon of flour with all but the first. Fold in the remaining flour with the fruits and orange juice.
4. Turn the mixture into the prepared tin, smooth the surface and sprinkle with the walnuts.
5. Bake in a preheated oven, 160°C/325°F/Gas Mark 3, for 1–1¼ hours, until a skewer pierced through the centre comes out clean.
6. Cool on a wire rack, then cut into fingers.

Date and Orange Teabread

Makes one 500 g (1 lb) loaf
Preparation time: 15 minutes,   *Cooking time: 55–60 minutes*
plus soaking time   *Freezing: Recommended*

125 g (4 oz) High Fibre Bran   *50 g (2 oz) sunflower seeds*
125 g (4 oz) dried chopped   *125 g (4 oz) plain wholemeal*
   dates   *flour*
300 ml (¹/₂ pint) orange juice   *2 teaspoons baking powder*
1 tablespoon clear honey

1. Grease and line a 500 g (1 lb) loaf tin.
2. Put the Breakfast Bran, dates, orange juice and honey in a mixing bowl. Stir well and leave for 1 hour.
3. Add the sunflower seeds and flour, then sift in the baking powder and mix together thoroughly.
4. Turn into the prepared tin and bake in a preheated oven, 180°C/350°F/Gas Mark 4, for 55–60 minutes, or until a skewer inserted into the centre comes out clean.
5. Turn onto a wire rack to cool.

Spiced Apple Scones

Makes 12   *Cooking time: 12–15 minutes*
Preparation time: 15 minutes   *Freezing: Recommended*

Use soft margarine to avoid the rubbing-in process. Don't peel the apples – the skin adds extra fibre.

250 g (8 oz) plain wholemeal   *50 g (2 oz) soft margarine*
   flour   *1 dessert apple, cored and grated*
1 teaspoon cream of tartar, sifted   *6 tablespoons milk*
¹/₂ teaspoon bicarbonate of soda,   *1 tablespoon clear honey*
   sifted   *milk and sesame seeds to glaze*
1 teaspoon ground cinnamon,
   sifted

1. Place all the ingredients in a bowl and mix with a fork to form a soft dough.
2. Turn onto a well floured surface, knead lightly and roll out to a 2 cm (³/4 inch) thickness.
3. Cut into 5 cm (2 inch) rounds with a fluted cutter.
4. Place on a floured baking sheet, brush with milk and sprinkle with sesame seeds. Bake in a preheated oven, 220°C/425°F/Gas Mark 7, for 12–15 minutes. Transfer to a wire rack to cool.

Orange Pancakes

Serves 5–6
Preparation time: 15 minutes,
plus making pancakes

Cooking time: 15 minutes
Freezing: Recommended for
pancakes only

If you have pancakes in the freezer, take out the number you need and adjust the amount of the filling.

12 Wholemeal Pancakes
*   (page 118)*
FOR THE FILLING:
2 oranges
250 g (8 oz) natural fromage
*   frais*

1 tablespoon clear honey
TO FINISH:
2 tablespoons apricot jam,
*   warmed*

1. To make the filling, first grate the zest of 1 orange finely and mix with the fromage frais and honey.
2. Peel the skin and pith from both oranges and cut into segments; reserve a few segments for decoration.
3. Spread a spoonful of filling on each pancake, place a few orange segments on top and roll up. Arrange on a heatproof dish and brush with a little apricot jam.
4. Bake in a preheated oven, 190°C/375°F/Gas Mark 5, for 15 minutes. Top with the reserved orange segments.

Raspberry Crumble

Serves 4
Preparation time: 20 minutes
Cooking time: 45 minutes

Freezing: Recommended at
end of stage 3

This dessert is so sumptuous when served that few would believe it is so easily made. A treat by itself, but some might like a topping of smetana.

175 g (6 oz) plain wholemeal
*   flour*
75 g (3 oz) margarine
50 g (2 oz) muscovado sugar
25 g (1 oz) hazelnuts, chopped
*   (optional)*

250 g (8 oz) dessert apples,
*   cored*
250 g (8 oz) raspberries
2 tablespoons clear honey

1. Place the flour in a bowl and rub in the margarine until the mixture resembles breadcrumbs, then mix in the sugar and nuts.
2. Slice the apples thinly and mix with the raspberries. Arrange in a 900 ml (1½ pint) pie dish and drizzle over the honey.
3. Sprinkle the crumb mixture over the top to cover the fruit completely and press down lightly.
4. Bake in a preheated oven, 180°C/350°F/Gas Mark 4, for 45 minutes, until golden. Serve hot.

Sunflower Crunchies

Makes about 20   *Cooking time: 15 minutes*
Preparation time: 15 minutes   *Freezing: Recommended*

175 g (6 oz) porridge oats   *125 ml (4 fl oz) sunflower oil*
25 g (1 oz) sunflower seeds,   *1 egg, beaten*
* roasted*   *1 tablespoon sesame seeds*
4 tablespoons clear honey

1. Place all the ingredients in a mixing bowl and mix together thoroughly.
2. Place teaspoonfuls of the mixture well apart on a baking sheet and flatten with a dampened palette knife.
3. Bake in a preheated oven, 180°C/350°F/Gas Mark 4, for 15 minutes, until golden brown.
4. Leave to cool for 2 minutes, then transfer to a wire rack to cool completely.

Apricot and Almond Tartlets

Makes 14
Preparation time: 30 minutes,   *Cooking time: 20–25 minutes*
plus chilling time   *Freezing: Recommended*

Moist and fruity little tartlets, ideal to keep in the freezer as they thaw in about 15 minutes.

FOR THE PASTRY: *1 egg*
50 g (2 oz) margarine   *25 g (1 oz) wholemeal flour*
2 tablespoons water   *50 g (2 oz) ground almonds*
125 g (4 oz) plain wholemeal   *few drops almond essence*
* flour*   *75 g (3 oz) ready-to-eat dried*
FOR THE FILLING: * apricots, chopped*
50 g (2 oz) margarine   *25 g (1 oz) flaked almonds*
2 tablespoons clear honey

1. Place the margarine, water and 2 tablespoons of the flour in a mixing bowl and blend with a fork. Add the remaining flour and mix together to form a stiff dough.
2. Turn onto a floured surface and knead lightly until smooth. Chill for 20 minutes.
3. To prepare the filling, mix the margarine, honey, egg, flour, ground almonds and essence together until blended. Mix the apricots into the almond mixture.
4. Roll out the pastry very thinly, cut into 7 cm (3 inch) rounds and use to line 14 tartlet tins.
5. Spoon the filling into the pastry cases, sprinkle with the flaked almonds and bake in a preheated oven, 190°C/375°F/Gas Mark 5, for 20–25 minutes. Serve warm or cold.

Banana Cake

Makes one 18 cm (7 inch) cake
Preparation time: 15 minutes
Cooking time: 20–25 minutes

Freezing: Recommended,
without the filling

125 g (4 oz) soft margarine	FOR THE FILLING:
4 tablespoons clear honey	1 small banana, mashed with
2 ripe bananas, mashed	1 teaspoon lemon juice
2 eggs	50 g (2 oz) curd cheese
125 g (4 oz) plain wholemeal	2 tablespoons ground
flour	almonds
2 teaspoons baking powder,	1 teaspoon clear honey
sifted	

1. Grease and line two 18 cm (7 inch) sandwich tins.
2. Place the margarine, honey and bananas in a bowl and blend with a fork. Add the eggs, flour and baking powder and beat together thoroughly until smooth.
3. Turn into the prepared tins and bake in a preheated oven, 180°C/350°F/Gas Mark 4, for 20–25 minutes, until the cakes are springy to the touch. Cool on a wire rack.
4. To make the filling, mix all the ingredients together until smooth. Use to sandwich the cakes together. This cake is best eaten within 48 hours.

Banana Brownies

Makes about 16
Preparation time: 15 minutes

Cooking time: 25–30 minutes
Freezing: Recommended

75 g (3 oz) unsweetened carob	125 g (4 oz) self-raising
or plain chocolate, in pieces	wholemeal flour
4 tablespoons corn oil	2 tablespoons cold water
4 tablespoons clear honey	1 banana, mashed
	2 eggs

1. Grease and line an 18 cm (7 inch) square shallow cake tin.
2. Place the carob or chocolate pieces, oil and honey in a small pan and heat gently until melted.
3. Place the flour in a mixing bowl and make a well in the centre. Beat in the carob mixture with the water, banana and eggs until smooth.
4. Pour into the prepared tin and bake in a preheated oven, 180°C/350°F/Gas Mark 4, for 25–30 minutes, until just beginning to shrink from the sides of the tin.
5. Cool on a wire rack. Cut into small pieces to serve.

Spicy Apple Pies

Makes about 10
Preparation time: 50 minutes

Cooking time: 15–20 minutes
Freezing: Recommended

These are lovely served warm with smetana. They are also good cold, and are useful for packed lunches.

375 g (12 oz) dessert apples, peeled, cored and sliced
2 tablespoons pure apple juice
1 teaspoon ground cinnamon
2 tablespoons sultanas
FOR THE PASTRY:
175 g (6 oz) plain wholemeal

flour
75 g (3 oz) margarine
2 tablespoons iced water (approximately)
milk to glaze
1 tablespoon sesame seeds

1. Place the apples, apple juice and cinnamon in a saucepan, cover and simmer gently for 15 minutes, stirring occasionally. Add the sultanas and leave to cool, with the lid on.
2. Meanwhile make the pastry: place the flour in a bowl and rub in the margarine until the mixture resembles breadcrumbs. Add enough water to mix to a firm dough, then turn onto a lightly floured surface and knead lightly. Chill for 15 minutes.
3. Roll out the pastry thinly on a floured surface. Cut out about ten 7.5 cm (3 inch) and ten 5 cm (2 inch) circles.
4. Use the larger circles to line 10 patty tins. Place a spoonful of the apple mixture in each. Dampen the edge and top with the remaining circles.
5. Press the edges to seal, make a hole in the centre and brush with milk. Sprinkle with the sesame seeds.
6. Bake in a preheated oven, 200°C/400°F/Gas Mark 6, for 15–20 minutes, until golden. Serve warm or cold.

Raspberry Roll

Serves 6–8
Preparation time: 30 minutes

Cooking time: 8–10 minutes
Freezing: Not recommended

Chocolate roulades are popular with all ages, but are hardly healthy eating! If you want your family to eat healthily, try this version using carob. You could use cocoa powder if you prefer.

3 eggs
75 g (3 oz) dark brown soft sugar
75 g (3 oz) plain wholemeal flour
3 tablespoons carob powder, sifted

1 tablespoon caster sugar
FOR THE FILLING:
227 g (8 oz) carton curd cheese
2 tablespoons clear honey
125 g (4 oz) raspberries, crushed

1. Grease and line a 30 × 20 cm (12 × 8 inch) Swiss roll tin, then grease the paper.
2. Whisk the eggs and sugar together for 10 minutes or until thick and mousse-like, using an electric whisk.
3. Carefully fold in the flour and carob powder with a metal spoon, then turn into the prepared tin.
4. Bake in a preheated oven, 200°C/400°F/Gas Mark 6, for 8–10 minutes, until the sponge springs back when pressed in the centre.
5. Wring out a clean tea towel in hot water, lay it on a work surface, place a sheet of greaseproof paper on top and sprinkle with the caster sugar.
6. Turn the sponge out onto the paper, carefully peel off the lining paper and trim off the crisp edges on the long sides.
7. Roll up the sponge with the sugared paper inside, remove the cloth, then place on a wire rack with the join underneath, to cool.
8. Mix the curd cheese with the honey and raspberries.
9. Unroll the sponge and remove the paper. Spread with the filling and roll up again. Cut into slices to serve.

1. Place the sugar, eggs, oil, water and malt extract in a bowl and mix together thoroughly.
2. Sift in the flour and carob powder and beat until smooth.
3. Arrange 12–15 paper bun cases on a baking sheet and three-quarter fill each one. Bake in a preheated oven, 180°C/350°F/Gas Mark 4, for 15 minutes. Cool on a wire rack.
4. To make the topping, beat the curd cheese in a bowl until smooth. Add the melted carob and orange rind and beat thoroughly. Place in a piping bag fitted with a large fluted nozzle and pipe a rosette onto each cake, or spread using a knife.

Gingerbread

Makes one 18 cm (7 inch) cake	Cooking time: 1–1¼ hours
Preparation time: 20 minutes	Freezing: Recommended

Store this cake in an airtight tin for several days before eating: the flavour improves and it becomes moist.

250 g (8 oz) plain wholemeal flour	90 ml (3 ½ fl oz) molasses
4 teaspoons ground ginger	125 ml (4 fl oz) clear honey
1 teaspoon each ground mixed spice and bicarbonate of soda	150 ml (¼ pint) pure apple juice
125 ml (4 fl oz) sunflower oil	2 eggs, beaten
	2 tablespoons flaked almonds (optional)

1. Grease and line an 18 cm (7 inch) square cake tin.
2. Place the flour in a mixing bowl, then sift in the spices and soda.
3. Make a well in the centre and add the oil, molasses, honey, apple juice and eggs. Beat thoroughly, gradually incorporating the flour until smooth.
4. Turn into the prepared tin and sprinkle with the almonds if using.
5. Bake in a preheated oven, 160°C/325°F/Gas Mark 3, for 1–1¼ hours, until a skewer pierced through the centre of the cake comes out clean.
6. Leave in the tin for 5 minutes, then turn onto a wire rack to cool. Cut into slices to serve.

Carob Cup Cakes

Makes about 15	Cooking time: 15 minutes
Preparation time: 25 minutes	Freezing: Recommended

These look just like little chocolate cakes, but as carob is naturally sweet, they contain far less sugar. The flavour is slightly different from chocolate, but still delicious. If you prefer, cocoa and chocolate can be substituted.

50 g (2 oz) molasses sugar	25 g (1 oz) carob powder
2 eggs	FOR THE TOPPING:
125 ml (4 fl oz) sunflower oil	50 g (2 oz) curd cheese
125 ml (4 fl oz) water	25 g (1 oz) unsweetened carob bar, melted
1 rounded tablespoon malt extract	grated rind of 1 orange
175 g (6 oz) wholemeal self-raising flour	

Apple Jalousie

Serves 4
Preparation time: 25 minutes
Cooking time: 20–25 minutes
Freezing: Recommended

Use dessert apples rather than cookers, so that extra sugar is unnecessary. The dates and spices also add natural sweetness to the dessert.

500 g (1 lb) dessert apples, cored and chopped
125 g (4 oz) chopped dates
1 teaspoon ground mixed spice
375g (12 oz) wholemeal or white puff pastry
beaten egg to glaze
1 tablespoon sesame seeds

1. Place the apples, dates and spice in a mixing bowl and mix thoroughly.
2. Cut the pastry in half and roll out one piece on a lightly floured surface to a rectangle measuring 30 × 23 cm (12 × 9 inches).
3. Place on a baking sheet and spread the apple mixture over the pastry to within 2.5 cm (1 inch) of the edges. Dampen the edges with water.
4. Roll out the remaining pastry to a rectangle slightly larger than the first. Flour the pastry lightly and fold in half lengthways.
5. Cut through the folded edge of the pastry at 1 cm ($^1/_2$ inch) intervals to within 2.5 cm (1 inch) of the edges.
6. Unfold and place over the apple. Seal the pastry edges, then knock up with the back of a knife.
7. Brush with beaten egg and sprinkle with the sesame seeds. Bake in a preheated oven, 200°C/400°F/Gas Mark 6, for 20–25 minutes, until golden.
8. Serve warm or cold.

Strawberry Nut Sponge

Serves 6
Preparation time: 15 minutes
Cooking time: 18–20 minutes
Freezing: Recommended, at end of stage 6

A luscious strawberry cake which is equally good eaten as a dessert or at teatime.

2 eggs
3 tablespoons clear honey
$^1/_2$ teaspoon ground cinnamon, sifted
50 g (2 oz) plain wholemeal flour
25 g (1 oz) ground almonds
1 tablespoons chopped almonds
175 g (6 oz) strawberries
200 g (7 oz) fromage frais

1. Grease and line a 20 cm (8 inch) sandwich tin.
2. Whisk the eggs and honey together until thick and mousse-like, using an electric whisk.

3. Carefully fold in the cinnamon, flour and ground almonds, using a metal spoon. Turn into the prepared tin and sprinkle with the chopped almonds.
4. Bake in a preheated oven, 190°C/375°F/Gas Mark 5, for 18–20 minutes, until the cake springs back when lightly pressed.
5. Carefully remove from the tin and cool on a wire rack.
6. Chop half the strawberries and mix into the fromage frais. Slice the remaining strawberries.
7. Split the cake in half horizontally and sandwich together with the fromage frais and sliced strawberries.

Fruit Flip

Serves 2
Preparation time: 4 minutes   *Freezing: Not recommended*

Natural fromage frais is a soft cheese which is delicious served with soft fruits.

200 g (7 oz) fromage frais
411 g (14½ oz) can apricot
  halves in fruit juice, drained
300 ml (½ pint) milk

1 teaspoon clear honey
  (optional)
1 tablespoon chopped roasted
  hazelnuts to decorate

1. Place all the ingredients in a blender or food processor and work until smooth; add the honey to taste, if you wish.
2. Pour into 2 glasses and sprinkle with the hazelnuts.
VARIATION
Replace the apricots with 250 g (8 oz) fresh strawberries.

Cottage Cheese with Fruit

Serves 1
Preparation time: 3 minutes   *Freezing: Not recommended*

This is a delicious summer lunchtime snack that looks pretty as well. Any combination of fruit can be used, e.g. apple quarters with sliced bananas and kiwi fruit. Use the fruit to scoop up the cottage cheese.

1 slice water melon, sliced
125 g (4 oz) strawberries
1 nectarine or peach, sliced

113 g (4 oz) carton cottage
  cheese
mint sprig to garnish (optional)

Arrange the fruit and cottage cheese on individual serving plates. Garnish with mint, if you wish, to serve.

Apricot Fool

Serves 6
Preparation time: 15 minutes

Cooking time: 20 minutes
Freezing: Not recommended

125 g (4 oz) dried ready-to-eat apricots
250 ml (8 fl oz) orange juice

2 × 150 g (5 oz) cartons natural yogurt
4 tablespoons smetana

1. Place the apricots and orange juice in a pan, bring to the boil, cover and simmer for 20 minutes. Allow to cool.
2. Purée in a food processor or blender.
3. Mix the yogurt until smooth, then fold in all but 1 tablespoon of the apricot purée.
4. Spoon into individual dishes. Swirl a spoonful of smetana on top of each one, then swirl in the remaining apricot purée.
Pictured on page 115

Summer Peaches

Serves 4
Preparation time: 15 minutes

Freezing: Not recommended

A delicious combination of peaches, strawberries and raspberries. Serve this in the strawberry season as it's so quick to prepare. It can be served without the addition of the liqueur, but this does impart a particularly good flavour!

50 g (2 oz) raspberries
2 tablespoons Crème de Framboise or Cointreau

2 peaches, peeled and stoned
175 g (6 oz) strawberries, sliced

1. Sieve the raspberries into a bowl, then stir in the liqueur.
2. Slice the peaches into the raspberry purée. Add the strawberries and turn gently to coat the fruit completely.
3. Chill until required. Serve with smetana or yogurt.
Pictured on page 115

Cranberry and Apple Crumble

Serves 6
Preparation time: 25 minutes

Cooking time: 25–30 minutes
Freezing: Not recommended

This is a Canadian-inspired recipe. Try substituting plums for cranberries and pears for apples.

250 g (8 oz) fresh cranberries
6 tablespoons water
4 tablespoons granulated sugar
500 g (1 lb) cooking apples, peeled, cored and sliced thinly
75 g (3 oz) plain wholemeal flour

pinch of salt
75 g (3 oz) butter or margarine
25 g (1 oz) skimmed milk powder
40 g (1½ oz) porridge oats
75 g (3 oz) light brown soft sugar
1 teaspoon ground cinnamon

1. Place the cranberries, water and sugar in a pan, bring to the boil and cook for 5 minutes. Leave to cool, then place in a greased 1.5 litre (2½ pint) shallow ovenproof dish with the apples.
2. Sift the flour and salt into a bowl and rub in the butter or margarine until the mixture resembles coarse crumbs. Stir in the remaining ingredients, then spoon evenly over fruit.
3. Bake in preheated oven, 180°C/350°F/Gas Mark 4, for 25–30 minutes, until the topping is crisp and the fruit is tender. Serve hot.

Yogurt Ice Cream

Serves 4
Makes 450 ml (³/4 pint)
Preparation time: 10 minutes, plus freezing
Freezing: Recommended

For children who are ice cream or yogurt addicts, this will be a winner – make it into ice lollies for fun.

250 g (8 oz) raspberries, plums,	*4 teaspoons sugar*
peaches or other soft fruit	*few drops vanilla essence*
300 g (10 oz) natural set yogurt	*mint sprigs to decorate*

1. Prepare the fruit as necessary, peeling plums and peaches; set aside a little to decorate. Purée the fruit in a blender or food processor with the remaining ingredients.
2. Spoon into a rigid freezerproof container, cover, seal and freeze for 2–3 hours, until partially frozen. Whisk well, then freeze until firm.
3. Transfer to the refrigerator 30 minutes before serving to soften. Scoop into chilled glass dishes and decorate with the reserved fruit and mint.
VARIATION
Use honey to sweeten for a pleasant change of flavour.

Raspberry Dream

Serves 6   *Freezing: Not recommended*
Preparation time: 35 minutes

50 g (2 oz) wholemeal	*200 g (7 oz) natural low fat*
breadcrumbs, toasted	*yogurt*
75 g (3 oz) oatmeal biscuits or	*175 g (6 oz) fresh or frozen*
muesli biscuits, broken	*raspberries, thawed*
1 packet black cherry jelly	

1. Mix half of the breadcrumbs with the biscuits and place in a large glass dish or 6 individual dishes.
2. Make up half of the jelly with water according to packet instructions and pour onto the crumbs. Leave to set completely in the refrigerator.
3. Make up the remaining jelly with 6 tablespoons water and chill until beginning to set. Whip until frothy, then stir in 50 g (2 oz) of the yogurt.
4. Mix three quarters of the raspberries into the yogurt jelly and spoon over the crumb base. Leave to set.
5. Spread the remaining yogurt over the top and sprinkle with the rest of the breadcrumbs. Chill well.
6. Decorate with the remaining raspberries to serve.

Pear Mousse

Serves 4
Preparation time: 15 minutes,   Cooking time: 30 minutes
plus soaking time   Freezing: Not recommended

A simple mousse with a stronger flavour than you can achieve with fresh pears.

125 g (4 oz) ready-to-eat dried   1 egg white
   pears   1 tablespoon clear honey
113 g (4 oz) carton curd cheese   1 pear, sliced thinly to
1 tablespoon lemon juice   decorate

1. Cook the pears in 450 ml (³/4 pint) of the soaking liquid for 30 minutes. Drain, reserving 2 tablespoons liquid.
2. Cool, then place the pears and reserved liquid in a food processor or blender with the cheese and 2 teaspoons of the lemon juice and work until smooth.
3. Whisk the egg white until stiff, then whisk in the honey.
4. Fold the egg white into the pear mixture, then spoon into individual glasses. Decorate with pear slices, brushed with the remaining lemon juice, to serve.
VARIATION
Prune Mousse: Use 125 g (4 oz) pitted prunes instead of the dried pears and cook for 15 minutes only. Use 1 tablespoon chopped nuts to decorate the mousse.

Paradise Pudding

Serves 4
Preparation time: 15 minutes   Freezing: Not recommended

As you'll guess from the name, this is one of everyone's favourites. When strawberries are not in season, use other fresh fruits. The oatmeal gives a lovely chewy texture and added fibre.

40 g (1¹/2 oz) almonds,   1 tablespoon Cointreau
   chopped finely   250 g (8 oz) Greek-style yogurt
40 g (1¹/2 oz) medium or fine   175 g (6 oz) strawberries,
   oatmeal   sliced
1 tablespoon clear honey

1. Place the almonds and oatmeal under a preheated moderate grill, turning frequently, until brown; cool.
2. Mix the honey and Cointreau together, fold into the yogurt, then fold in the almond mixture.
3. Divide the strawberries between 4 glasses, reserving a few slices for decoration.
4. Spoon the oat cream over the strawberries and decorate with the reserved strawberry slices.

Apricot Yogurt Ice

Serves 6

Preparation time: 15 minutes,   Cooking time: 20 minutes
plus soaking time   Freezing time: 4 hours

A very easy ice cream to make, using Greek yogurt instead of cream. It can also be made, very successfully, with other dried fruits, especially prunes.

250 g (8 oz) ready-to-eat dried   2 tablespoons clear honey
*   apricots   250 g (8 oz) Greek-style yogurt*
375 ml (12 fl oz) apple juice   sliced strawberries to decorate
2 egg whites

1. Place the apricots and apple juice in a pan, cover and cook gently for 20 minutes.
2. Cool slightly, then purée in a food processor or blender. Leave to cool completely.
3. Whisk the egg whites until stiff, then gradually whisk in the honey.
4. Beat the yogurt until smooth, then fold into the apricot purée. Fold in the egg white mixture.
5. Turn into a rigid freezerproof container, cover, seal and freeze until solid.
6. Transfer to the refrigerator 40 minutes before serving, to soften. Scoop into individual dishes and decorate with sliced strawberries to serve.

Orange Chartreuse

Serves 6   Setting time: 2 hours
Preparation time: 30 minutes   Freezing: Not recommended

A refreshing dessert, easy to prepare and ideal to serve at a dinner party as it looks so attractive.

4 oranges   125 g (4 oz) strawberries
300 ml (¹/2 pint) apple juice   1 tablespoon clear honey
15 g (¹/2 oz) gelatine   strawberry leaves (optional)
2 tablespoons Cointreau

1. Peel and segment the oranges, discarding all the pith and pips. Divide the orange segments and any juice between 6 small ramekins or individual moulds.
2. Put half the apple juice in a small pan, sprinkle over the gelatine and leave to soak for 5 minutes.
3. Heat gently until dissolved, then add the remaining apple juice and Cointreau. Pour over the oranges and leave in the refrigerator until set.
4. Purée the strawberries in a blender or food processor and mix with the honey. Spoon a little strawberry purée onto each serving plate.
5. Dip the ramekins or moulds quickly in hot water, then invert each dessert onto the strawberry purée.
6. Decorate with strawberry leaves, if you have any.

Lebanese Fruit Salad

Serves 4
Preparation time: 15 minutes
Cooking time: 15 minutes

Freezing: Recommended, at end of stage 2

An attractive dessert which is delicious on its own or served with yogurt or smetana. Any left over is very good served with Granola (page 94) for breakfast.

125 g (4 oz) dried apricots
125 g (4 oz) pitted prunes
450 ml (¾ pint) apple juice
1 large orange

125 g (4 oz) fresh dates, halved and stoned
1 tablespoon pumpkin seeds
2 tablespoons pine kernels

1. Place the apricots, prunes and apple juice in a pan and bring to the boil. Cover and simmer for 15 minutes. Leave to cool, with the lid on the pan.
2. Peel the orange and divide into segments, discarding all pith and pips. Add the orange segments and dates to the other fruit and toss gently. Divide between individual serving dishes and chill until required.
3. Put the seeds and pine kernels in a heavy-based pan and place over a high heat, shaking the pan constantly, until they begin to pop and brown.
4. Sprinkle over the fruit and serve immediately.

Prune and Cheese Pancakes

Serves 4
Preparation time: 5 minutes, plus pancake making

Cooking time: 25 minutes
Freezing: Recommended, at end of stage 2

This dessert is also very good made with dried apricots, or with stewed apples and raisins. They are all quite sweet enough to make the addition of sugar unnecessary.

250 g (8 oz) pitted prunes, chopped
300 ml (½ pint) apple juice
12 Wholemeal Pancakes (page 118)

175 g (6 oz) natural fromage frais
1 tablespoon clear honey
15 g (½ oz) flaked almonds, browned

1. Place the prunes and apple juice in a pan, cover and simmer for 15 minutes, stirring occasionally, until the liquid has been absorbed.
2. Place a little of the prune mixture on each pancake, then top with a spoonful of fromage frais. Roll up and arrange in an ovenproof dish.
3. Warm the honey and brush over the pancakes to glaze. Place in a preheated oven, 180°C/350°F/Gas Mark 4, for about 10 minutes, to heat through. Sprinkle with the almonds to serve.

Sunrise Sundae

| Serves 4 | Cooking time: 15 minutes |
| Preparation time: 10 minutes | Freezing: Not recommended |

A fresh start to the day, but a little more filling than the citrus fruits usually served at breakfast.

125 g (4 oz) dried apricots	2 oranges
125 g (4 oz) pitted prunes	4 tablespoons smetana
450 ml (¾ pint) water	4 tablespoons Granola (page 94)

1. Place the apricots, prunes and water in a saucepan and bring to the boil. Cover and simmer for 15 minutes, then leave to cool, with the lid on the pan.
2. Peel the oranges and divide into segments, discarding all the pith and pips. Mix with the other fruit, then turn into 4 individual shallow dishes.
3. Top each with a spoonful of smetana, then sprinkle with a spoonful of granola.

Date and Oat Fingers

| Makes 14 | Cooking time: 35 minutes |
| Preparation time: 15 minutes | Freezing: Recommended |

These fingers are particularly high in fibre. Use dried figs or prunes instead of dates sometimes for a change.

250 g (8 oz) dried chopped dates	175 g (6 oz) porridge oats
3 tablespoons apple juice	175 g (6 oz) plain wholemeal flour
175 ml (6 fl oz) sunflower oil	50 g (2 oz) walnuts, chopped
4 tablespoons clear honey	

1. Grease and line a 20 cm (8 inch) square shallow cake tin.
2. Place the dates and apple juice in a small pan and simmer for about 5 minutes, until soft.
3. Place the oil and honey in a saucepan and stir over low heat until evenly blended. Add the oats, flour and walnuts and mix together thoroughly.
4. Turn half the mixture into the prepared tin, pressing down firmly.
5. Cover evenly with the date mixture, sprinkle over the remaining oat mixture and press down firmly with a palette knife.
6. Bake in a preheated oven, 190°C/375°F/Gas Mark 5, for 35 minutes, until golden brown.
7. Leave to cool for 5 minutes, then cut into 14 fingers. Allow to cool completely before removing the fingers carefully from the tin.

Strawberry Romanoff

Serves 4
Preparation time: 20 minutes
Freezing: Not recommended

This light, creamy dessert is perfect for warm summer days. It is best served with crisp biscuits.

142 ml (5 fl oz) carton double cream
2 tablespoons Grand Marnier
1 egg white
1 tablespoon clear honey
150 g (5 oz) smetana
375 g (12 oz) strawberries, halved
4 frosted strawberry leaves to decorate

1. Combine the cream and Grand Marnier, then whip until it holds its shape.
2. Whisk the egg white until stiff, then whisk in the honey. Fold into the cream with the smetana.
3. Set aside a few strawberry halves for decoration. Fold the rest into the cream mixture.
4. Spoon into 4 glass serving dishes and chill until required. Decorate with the reserved strawberries and the frosted leaves.

Spiced Apple Layer

Serves 4
Preparation time: 10 minutes, plus cooling
Cooking time: 15–20 minutes
Freezing: Not recommended

Choose tall glasses so that the layers in this delicious dessert are more obvious. The dates may be replaced with other dried fruits if you prefer.

4 tablespoons pure apple juice
500 g (1 lb) dessert apples, peeled and sliced
1/2 teaspoon ground cinnamon
125 g (4 oz) chopped dates
150 g (5 oz) carton natural set yogurt
4 tablespoons smetana
2 tablespoons flaked almonds, toasted

1. Place the apple juice with the apples, cinnamon and dates in a heavy-based pan, cover and cook gently for 15–20 minutes until softened, stirring occasionally. Leave to cool.
2. Mix the yogurt and smetana together until smooth.
3. Place half of the apple mixture in 4 individual glasses and cover with half of the yogurt mixture. Repeat the layers. Chill until required.
4. Sprinkle with the almonds to serve.

Prunes in Brandy

Serves 6
Preparation time: 10 minutes, plus soaking time
Cooking time: 20 minutes
Freezing: Not recommended

250 g (8 oz) pitted dried prunes
350 ml (12 fl oz) orange juice
2 tablespoons brandy
2 oranges

1. Place the prunes and orange juice in a pan and leave to soak for 30 minutes. Bring to the boil, then cover and cook for 20 minutes. Add the brandy and leave to cool.
2. Meanwhile, peel the zest from the oranges and use to make orange rind shreds. Peel the pith from the oranges, then cut the flesh into segments, discarding all pith, and add to the prunes.
3. Spoon into individual glass dishes, sprinkle with the orange shreds and chill until required.
4. Serve with Greek yogurt or smetana if you wish.

Apricot Compote

Serves 4

Preparation time: 10 minutes, plus soaking time	Cooking time: 15 minutes
	Freezing: Not recommended

250 g (8 oz) ready-to-eat dried apricots	8 kumquats, sliced thinly
	sugar to taste
150 ml (1/4 pint) pure orange juice	2 tablespoons toasted flaked almonds (optional)
300 ml (1/2 pint) water	

1. Soak the apricots in the orange juice and water for 2 hours.
2. Bring to the boil, then simmer gently for 10 minutes. Add the kumquats and simmer for 5 minutes. Taste and sweeten to taste with sugar.
3. Turn into a serving bowl and sprinkle with the almonds if using. Serve with smetana, yogurt or whipped cream.

Blackcurrant Crumble

Serves 4	Cooking time: 25–30 minutes
Preparation time: 15 minutes	Freezing: Recommended

500 g (1 lb) blackcurrants	75 g (3 oz) margarine
3 tablespoons clear honey	50 g (2 oz) muscovado sugar
175 g (6 oz) plain wholemeal flour	50 g (2 oz) hazelnuts, chopped

1. Place the blackcurrants in a 900 ml (1 1/2 pint) oven-proof dish and drizzle over the honey.
2. Place the flour in a bowl and rub in the margarine until the mixture resembles breadcrumbs. Stir in the sugar and hazelnuts, then sprinkle over the fruit.
3. Bake in a preheated oven, 200°C/400°F/Gas Mark 6, for 25–30 minutes, until golden. Serve with smetana, yogurt or single cream.

Brochettes des Fruits

Serves 6	Cooking time: 1 minute
Preparation time: 15 minutes	Freezing: Not recommended

A very quick dessert, but most attractive to serve. Especially delicious if served flambéd, but also good with a fruit sauce.

1/2 pineapple	125 g (4 oz) black grapes, seeded
12 strawberries	2 tablespoons caster sugar
1/2 × 425 g (15 oz) can lychees in syrup, drained	3 tablespoons brandy
	strawberry leaves to decorate

1. Peel the pineapple, remove and discard the central hard core, then cut the flesh into chunks.
2. Thread all of the fruit, alternately, onto 12 wooden skewers. Place in a grill pan and sprinkle with the sugar.
3. Place under a preheated hot grill for about 1 minute until heated; do not overcook. Arrange on a heatproof dish.
4. Warm the brandy in a ladle or small saucepan, ignite and pour over the fruit. Decorate with strawberry leaves and serve immediately.

Poires aux Cassis

Serves 6
Preparation time: 20 minutes
Cooking time: 10 minutes

Freezing: Recommended for sauce only

A popular dessert in Burgundy, where crème de cassis originates. You can poach the pears lightly if you prefer, but it's best to use really juicy William pears and serve them as they are. Frozen blackcurrants could be used.

375 g (12 oz) blackcurrants
50 g (2 oz) caster sugar
125 ml (4 fl oz) water

2 tablespoons crème de cassis
  (optional)
6 William pears

1. Place the blackcurrants, sugar and water in a pan and cook gently for about 10 minutes, stirring occasionally, until soft.
2. Purée in a food processor or blender, then sieve to remove the seeds. Leave to cool, then add the crème de cassis, if using.
3. Peel, halve and core the pears; arrange on individual dishes. Spoon over the sauce and serve immediately.

Summer Fruit Compote

Serves 4
Preparation time: 15 minutes,
plus cooling

Cooking time: 10 minutes
Freezing: Not recommended

250 g (8 oz) mixed
  blackcurrants and
  redcurrants
2 tablespoons clear honey

4 tablespoons pure orange juice
1 teaspoon arrowroot
250 g (8 oz) strawberries,
  quartered

1. Place the blackcurrants and redcurrants, honey and orange juice in a pan, bring to the boil, then cover and simmer gently for 10 minutes, until softened.
2. Strain the fruit and place in a bowl. Return the syrup to the pan.
3. Blend the arrowroot with a little water until smooth, then stir into the syrup. Bring to the boil, stirring constantly until thickened and clear.
4. Pour over the currants, add the strawberries and Grand Marnier, mix together gently and leave to cool.
5. Turn into a glass serving bowl and chill until required. Serve with yogurt or cream.

Strawberry Chartreuse

Serves 6
Preparation time: 35 minutes, plus setting time
Freezing: Not recommended

1 mango
1 kiwi fruit, peeled and sliced
125 g (4 oz) strawberries, halved
1 William pear, peeled and chopped
300 ml (1/2 pint) pure orange juice

1 sachet gelatine
2 tablespoons Grand Marnier
FOR THE STRAWBERRY SAUCE:
250 g (8 oz) strawberries
1 tablespoon icing sugar, sifted
2 tablespoons framboise liqueur or cointreau

1. Cut the mango either side of the stone. Scoop out and chop all the flesh. Place in a 900 ml (1 1/2 pint) ring mould or 500 g (1 lb) loaf tin with the kiwi fruit, strawberries and pear.
2. Place 150 ml (1/4 pint) of the orange juice in a small pan and sprinkle over the gelatine. Leave to soak for 5 minutes, then heat very gently until dissolved.
3. Add the remaining orange juice and Grand Marnier, pour into the mould or tin and chill for 2 hours, until set.
4. To make the sauce, blend or process the strawberries and sugar. Sieve and add the liqueur.
5. To turn out, dip the mould or tin quickly into hot water, then invert onto a serving plate. Cut into slices, and serve with the strawberry sauce.

Raspberry Yogurt Drink

Makes 450 ml (3/4 pint)
Preparation time: 5 minutes
Freezing: Not recommended

Refreshing and filling – ideal when you're in a hurry. Substitute blackberries, when in season, as they are very high in fibre. Experiment with other fruits of your choice – for sweeter fruits you will probably need less honey.

50 g (2 oz) raspberries
150 g (5 oz) carton natural yogurt

125 ml (4 fl oz) milk
2 teaspoons clear honey

1. Place all the ingredients in a blender or food processor, and work until smooth.
2. Pour into glasses to serve.

Summer Sundaes

Serves 8
Preparation time: 30 minutes,
plus chilling

Cooking time: 10 minutes
Freezing: Recommended, if
made in freezerproof dishes

A variation of summer pudding, served in wine glasses.
Ideal to serve at an 'al fresco' meal in the summer.

500 g (1 lb) mixed
blackberries, blackcurrants
and redcurrants
2 tablespoons clear honey

250 g (8 oz) strawberries,
sliced, or raspberries
8 slices wholemeal bread

1. Place the blackberries, blackcurrants and redcurrants,
honey and 2 tablespoons water in a heavy-based pan and
cook gently for 10 minutes until tender, stirring occasionally.
2. Add the strawberries or raspberries and leave to cool.
Strain, reserving the juice.
3. Cut out 16 circles of bread to fit inside the wine
glasses and soak in the reserved juice.
4. Place a third of the fruit in 8 wine glasses and top
with a circle of bread. Place another third of the fruit on
top and cover with another circle of bread. Top with the
remaining fruit. Chill for 30 minutes or until required.
5. Serve with smetana or cream if you wish.

Star Fruit Salad

Serves 6
Preparation time: 20 minutes

Freezing: Not recommended

Star fruit, sometimes called Carambola, should be yellowish
when ripe. The fluted edges begin to go brown, so are best
trimmed away with scissors. If unavailable, kiwi fruit
makes an equally good addition to this fruit salad.

425 g (15 oz) can lychees in
syrup
juice of 1 lime
2 tablespoons Cointreau
2 oranges

1 small Ogen melon, halved
and seeded
3 star fruit
1/2 tablespoon shredded mint

1. Place the lychees with their syrup, lime juice and
Cointreau in a bowl.
2. Peel the oranges and cut into segments, discarding
all pith. Cut the melon flesh into cubes or scoop into
balls, then add to the bowl with the oranges.
3. Cut the brown ribs from the star fruit, using scissors.
Cut the star fruit into slices and add to the bowl.
4. Mix together well, turn into a glass serving dish and
sprinkle with the mint. Chill until required.

Microwave Wholefoods

Microwave ovens and wholefoods are not normally thought of as natural partners, but in fact a microwave can be a boon in the kitchen of the wholefood cook. Although their cooking times may be only a little shorter than conventional, the 'classic' wholefoods – rice, pasta and pulses – are often cooked more conveniently by microwave, with less chance of the pan burning dry and the contents becoming soggy or sticking to the bottom. Brown rice and wholewheat pasta microwave particularly well, and take only fractionally longer than the refined, white versions.

Of course, the advantages of taste and nutrition in microwaving vegetables and fish are well known, and this simple way of preparing fresh ingredients is ideal for the wholefood way of cooking. All recipes have been tested in 650 watt microwave ovens. Adjust timings according to manufacturer's recommendations, and follow the manufacturer's instructions.

Right (clockwise from top left): Flageolets à la Française, Ginger Prawns (page 142), Middle Eastern Kebabs, Tipsy Bread Pudding (page 142), Orange Tart in Ginger pastry (page 157)

Flageolets à la Française

Serves 6

Preparation time: 10 minutes, plus soaking time	*Cooking time: 64 minutes*
	Standing time: 15 minutes
Power setting: HIGH	*Freezing: Recommended*

25 g (1 oz) butter	*bacon, derinded and chopped*
300 g (10 oz) dried flageolets, soaked overnight in hot water	*1 litre (1³/4 pints) hot vegetable stock*
6 spring onions, white part only, halved	*6 lettuce leaves, or 1 lettuce heart, quartered*
5 rashers unsmoked streaky	*1¹/2 teaspoons sugar*
	salt and pepper to taste

1. Place the butter in a casserole and microwave on HIGH for 30 seconds. Stir in the drained beans, spring onions, bacon and 300 ml (¹/2 pint) of the stock. Cover and cook on HIGH for 4 minutes, stirring halfway through cooking.
2. Stir in the remaining stock, and salt and pepper, cover and cook for 55 minutes, stirring every 10 minutes. Stir in the lettuce and sugar, cover and cook for 5 minutes, stirring halfway through cooking. Leave to stand for 15 minutes before serving.

Middle Eastern Lamb Kebabs

Serves 4	*Power setting: MEDIUM*
Preparation time: 15 minutes, plus marinating	*Cooking time: 10 minutes*
	Freezing: Not recommended

750 g (1¹/2 lb) boneless leg of lamb or neck fillet, cut into 2.5 cm (1 inch) cubes	*1 tablespoon wine vinegar*
	1 teaspoon ground cumin
125 g (4 oz) ready-to-eat dried apricots	*1 small onion, chopped finely*
	1 clove garlic, chopped finely
FOR THE MARINADE:	*1 tablespoon finely chopped parsley*
4 tablespoons olive oil	*salt and pepper to taste*

1. Combine the marinade ingredients together in a bowl. Add the lamb, tossing to make sure each piece is covered. Cover and chill for about 8 hours, stirring occasionally.
2. Thread the lamb and apricots alternately on 4 wooden or bamboo skewers and arrange on a microwave roasting rack or large dish. Cover with greaseproof paper and cook on MEDIUM for 10 minutes.
3. Serve with brown or saffron rice with wild rice folded through and a salad.

Ginger Prawns

Serves 4
Preparation time: 10 minutes   *Cooking time: 2 minutes*
Power setting: HIGH   *Freezing: Not recommended*

250 g (8 oz) peeled prawns   *1 teaspoon finely chopped*
250 g (8 oz) bean sprouts   *fresh root ginger*
3 spring onions, shredded   *2 teaspoons oyster sauce*
1/2 red pepper, sliced finely   *2 teaspoons sesame oil*
                                    1 tablespoon soy sauce

Place all the ingredients in a large bowl, then cook on HIGH for 2 minutes. Stir and serve immediately.
Pictured on page 141

Tipsy Bread Pudding

Serves 4–6
Preparation time: 10 minutes,   *Cooking time: 12 minutes*
plus soaking time   *Standing time: 2 minutes*
Power setting: HIGH   *Freezing: Not recommended*

250 g (8 oz) wholemeal bread,   *4 tablespoons dark rum*
  broken into pieces   *450 ml (3/4 pint) milk*
125 g (4 oz) raisins   *50 g (2 oz) butter*
75 g (3 oz) demerara sugar   *3 eggs, beaten*
pinch of mixed spice

1. Place the bread, raisins, half of the sugar and the mixed spice in a bowl.
2. Mix the rum and milk together, pour over the bread and leave to soak for 30 minutes.
3. Place the butter in a bowl and microwave on HIGH for 2 minutes.
4. Stir the beaten eggs and melted butter into the bread mixture, then pour into 4 or 6 greased ovenproof dishes. Cook on HIGH for 10 minutes.
5. Remove from the oven and sprinkle with the remaining sugar. Leave to stand for 2 minutes. Serve hot or cold with yogurt or whipped cream.
Pictured on page 141

Lamb Fillet with Rosemary Vinegar

Serves 4   *Cooking time: 9 1/2–11 1/2 minutes*
Preparation time: 5 minutes   *Standing time: 4 minutes*
Power setting: HIGH   *Freezing: Not recommended*

To make rosemary vinegar, place 2 large rosemary sprigs in a bottle of wine vinegar and leave for several weeks.

25 g (1 oz) butter   *1 teaspoon cornflour blended*
2 shallots, chopped finely   *with 1 tablespoon water*
2 1/2 tablespoons rosemary   *2–3 lamb shoulder or neck*
  vinegar   *fillets, weighing about 625 g*
3 tablespoons freshly squeezed   *(1 1/4 lb)*
  orange juice   *1 tablespoon sunflower oil*
125 ml (4 fl oz) dry white wine *salt and pepper to taste*
1 tablespoon demerara sugar

1. Place half of the butter in a bowl with the shallots and cook on HIGH for 1 minute. Stir in the vinegar and cook for 2 minutes. Add the orange juice, wine and sugar, stir well, cover and cook for 2 minutes. Stir in the blended cornflour, and salt and pepper and cook for 1 minute. Stir well, cover with foil and set aside.
2. Melt the remaining butter on HIGH for 15–20 seconds. Brush over the lamb and sprinkle with salt and pepper.
3. Heat a browning dish according to the manufacturer's instructions. Without removing from the oven, add the oil and lamb, pressing down well to brown. Cover with kitchen paper and cook on HIGH for 2 minutes. Turn the fillets and cook for 1 1/2 minutes for medium rare and 3 1/2 minutes for well done. Cover with foil and leave to stand for 4 minutes.
4. Cut the fillets into thick slices and arrange on a warmed serving dish. Pour over the sauce, or hand separately, and serve with steamed courgettes and new potatoes.
Pictured on page 143

Lamb Steaks en Daube

Serves 4
Preparation time: 15 minutes, plus marinating
Power setting: HIGH and LOW

Cooking time: 47 minutes
Standing time: 10 minutes
Freezing: Recommended at end of stage 4

A daube is usually made with beef, but this version makes a pleasant change. The word *daube* comes from *daubière*, which is a covered casserole dish.

1 onion, halved and sliced thinly
2 cloves garlic, sliced thinly
2 small carrots, sliced thinly
2 × 2.5 cm (1 inch) pieces orange peel
2–3 lamb steaks, total weight 625 g (1¼ lb)
1 tablespoon olive oil
1 bouquet garni
125 ml (4 fl oz) red wine
2 tablespoons brandy (optional)

15 g (½ oz) butter
1 tablespoon wholemeal flour
2 tablespoons tomato purée
230 g (8 oz) can peeled tomatoes
1 teaspoon demerara sugar
125 ml (4 fl oz) hot chicken stock
2 rashers rindless smoked streaky bacon, chopped
8 small black olives (optional)
salt and pepper to taste

1. Put half the onion, garlic and carrots, and 1 piece of orange peel in a large dish. Season with a little salt and pepper. Add the lamb. Put the remaining onion, carrots and orange peel on top and season again. Drizzle over the oil, add the bouquet garni and pour on the wine, and brandy if using. Cover and leave to marinate for 3–4 hours or overnight, turning the meat 2 or 3 times.
2. Remove the lamb and set aside. Strain the marinade into a jug and set aside. Reserve the vegetables and bouquet garni.
3. Place the butter in a bowl and microwave on HIGH for 20 seconds. Stir in the flour, then stir in the tomato purée. Gradually add the reserved marinade stirring constantly, then stir in the tomatoes with their juice, sugar and stock. Cook on HIGH for 4 minutes, stirring thoroughly halfway through cooking. Check the seasoning.
4. Place the lamb steaks side by side in a casserole. Add the bacon, reserved vegetables and bouquet garni and pour on the sauce. Cover and cook on HIGH for 8 minutes, turning the dish round halfway through cooking if necessary. Turn the setting to LOW and cook for 30 minutes, turning the dish round several times during cooking if necessary.
5. Add the olives if using, and cook for 5 minutes. Leave to stand for 10 minutes before serving.

Bottom: Lamb fillet with Rosemary Vinegar (page 142)

Lemon Chicken

Serves 4

Preparation time: 15 minutes	Cooking time: 12 minutes
Power setting: HIGH	Freezing: Not recommended

1 tablespoon oil	shredded rind of 1 lemon
500 g (1 lb) boneless skinned chicken breasts, cut into thin strips	5 spring onions, chopped
	2 tablespoons dry sherry
4 small courgettes, sliced thinly	2 tablespoons soy sauce
2 carrots, sliced thinly	juice of ½ lemon
1 teaspoon grated fresh root ginger	2 teaspoons cornflour

1. Place the oil in a bowl and microwave on HIGH for 1 minute, add the chicken and cook on HIGH for 2 minutes.
2. Add the courgettes, carrots and ginger and cook on HIGH for 3 minutes.
3. Stir in the lemon rind, spring onions, sherry and soy sauce, cover and cook on HIGH for 3 minutes.
4. Blend the lemon juice and cornflour together, stir into the dish, cover and cook on HIGH for 3 minutes, until the sauce thickens.
5. Serve with boiled brown rice and prawn crackers.

Mustard Pork

Serves 6

Preparation time: 10 minutes	Standing time: 15 minutes
Power setting: HIGH	Freezing: Recommended only if it is to be eaten cold; freeze sauce and meat separately
Cooking time: 26 minutes	

1.25 kg (2½ lb) boneless pork joint, rind removed	2 dessert apples, peeled, cored and sliced
3 tablespoons coarse grain mustard	2 teaspoons dark brown soft sugar
1 onion, sliced thinly	250 ml (8 fl oz) dry cider
	salt and pepper to taste

1. Rub a little salt and pepper all over the pork. Spread the top and sides with the mustard. Set aside.
2. Place the onion and apples in a baking dish, sprinkle with the sugar and add the cider. Season with a little salt and pepper and cook on HIGH for 4 minutes, stirring halfway through cooking.
3. Add the pork, cover loosely with kitchen paper and cook on HIGH for 22 minutes, turning the dish round several times during cooking if necessary. Remove the meat, wrap in foil and leave to stand for 15 minutes.
4. Meanwhile, purée the cooking sauce in a blender or food processor. Check the seasoning.
5. Transfer the meat to a warmed serving dish and carve into slices. Hand the sauce separately and serve with duchesse potatoes and a green vegetable such as brussels sprouts.

Roast Pheasant with Kumquats

Serves 6
Preparation time: 15 minutes
Power setting: HIGH

Cooking time: 25 minutes
Standing time: 10 minutes
Freezing: Not recommended

Choose hen pheasants if you can, as they are more tender.

2 oven-ready pheasants
6 large tarragon sprigs
175 g (6 oz) kumquats
25 g (1 oz) butter, melted

2 tablespoons clear honey
1 tablespoon brandy
salt and pepper to taste
watercress to garnish

1. Sprinkle the insides of the pheasants with salt and pepper. Place 2 tarragon sprigs and 3 kumquats inside each bird.
2. Place the pheasants on a microwave roasting rack over a dish, leg tips towards the centre. Brush with half of the melted butter, sprinkle with salt and pepper and place the remaining tarragon sprigs on top. Cook on HIGH for 10 minutes, turning the dish round twice during cooking if necessary. Turn the pheasants onto their breasts, brush with melted butter and cook for 6 minutes. Turn the pheasants onto their backs again, brush with any remaining butter, and cook for 6 minutes. Wrap in foil and leave to stand for 10 minutes.
3. Meanwhile, place the honey and brandy in a bowl and microwave on HIGH for 30 seconds. Cut the remaining kumquats in half lengthways and add to the bowl, stirring well to coat. Cook on HIGH for 3 minutes, stirring once during cooking.
4. Drain off any liquid from inside the pheasants. Arrange the pheasants on a warmed serving dish, surrounded with the kumquats. Garnish with watercress and serve with matchstick or game chips and steamed brussels sprouts.

Cabbage-Wrapped Chicken

Serves 4
Preparation time: 25 minutes
Power setting: HIGH

Cooking time: 14 minutes
Freezing: Recommended

125 ml (4 fl oz) each dry cider and hot chicken stock
1 small onion, sliced thinly
1 bay leaf
4 peppercorns
4 parsley stalks
4 small boneless chicken breasts, skinned

2 tablespoons finely chopped parsley
8 rashers streaky bacon, derinded
4 large green or Savoy cabbage leaves, blanched
2 tablespoons tomato purée
1 teaspoons demerara sugar
salt and pepper to taste

1. Place the cider and stock in a large dish. Add the onion, bay leaf, peppercorns and parsley stalks and cook on HIGH for 3 minutes or until boiling. Cover and set aside.
2. Lay the chicken breasts on a board. Using a sharp knife, make 3 diagonal cuts on top of each breast. Rub with salt and pepper and spoon the chopped parsley into each cut.
3. Wrap 2 bacon rashers round each chicken breast, then roll up in the cabbage leaves, tucking in the ends to form 'parcels'. Arrange in the dish with the fold underneath, cover and cook on HIGH for 4 minutes. Rearrange the 'parcels', baste with the liquid, cover and cook for 4 minutes. Remove with a slotted spoon, wrap in foil and set aside.
4. Strain the flavoured stock into a bowl and cook on HIGH for 1 minute. Blend the tomato purée and sugar with some of the hot liquid, then stir back into the bowl. Check the seasoning and cook on HIGH for 2 minutes.
5. Serve the 'parcels' with the sauce and accompany with creamed celeriac.

Onion and Stilton Tartlets

Serves 4
Preparation time: 15 minutes   Cooking time: 12 minutes
Power setting: HIGH   Freezing: Not recommended

If you use the plastic microwave individual tartlet dishes now available, the cooked pastry cases will be easier to unmould. You can, of course, use ready-cooked pastry cases and just warm through.

375 g (12 oz) Wholemeal Pastry (page 118)
1 onion, halved and sliced
125 g (4 oz) Stilton cheese, crumbled
1 teaspoon cornflour
1 egg yolk
142 ml (5 fl oz) carton single cream
salt and pepper to taste

1. Grease 4 tartlet dishes and line the bases with lightly oiled greaseproof paper or baking parchment.
2. Roll out the pastry to a 5 mm (¼ inch) thickness and use to line the dishes. Prick the pastry all over with a fork, cover loosely with kitchen paper and cook on HIGH for 4 minutes or until dry, turning the dishes round halfway through cooking if necessary. Leave to stand while preparing the filling.
3. Place the onion and 3 tablespoons water in a bowl and cook on HIGH for 4 minutes, stirring halfway through cooking. Stir in the cheese.
4. Mix the cornflour, egg yolk and cream together and stir into the onion and cheese mixture. Season with salt and pepper and cook on HIGH for 2 minutes, stirring each minute.
5. Line a flat dish with kitchen paper, unmould the pastry cases onto it and reheat on HIGH for 2 minutes.
6. Place the tartlets on 4 individual plates and divide the filling between them. Garnish with salad leaves and serve warm.

Sesame Carrots

Serves 4   Cooking time: 12 minutes
Preparation time: 10 minutes   Standing time: 2 minutes
Power setting: HIGH   Freezing: Not recommended

Sesame seeds give the carrots a crunchy texture, and have a nutty flavour.

500 g (1 lb) carrots, cut into thin slices
1 tablespoon sesame seeds
25 g (1 oz) butter
salt and pepper to taste

1. Place the carrots and 3 tablespoons water in a dish, cover and cook on HIGH for 8 minutes, stirring halfway through cooking. Leave to stand for 2 minutes.
2. Put the sesame seeds in a shallow container and cook on HIGH for 2 minutes. Set aside.
3. Drain the carrots, add the butter and cook on HIGH for 2 minutes. Season with salt and pepper and toss well.
4. Spoon into a warmed serving dish and sprinkle with the sesame seeds to serve.

Magrets of Duck with Mango Sauce

Serves 4
Preparation time: 20 minutes
Power setting: HIGH

Cooking time: 11 minutes
Standing time: 4 minutes
Freezing: Not recommended

A 'magret' is the boneless breast of duck. It is usually served medium rare but if you prefer it well done, add 2 minutes to the final cooking time. If you like the skin browned and crisp, place under a conventional preheated hot grill for 2–3 minutes before serving.

4 duck magrets
salt and pepper to taste
tarragon sprigs to garnish
FOR THE SAUCE:
2 ripe mangoes
15 g (½ oz) butter

2 shallots or 1 small onion,
   chopped finely
2 tablespoons wine vinegar
175 ml (6 fl oz) hot chicken
   stock
2 teaspoons redcurrant jelly

1. First prepare the sauce. Peel the mangoes and cut away from the stone. Slice one mango, cover and set aside for the garnish. Chop the other one coarsely.
2. Place the butter, shallots or onion and vinegar in a large jug and cook on HIGH for 2 minutes. Add the chicken stock and chopped mango and cook for 3 minutes, stirring once during cooking.
3. Purée in a blender or food processor, then rub through a sieve into a jug. Stir in the redcurrant jelly until thoroughly blended; if necessary, return to the microwave oven for 30 seconds. Check the seasoning, cover and set aside.
4. Prick the duck skin all over and rub with the salt and pepper.
5. Heat a browning dish according to the manufacturer's instructions. Without removing from the oven, add the duck, skin side down. Press down well to brown, then cook on HIGH for 3 minutes. Drain off the fat, turn the breasts and cook for 3 minutes. Drain off any fat, cover with foil and leave to stand for 4 minutes.
6. Transfer to warmed individual plates and carve into slices. Garnish with the reserved mango slices and tarragon and serve with the sauce and a crisp salad.

liquid as possible, then add to the onion. Add the soft cheese in pieces and mix thoroughly, mashing the cheese with a fork. Season carefully with salt, pepper and nutmeg and use to stuff the cannelloni tubes.

3. Pour half of the tomato sauce into a large baking dish and arrange the cannelloni in one layer. Pour on the remaining tomato sauce, sprinkle with the grated cheese and cook on HIGH for 10 minutes, turning the dish round 2 or 3 times during cooking if necessary. Cover with foil and leave to stand for 10 minutes. Serve with a crisp salad.

Couscous-Filled Tomatoes

Serves 4	
Preparation time: 10 minutes, plus soaking time	Cooking time: 12 minutes
	Standing time: 8 minutes
Power setting: HIGH	Freezing: Not recommended

Choose good red, firm tomatoes with their stalks still on. Use the discarded seeds and flesh in a soup or sauce.

4 extra-large tomatoes, total weight about 1 kg (2 lb)	seeded and chopped finely
75 g (3 oz) couscous or bulgar wheat	8 small button mushrooms, sliced thinly
25 g (1 oz) butter	1 tablespoon chopped parsley (optional)
1/2 small onion, chopped finely	2 teaspoons demerara sugar
1 clove garlic, crushed	salt and pepper to taste
1/2 small green pepper, cored,	

1. Leaving the stalks on, cut a slice off the top of each tomato and set aside. Carefully scoop out the seeds and some flesh from the tomatoes, leaving a thick shell. Sprinkle the insides with salt and pepper. Place upside down on kitchen paper and leave to drain.

2. Place the couscous or bulgar wheat in a bowl, add 6 tablespoons hot water and leave to soak for 10 minutes.

3. Place half of the butter, the onion, garlic, green pepper, mushrooms and 2 tablespoons water in a bowl and cook on HIGH for 4 minutes, stirring halfway through cooking. Add the parsley if using, couscous or bulgar wheat, and salt and pepper and stir well.

4. Place the tomatoes, touching, in a baking dish. Sprinkle 1/2 teaspoon of the sugar inside each tomato and spoon in the filling. Dot with the remaining butter and cook on HIGH for 3 minutes. Give the tomatoes a quarter turn in the dish and cook for 3 minutes. Replace the tops, give the tomatoes another quarter turn and cook for 2 minutes. Cover with foil and leave to stand for 8 minutes. Serve with a lettuce and avocado salad.

Spinach and Cheese Cannelloni

Serves 4–6	Cooking time: 14 minutes
Preparation time: 20 minutes	Standing time: 10 minutes
Power setting: HIGH	Freezing: Recommended

Use the cannelloni tubes which require no pre-cooking.

12 cannelloni tubes	1 clove garlic, crushed
600 ml (1 pint) Tomato Sauce (page 18)	500 g (1 lb) frozen chopped spinach, thawed
50 g (2 oz) grated Cheddar cheese	142 g (5 oz) packet full fat soft cheese with garlic and herbs
FOR THE FILLING:	salt, pepper and grated nutmeg to taste
25 g (1 oz) butter	
1 small onion, chopped finely	

1. First prepare the filling. Place the butter, onion, garlic and 2 tablespoons water in a bowl and cook on HIGH for 4 minutes. Stir and set aside.

2. Drain the spinach thoroughly, squeezing out as much

Tomato and Potato Bake

Serves 4–6
Preparation time: 15 minutes
Power setting: HIGH
Cooking time: 16 minutes
Freezing: Not recommended

375 g (12 oz) potatoes, sliced
    thinly
1 large onion, sliced
40 g (1½ oz) butter
500 g (1 lb) tomatoes, skinned
    and sliced
4 tablespoons single cream
½ teaspoon chopped basil
salt and pepper to taste

1. Place the potatoes in a large shallow dish with 4 tablespoons water. Place another fitting dish on top and put into it the onion and butter. Place the 2 dishes in the oven and cook on HIGH for 6 minutes, stirring the onion twice during cooking.
2. Arrange half of the potatoes in a serving dish. Cover with half of the tomatoes, then two thirds of the onion. Spoon over half of the cream and basil, then season with salt and pepper.
3. Repeat the potato and tomato layers, pile the remaining onion in the centre and spoon the remaining cream over the tomatoes. Season with the remaining basil, and salt and pepper, then cook on HIGH for 10 minutes.

Stuffed Peppers

Serves 4
Preparation time: 15 minutes
Power setting: HIGH
Cooking time: 15 minutes
Standing time: 2 minutes
Freezing: Not recommended

These stuffed peppers make an ideal vegetarian meal.

4 large peppers
2 tablespoons oil
1 onion, chopped
3 celery sticks, chopped
125 g (4 oz) mushrooms, chopped
125 g (4 oz) wholemeal
    breadcrumbs
50 g (2 oz) Brazil nuts, chopped
½ teaspoon dried mixed herbs
125 g (4 oz) Cheddar cheese,
    grated
salt and pepper to taste

1. Slice the tops off the peppers and remove the seeds.
2. Place the oil in a bowl with the onion, cover and cook on HIGH for 3 minutes. Add the celery and mushrooms and cook for 2 minutes.
3. Mix in the remaining ingredients, then spoon into the peppers. Replace the tops and stand the peppers upright close together in a dish.
4. Pour in 3 tablespoons water, cover and cook on HIGH for 10 minutes. Stand for 2 minutes before serving.

1. Drain the gammon joint and place in a roasting bag. Tie loosely with string and cook on MEDIUM, allowing 12 minutes per 500 g (1 lb); turn the joint over halfway through cooking.

2. Snip a corner from the roasting bag and pour off the juices into a measuring jug. Skim off any fat from the surface and make up to 150 ml (¼ pint) with water. Leave the joint to stand for 20 minutes.

3. Meanwhile, place the butter in a bowl and microwave on HIGH for 1 minute. Stir in the flour, then the gammon juices and cream. Cook on HIGH for 2 minutes, stirring every 30 seconds. Add the peppercorns and keep warm.

4. Remove the rind from the joint and carve the meat into slices. Arrange on a warmed serving plate, pour over a little sauce and serve the remaining sauce separately.

Lamb in Red Wine

Serves 4	Power setting: HIGH
Preparation time: 25 minutes,	Cooking time: 15 minutes
plus marinating	Freezing: Not recommended

Boning and rolling lamb is not too difficult but it is quicker and easier to buy ready-prepared noisettes.

1 kg (2 lb) best end of neck of lamb, or 8 noisettes of lamb, each 2.5 cm (1 inch) thick	1 tablespoon tomato purée
	15 g (½ oz) butter
	15 g (½ oz) plain flour
250 ml (8 fl oz) red wine	salt and pepper to taste
1 clove garlic, crushed	parsley sprigs to garnish
few rosemary sprigs	

1. To prepare noisettes yourself, skin the best end of neck, then place fat side down on a board and cut the meat from the bones with a sharp knife. Season with salt and pepper, roll up tightly and tie at 2.5 cm (1 inch) intervals with fine string. Cut through the meat between the string to make noisettes. Place in a shallow bowl.

2. Mix the wine, garlic, rosemary, tomato purée, and salt and pepper together, then pour over the lamb. Cover and leave to marinate for 3 hours.

3. Cook on HIGH for 8 minutes. Remove lamb, return dish to oven and cook for 5 minutes. Discard the rosemary.

4. Meanwhile, remove string from the lamb and arrange on a warmed serving dish; cover with foil to keep warm.

5. Mash the butter and flour together with a fork, then whisk into the sauce. Cook on HIGH for 2 minutes.

6. Pour over the lamb and garnish with parsley. Serve with new potatoes and a julienne of vegetables.

Gammon with Green Pepper Sauce

Serves 4–6	Cooking time: 27–39 minutes
Preparation time: 10 minutes,	Standing time: 20 minutes
plus overnight soaking	Freezing: Not recommended
Power setting: HIGH and MEDIUM	

Green peppercorns are available fresh or preserved in brine for future use.

1–1.5 kg (2–3 lb) smoked gammon joint, soaked overnight	25 g (1 oz) plain flour
	142 ml (5 fl oz) carton single cream
25 g (1 oz) butter	1 tablespoon green peppercorns

Lentil Curry

Serves 4–6
Preparation time: 10 minutes   *Cooking time: 23 minutes*
Power setting: HIGH   *Freezing: Not recommended*

Serve as an accompaniment to a meat or chicken curry, or as a main course for a vegetarian meal.

1 onion, chopped	*750 ml (1¼ pints) hot*
2 tablespoons oil	*vegetable stock*
2 teaspoons hot curry powder	*2 tablespoons mango chutney*
250 g (8 oz) red lentils	*salt and pepper to taste*

1. Place the onion and oil in a bowl, cover and cook on HIGH for 2 minutes. Add the curry powder and cook for 1 minute.
2. Stir in the remaining ingredients, cover and cook on HIGH for 20 minutes. Check the seasoning, stir well then transfer to a warmed serving dish.

Aubergine Layer

Serves 4–6   *Power setting: HIGH*
Preparation time: 25 minutes,   *Cooking time: 32 minutes*
plus standing time   *Standing time: 5 minutes*

500 g (1 lb) aubergines, cut into	*2 teaspoons tomato purée*
5 mm (¼ inch) slices	*1 teaspoon dried oregano*
1 onion, chopped	*75 g (3 oz) no pre-cook lasagne*
2 tablespoons oil	*150 g (5 oz) carton natural*
1 clove garlic, crushed	*yogurt*
250 g (8 oz) mushrooms,	*1 egg, beaten*
chopped	*2 teaspoons grated Parmesan*
375 g (12 oz) tomatoes, skinned	*cheese*
and chopped	*salt and pepper to taste*

1. Sprinkle the aubergine slices with salt, place in a colander and leave to stand for 1 hour. Rinse well, pat dry on kitchen paper, then place in a bowl, cover and cook on HIGH for 4 minutes. Set aside.
2. Place the onion and oil in another bowl and cook on HIGH for 3 minutes. Add the garlic, mushrooms, tomatoes, tomato purée, oregano, and salt and pepper, cover and cook on HIGH for 5 minutes.
3. Arrange a third of the lasagne in a shallow dish, cover with a third of the tomato sauce, and finish with a third of the aubergine slices. Repeat these layers twice.
4. Beat the yogurt and egg together, season with salt and pepper, then spoon over the aubergines. Sprinkle with the Parmesan and cook on HIGH for 20 minutes.
5. Leave to stand for 5 minutes. Serve with salad.

Skate with Leeks and Capers

Serves 2	*Cooking time: 7 minutes*
Preparation time: 10 minutes	*Standing time: 3 minutes*
Power setting: HIGH	*Freezing: Not recommended*

¹/₂ very small leek, cut into	*2 tablespoons capers*
thin strips	*500 g (1 lb) skate wings*
25 g (1 oz) butter	*2 tablespoons sunflower oil*
3 tablespoons dry white wine	*salt and pepper to taste*
or water	

1. Place the leek, half of the butter and the wine or water in a bowl and cook on HIGH for 2¹/₂ minutes. Stir in the capers, cover and set aside.
2. Melt the remaining butter on HIGH for a few seconds.
3. If the skate is in one piece, cut in half vertically. Brush the flesh with the butter, then sprinkle lightly with salt and liberally with pepper.
4. Heat a large browning dish according to manufacturer's instructions. Without removing from the oven, quickly add the oil and fish, skin side up. Cover with kitchen paper and cook on HIGH for 2 minutes. Turn the fish, cover and cook for 1¹/₂ minutes. Cover with foil and leave to stand for 3 minutes. Meanwhile, reheat the sauce on HIGH for 1 minute.
5. Transfer the fish to a warmed serving dish and spoon over the sauce. Serve with boiled potatoes.

Creamy Watercress Soup

Serves 4	*Cooking time: 16 minutes*
Preparation time: 10 minutes	*Freezing: Recommended after*
Power setting: HIGH	*Step 4*

This fresh-tasting soup can be served chilled for a summer meal or hot with croûtons.

50 g (2 oz) butter	*1 teaspoon lemon juice*
2 large bunches watercress,	*25 g (1 oz) cornflour*
chopped	*300 ml (¹/₂ pint) milk*
1 onion, chopped	*pinch of grated nutmeg*
600 ml (1 pint) hot vegetable	*salt and pepper to taste*
stock	*4 tablespoons single cream*

1. Place the butter in a large bowl and microwave on HIGH for 1 minute. Add the watercress and onion, cover the bowl and cook for 5 minutes.
2. Add the stock, lemon juice, and salt and pepper, cover the bowl and cook on HIGH for 5 minutes.
3. Cool a little, then pour into a blender or food processor and work until smooth.
4. Blend the cornflour with a little of the milk to a smooth paste, then stir in the remaining milk and the nutmeg. Add to the soup, return to the bowl, cover and cook on HIGH for 5 minutes. Serve with a swirl of cream on each portion.

Tarragon Trout

Serves 4
Preparation time: 10 minutes
Power setting: HIGH

Cooking time: 16 minutes
Freezing: Not recommended

50 g (2 oz) butter
1 small onion, chopped
250 g (8 oz) button
  mushrooms, chopped
1 tablespoon chopped tarragon

4 trout, cleaned
2 tablespoons dry white wine
salt and pepper to taste
lemon slices and tarragon
  sprigs to garnish

1. Place the butter in a bowl and microwave on HIGH for 1 minute. Add the onion and cook on HIGH for 1 minute. Stir in the mushrooms and cook for 2 minutes. Add the tarragon, and salt and pepper.
2. Make 2 slits on each side of each fish to prevent the skin from bursting during cooking. Divide the mushroom mixture between the trout, stuffing it into the body cavity. Shield the tails with foil.
3. Place the fish in a shallow dish, pour over the wine, cover and cook on HIGH for 12 minutes, changing the position of the fish halfway through cooking.
4. Garnish with the lemon slices and tarragon to serve.

Salmon with Dill Sauce

Serves 4
Preparation time: 10 minutes
Power setting: HIGH

Cooking time: 8 minutes
Freezing: Not recommended

4 salmon steaks, about 2.5 cm
  (1 inch) thick
4 tablespoons water
juice of ½ lemon
2 egg yolks

125 g (4 oz) butter
1 tablespoon chopped dill
salt and pepper to taste
dill sprigs to garnish

1. Arrange the salmon in a large shallow dish. Mix the water with 1 tablespoon of the lemon juice, season with salt, then pour over the fish.
2. Cover with greaseproof paper and cook on HIGH for 6 minutes. Set aside while making the sauce.
3. Place the egg yolks in a blender or food processor and blend for 30 seconds. Microwave the butter in a dish on HIGH for 1 minute, then add the remaining lemon juice.
4. With the motor running, pour the butter in a steady stream onto the egg yolks until combined. Pour into a bowl and stir in the chopped dill and salt and pepper.
5. Arrange the salmon on a warmed serving plate and spoon a little of the sauce over each portion. Garnish each with a sprig of dill.

Date Flapjacks

Makes 8
Preparation time: 15 minutes   *Cooking time: 10 minutes*
Power setting: HIGH   *Freezing: Not recommended*

250 g (8 oz) dates, stoned and chopped	*50 g (2 oz) demerara sugar*
3 tablespoons water	*125 g (4 oz) porridge oats*
75 g (3 oz) margarine	*125 g (4 oz) plain wholemeal flour*
1 tablespoon golden syrup	

1. Place the dates and water in a bowl, cover and cook on HIGH for 3 minutes. Mash with a fork, adding a little more water if needed to make a spreading consistency.
2. Place the margarine, syrup and sugar in a bowl and microwave on HIGH for 2 minutes, until the margarine has melted. Mix in the oats and the flour.
3. Spread one half of the oat mixture over the base of an 18 cm (7 inch) flan dish, then cover with the dates, spreading evenly. Spoon the remaining oat mixture on top and press down well.
4. Cook on HIGH for 5 minutes. Cut into wedges, while still slightly warm. Leave in the dish until cold.

Iced Gingerbread

Makes one 22 cm (8½ inch) cake   *Cooking time: 14 minutes*
Preparation time: 15 minutes   *Standing time: 10 minutes*
Power setting: HIGH   *Freezing: Not recommended*

Wholemeal flour gives this cake a nutty texture. Try adding some sultanas or chopped preserved ginger to the mixture.

175 g (6 oz) margarine	*1 teaspoon bicarbonate of soda*
4 tablespoons golden syrup	*1 teaspoon salt*
4 tablespoons black treacle	*1 egg, beaten*
175 g (6 oz) dark brown soft sugar	*300 ml (½ pint) milk*
	TO DECORATE:
375 g (12 oz) plain wholemeal flour	*250 g (8 oz) icing sugar, sifted*
1 tablespoon each ground ginger and baking powder	*2 tablespoons water*
	50 g (2 oz) crystallized ginger, chopped

1. Grease and base-line a 22 cm (8½ inch) square dish.
2. Place the margarine, syrup, treacle and sugar in a bowl and microwave on HIGH for 2 minutes, until the margarine has melted.
3. Place the flour in a large bowl, then sift in the ginger, baking powder, bicarbonate of soda and salt. Beat in the egg, milk and melted mixture.
4. Pour into the prepared dish and cook on HIGH for 12 minutes. Leave to stand for 10 minutes, then turn out onto a wire rack to cool.
5. Beat the icing sugar with the water to make a thick glacé icing, then spread over the top of the cake. Sprinkle with the chopped ginger. Leave to set, then cut into fingers.

Chocolate Coconut Brownies

Makes 16
Preparation time: 10 minutes
Power setting: HIGH

Cooking time: 9 minutes
Standing time: 5 minutes
Freezing: Not recommended

These are so quick you can make them within minutes of children arriving home with unexpected friends for tea.

150 g (5 oz) wholemeal self-raising flour
1/2 teaspoon bicarbonate of soda
175 g (6 oz) light brown soft sugar

125 g (4 oz) desiccated coconut
4 tablespoons cocoa powder
125 g (4 oz) margarine, diced
2 eggs, beaten
150 ml (1/4 pint) milk

1. Grease and line a 22 cm (8½ inch) square dish.
2. Mix together the flour, bicarbonate of soda, sugar, coconut and cocoa in a large bowl.
3. Place the margarine in a bowl and microwave on HIGH for 1 minute. Beat into the dry ingredients, with the eggs and milk, until smooth. Pour into the prepared dish.
4. Cook on HIGH for 8 minutes. Leave to stand for 5 minutes, then turn out onto a wire rack to cool.
5. Cut into squares to serve.

Apple and Walnut Loaf

Makes 10 slices
Preparation time: 15 minutes
Power setting: HIGH

Cooking time: 5 minutes
Standing time: 10 minutes
Freezing: Not recommended

175 g (6 oz) plain wholemeal flour
1 teaspoon baking powder
1/2 teaspoon mixed spice
75 g (3 oz) margarine
125 g (4 oz) light brown soft sugar

1 egg, beaten
250 g (8 oz) cooking apples, peeled and grated coarsely
50 g (2 oz) walnuts, chopped
3 tablespoons milk
25 g (1 oz) demerara sugar

1. Place the flour, baking powder and mixed spice in a bowl, mix together and set aside.
2. Beat the margarine and light brown sugar together until creamy, then add the egg, beating well.
3. Fold in the flour mixture, then the apple and walnuts. Stir in the milk.
4. Turn the mixture into a greased 12 × 18 cm (5 × 7 inch) loaf dish, level the top, then sprinkle with the demerara.
5. Cook on HIGH for 5 minutes. Leave to stand for 10 minutes, then turn out onto a wire rack to cool. Cut into slices to serve. Best eaten the same day as making.

Apple and Raspberry Charlotte

Serves 6–8   *Power setting: HIGH*
Preparation time: 15 minutes   *Cooking time: 18 minutes*

A family favourite, this dessert could be made with blackberries or loganberries instead of raspberries.

750 g (1½ lb) cooking apples,   *250 g (8 oz) wholemeal*
   peeled and chopped   *breadcrumbs*
50 g (2 oz) granulated sugar,   *75 g (3 oz) light brown soft*
   or to taste   *sugar*
375 g (12 oz) raspberries,   *142 ml (5 fl oz) carton double*
   thawed if frozen   *cream, whipped*
50 g (2 oz) butter   *25 g (1 oz) walnuts, chopped*

1. Place the apples in a bowl with 3 tablespoons water, cover and cook on HIGH for 5 minutes, stirring halfway through cooking.
2. Add the granulated sugar and mash with a fork. Leave to cool, then stir in the raspberries.
3. Place the butter in a large heatproof glass dish and microwave on HIGH for 1 minute. Stir in the breadcrumbs and brown sugar, spreading out evenly. Cook on high for 10–12 minutes, stirring every minute during cooking. Leave to cool, allowing the crumbs to become crisp.
4. Spread one third of the crumbs onto the base of a glass bowl. Cover with half of the fruit. Sprinkle with half of the remaining crumbs, then the remaining fruit. Finish with a layer of crumbs.
5. Pipe the cream around the edge of the charlotte and sprinkle with the nuts. Serve as soon as possible.

Moroccan Fruit Compote

Serves 6   *Cooking time: 15 minutes*
Preparation time: 5 minutes   *Standing time: Until cool*
Power setting: HIGH   *Freezing: Not recommended*

500 g (1 lb) dried mixed fruits, *450 ml (¾ pint) water*
   e.g. apricots, apples, pears, *2 tablespoons clear honey*
   prunes or figs   *1 cinnamon stick*
150 ml (¼ pint) pure orange   *pinch of ground allspice*
   juice   *25 g (1 oz) blanched almonds*

1. Place the fruits in a large bowl, pour in the orange juice and water, cover and cook on HIGH for 5 minutes.
2. Add the honey, cinnamon stick and allspice, cover and cook on HIGH for 10 minutes.
3. Leave to stand until cool, during which time the fruit will become plumper and more tender. Remove the cinnamon stick, stir in the almonds and chill until required. Serve with crisp biscuits.

Caribbean Crumble

Serves 4–6
Preparation time: 5 minutes   *Standing time: 10–15 minutes*
Power setting: HIGH   *Freezing: Recommended at*
Cooking time: 7 minutes   *end of stage 2*

1 large ripe mango, peeled   FOR THE TOPPING:
  and sliced   *75 g (3 oz) plain wholemeal*
1 paw-paw, peeled and cubed   *flour*
227 g (8 oz) can pineapple   *50 g (2 oz) oatmeal*
  pieces in natural juice   *25 g (1 oz) bran flakes, crushed*
grated rind of ¹/₂ lemon   *2 tablespoons demerara sugar*
2 teaspoons lemon juice   *¹/₂ teaspoon ground cinnamon*
2 tablespoons demerara sugar   *50 g (2 oz) butter*

1. Place all the fruit, with their juices, in a 1.2 litre (2 pint) dish. Stir in the lemon rind and juice, and the sugar.
2. Mix the dry topping ingredients together, rub in the butter until the mixture resembles breadcrumbs, then spoon over the fruit.
3. Cook on HIGH for 7 minutes. Leave to stand for 10–15 minutes before serving.

Orange Tart in Ginger Pastry

Serves 4–6
Preparation time: 25 minutes,   *Power setting:* HIGH
plus chilling pastry   *Cooking time: 18 or 21 minutes*
                                        Freezing: Recommended

1 tablespoon brandy   *75 g (3 oz) plain white flour,*
4 tablespoons sugar   *sifted*
1 large orange, sliced thinly   *1¹/₂ teaspoons ground ginger*
3 eggs   *75 g (3 oz) butter, softened*
65 g (2¹/₂ oz) ground almonds   *3 tablespoons caster sugar*
FOR THE PASTRY: *1 egg yolk*
150 g (5 oz) plain wholemeal   *4 tablespoons water*
  flour   *orange leaves to garnish*

1. Place the brandy and 3 tablespoons water in a large dish. Stir in half of the sugar and cook on HIGH for 4¹/₂ minutes. Add the orange slices, in a single layer, and cook on HIGH for 2 minutes. Turn and cook for 1 minute. Set aside while making the pastry.
2. Mix the flours and ginger together and place in a mound on a pastry board. Make a well in the centre and add the butter, sugar and egg yolk. Gradually work in the flour with your fingertips, adding the water gradually to form a smooth dough.
3. Roll out on a lightly floured surface to a 5 mm (¹/₄ inch) thickness and use to line a greased 20 cm (8 inch) flan dish. Prick the base. Place in the freezer for 15 minutes or until very firm. Cover loosely with kitchen paper and cook on HIGH for 5 minutes or until dry. Set aside while completing the filling.
4. Beat the eggs, ground almonds and remaining sugar together in a bowl and cook on HIGH for 1¹/₂ minutes, stirring well halfway through cooking. Spoon into the pastry case and cook on HIGH for 2 minutes. Arrange the orange slices over the top. Spoon over half of the syrup and cook on HIGH for 2 minutes. Leave until cold.
5. If you wish, cook the remaining syrup on HIGH for about 3 minutes, until very lightly caramelized, then drizzle over the tart to serve. Garnish with orange leaves.
Pictured on page 141